Manfred Eder
Hans Tilscher

Chiropractic Therapy
Diagnosis and Treatment

English Language Edition
Edited by
Marianne S. Gengenbach, D.C., CCSP
Logan College of Chiropractic
Chesterfield, Missouri

AN ASPEN PUBLICATION®
Aspen Publishers, Inc.
Rockville, Maryland
1990

Library of Congress Cataloging-in-Publication Data

Eder, Manfred, 1927— .
[Chirotherapie. English]
Chiropractic therapy: diagnosis and treatment/ Manfred Eder,
Hans Tilscher; English language edition edited by Marianne Gengenbach.
p. cm.
Translation of: Chirotherapie: vom Befund zur Behandlung.
Includes bibliographical references.
ISBN: 0-8342-0119-4
I. Chiropractic . II. Tilscher, Hans. II. Gengenbach, Marianne.
III. Title.
RZ241.E3413   1990   615.5′34--dc20   89-18119
CIP

Originally published *Chirotherapie*© 1988
Hippokrates Verlag

Editorial Services: Jane Coyle Garwood

Library of Congress Catalog Card Number: 89-18119
ISBN: 0-8342-0119-4

Printed and Bound in Canada

1 2 3 4 5

Table of Contents

Foreword

Chiropractic practitioners and students are in sore need of materials that integrate principles of biomechanics, manipulation, and neurophysiology. Only from such a solid framework can a true understanding of the value of chiropractic therapy be built. It has always made me feel sheepish to have to tell students that some of the most progressive literature in this regard comes to us not from within our own profession but from the fields of physical therapy or osteopathy.

During the course of my chiropractic education, I was inundated with the siren songs of the myriad "techniques" for chiropractic manipulation. Much like other students, I often longed for a basic source of information that would help me understand my choices. During the course of my career as a chiropractic educator, I have continued to wish for the emergence of texts on manipulation that are based not only on sound biomechanical principles but incorporate chiropractic principles and philosophy as well. Unfortunately, the trend thus far has been to find excellent texts on spinal biomechanics without directions for manipulation, or to find sources on manipulation that do not address its neurophysiological effects. This tends to promote a mechanistic reduction of chiropractic therapy in the general literature.

Imagine then my pleasant surprise at finding a text about *chiropractic* therapy that provides just such an integrative approach—and from a clinical perspective. In choosing to edit this foreign text it is my objective to bring to chiropractic a clearer understanding of chiropractic therapy. The authors offer clear elucidation of its biomechanical basis, its necessity in musculoskeletal dysfunction, and its neurophysiological roots, both in terms of symptom causation and potential treatment effects. In that sense I see this text as an ideal introduction for the chiropractic student seeking understanding of his or her art. It can also serve as a reaffirmation and summary for the experienced practitioner searching for newer scientific explanation and validation.

It is my hope that the publication of *Chiropractic Therapy: Diagnosis and*

Treatment in this country will provide a springboard for expansion of its content into increasing knowledge and an ever greater clarity of clinical thought for the chiropractic profession.

In editing this translation I have attempted to represent the authors' original language and intent as accurately as possible. I would like to thank CRS for giving me the courage to begin this project—and WRT for helping me find the courage to finish it.

Marianne S. Gengenbach, D.C., CCSP
Logan College of Chiropractic
Chesterfield, Missouri

Preface

Until recently, literature concerning manipulative medicine was limited to a few standard textbooks. The literature has proliferated in the past few years; but it has become difficult to supply a practical reading list to someone interested in this subject, because most publications touch only on fragmented areas of chiropractic therapy. In addition, concepts dealing with theoretical, diagnostic, and therapeutic problems that were developed during the advent of the academic-scientific analysis of manipulative therapy of the last 30 years are flavored by nationalistic orientations. Even though these concepts often supplement one another, some duplicate and contradict each other, impeding understanding and obscuring the subject orientation. Such contradictions are especially evident in certain manipulative techniques that are now being offered in an overabundance.

The authors of this work wish to contribute a greater clarity of vision to discussions of chiropractic therapy—a vision that is based on their experiences gained from many years of practice, their perception of the overall development of this field, and their extensive academic and postgraduate studies. It is therefore inevitable that the treatment of the subject matter is somewhat subjective. The necessary departure from hypothetical and traditional paths in favor of methods proven in practice and the occasional deviation from "pure doctrine" is not deliberate, but motivated by the desire not to suppress practical information. Therefore, the objective of the following discourse is to introduce simple, proven techniques of manipulation, whose performance is required on a daily basis.

It stands to reason that it is difficult to master manipulative medicine through books alone, and that all textbooks pertaining to certain techniques can only provide a foundation for learning and teaching. As in other fields, the ambiguity in chiropractic therapy lies in its inherently changing nature. Even manipulative techniques fluctuate with fashion; they are introduced and then slowly fade from sight. Moreover, because certain manipulative therapists stand out as teachers, the techniques being offered today are tinted with individualistic variations. To further complicate the matter, research in the admittedly difficult area of pure functional disturbances and their clinical significance is still being conducted. Physicians who are scientifically interested in the objective presentation of this material find it difficult to await the conclusion of research. An objective presentation, therefore, is often involuntarily replaced by speculation, compounded by a tendency to stick to a preferred teaching theory.

Because of the resulting confusion and the difficulties encountered during the conveyance of manipulative skills and abilities, there are still too few physicians who turn toward manipulation. The abundance of literature on the subject cannot change this deficiency by itself. Moreover, readers of this work may be disappointed to discover that even the most fastidious study of this book will not produce the perfect chiropractor. The mastery of any technique requires diligent practice. This practice consists of the automation of necessary movements to freely form a cortical picture of the overall clinical situation and to respond appropriately, without being impeded by technical difficulties. If the term *healing art* is justifiably to be applied to manipulation, technical difficulties must become insignificant.

Books are only a teaching aid in learning chiropractic therapy.

An additional difficulty facing the student during the use of chiropractic therapy is the problem of targeted application of learned techniques. In other words, when should you do what? In too many cases, no transitional concepts are offered to enable a movement from diagnosis to subsequent therapeutic results. This problem, which has been experienced for many years by physicians during their training in manipulative techniques, was our motivation in providing these aids to the student. We also encourage teaching staff to consider these proposed concepts and follow their course. We have covered certain areas—neurophysiological principles, pain mechanisms, and general principles of manipulation—in previous books and are again presenting them here. This reiteration is necessary because the processes involved in manipulation can be neither interpreted, nor understood without such an introduction. Also, it would be wrong to assume that the readers of this book are familiar with our other publications.

Many heartfelt thanks go to the publishers for their outstanding cooperation and for their consideration of our wishes where design was concerned. We thank the Ludwig-Boltzmann Society for their generous support and preparation of the material. We are especially grateful to those who, over the years, have shared their special knowledge of chiropractic details and who have conceptually contributed to the realization of this book.

Section I

1. Overview of the History of Manipulative Therapy in Europe

> Manipulative medicine is as old as mankind.

It may be safely assumed that the human hand, with its perfect harmony of sensory and motor abilities, is the most primordial source of diagnostic and therapeutic measures. It is not surprising that corresponding treatments of the human skeletal system are mentioned even in the oldest records, which may be traced back to 300 A.D. Many such records have been preserved by ancient cultures, including records by the prominent physicians of antiquity—Hippocrates, Apollonius or Citium, and Galen. These records contain passages that might be considered modern in their approach; they describe a stretching of the spinal column during which the therapists conducted a "proper therapy" with the help of their hands and feet. Mechanical treatment methods have continued to exist into the subsequent centuries up to our own time. Their importance, however, varied in scope.

Special consideration must be given here to two areas in the development of manipulative therapy in the late 19th century. One of these is a method developed by the Swiss physician Otto Naegeli, published in 1899 under the title *Nerve Disorders and Nerve Pains: Their Treatment and Healing Through Manipulations*. This work was mostly referred to for headache therapy. Naegeli claimed that his method resulted in better blood circulation through the use of manipulation. Another area—perhaps the most significant development of modern manipulative therapy—originated in the United States when Andrew Taylor Still (1830–1917) devised osteopathic theory. He himself suffered from migrainelike headaches from the time he was ten years old and supposedly cured the headaches by positioning himself with his neck in a lasso, which was hung close to the ground between two trees. Still studied medicine and, after this key experience and further observations, devoted his interest fully to spinal problems and their effects on human health. In 1894, he founded the American School of Osteopathy in Kirksville, Missouri. Even today, the subtle manipulative examination and treatment he recommended forms a basis for modern, scientifically oriented, manipulative medicine. During further development of osteopathy, several colleges specializing in this field obtained medical accreditation. As a result, doctors who graduate from these colleges enjoy equal status with practitioners from medical schools.

In a parallel development, another health practitioner movement spread throughout the United States. Its members called themselves chiropractors and also performed manipulation. This occupational group, which was founded and trained by a store merchant named David D. Palmer, showed sectarian traits and isolated itself from osteopathy and conventional medicine. The group developed its own concepts and theories concerning the mechanism and effect of chiropractic manipulation. Chiropractors, whose educational program was still in the early stages, began to arrive in Europe and not only spread their methods of treatment, but also propagated the theory of subluxation, asserting that vertebral displacements were responsible for a variety of ailments. For the most part, it was this rather general and unsubstantiated version of the subluxation theory that received a shattering evaluation in the so-called Swiss Assessments, which were issued by renowned hospitals and well publicized. As a result, not only were questionable theoretical ideas swept off the table, but manipulative theory per se was banished from many academic circles.

Present-day manipulative medicine carried the stigma of this assessment for a long time. In the 1950s, medical associations specializing in manipulative medicine were established in West Germany, Switzerland, and Austria. Only then, through thorough sifting of antiquated concepts and the application of neurophysiological research findings, could an adequate ideological concept begin to be developed. This new model has gained acceptance within academic environments holding stringent requirements for scientific fact and thought. In 1973, a chair for manipulative medicine was established for the first time in a German-speaking country at the neurological hospital in Graz, Austria. The full academic integration of this theory is being achieved by Tilscher and by Eder, who were appointed as university lecturers in 1982 and 1984, respectively, and, as the *vena legendi* for manipulative medicine, that is, vertebrology and arthrology.

Before discussing the technical details of diagnostic and therapeutic programs, we will consider several important aspects of the associated physiological processes.

2. The Ideological Model: Motor Unit (Vertebron and Arthron)

With the introduction into vertebrology of the concept of the motor seg-ment (Junghanns) came the first ideological structure for manipulative medicine that was not connected to mere descriptive anatomy and that could support the theoretical basis of chiropractic therapy. This functional model consists of the following: the two spinal bodies, the connective in-tervertebral disc, the vertebral articulations, and the cartilage system. Without this model, it is impossible to define the term *vertebral dysfunction,* which is the core and starting point of theoretical considerations. Simul-taneously, this functional model clears the way for a correction of the etiopathologic value of the traditional "wear and tear" concept and its in-evitable overestimation of the significance of degenerative, pathomorphol-ogical changes.

> The "wear and tear" concept is replaced by the principle "Disease is malfunction."

The logical consequence of this principle for manipulative medicine is the task of finding the location and type of malfunction and, subsequently, attempting to restore normal function through appropriate methods of treatment. The chosen formulation of this definition implies that the loca-tion and type of functional breakdown will require differential analysis. First, one must select the portions of the motor segment that are, in each case, the main causes of the functional disturbance. With the increasing recognition and understanding of neurophysiological and biocybernetic problems, the original motor-segment model proved too narrow, because the disc, facet joints, and ligaments are not the only possible causes of malfunction. Most other segmentally attached structures, including the muscular system, connective tissue, and vascular supply, also must be con-sidered. Gutzeit defined such an expanded concept as a "vertebron"; the

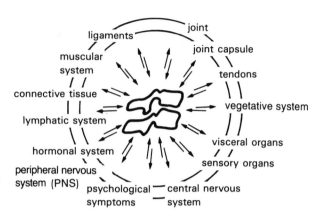

Figure 1 A schematic diagram of the cognitive model of the "Segmental-Reflexive Complex," which symbolizes the horizontal and vertical combinations of reactions of various structures and systems with the motor segment, or "vertebron."

peripheral joints and their associated structures were designated, in an analogical sense, as "arthrons."

Second, one must consider informational and regulative connections with other functional aspects of the body (see Figure 1). Just as viscerocutaneous, viscerovisceral, and viscerovertebral reflexes are known to exist, so too other segmental structures and systems can be assumed to be interconnected in an opposing or mirrored fashion. Not only are horizontally oriented reflexive interrelationships to be considered in understanding segmental reflexes, but also vertically oriented processes, whereby segmentally overlapping transverse connections are expanded on and complicated by the arrangement of the vegetative system. These interrelationships are also influenced by axonal reflexes, by the more central reticular formation, and by the limbic system. This almost inconceivable set of interactions behaves as an actual segmentally reflexive complex (Eder) in response to any irritation. Thus, correspondingly variable symptomatology can develop in response to malfunctions of a single component of the system.

> Joints, muscles, intervertebral discs, and ligaments are the most frequent causes of motor-segment malfunction.

For clinicians in manipulative medicine, a basic understanding of this complex structural, and reflexive mechanism provides the key to the comprehension of daily realities. The evaluation of the individual case will be aided by the fact that the actual origin of most malfunctions confines itself to a few, commonly affected main structures, which also predictably vary by specific body region. For example, discogenic disease is a prevalent problem in the lumbar area and radicular signs are frequent, but these developments are less common in the cervical region. Breakdowns in joint function are more dominant in cervical symptomatology and play a lesser role in lumbar syndromes. Ligamentous, muscular, and pseudoradicular pathomechanisms can also be ranked according to their frequency and regional distribution. The knowledge of such arrangements consequently

creates an initial basis for the use of chiropractic therapy, which also specifically addresses issues of indication and contraindication.

> Without a mastery of knowledge concerning spinal column disease
> and malfunction classification, chiropractic therapy remains limited
> to coincidental success.

An understanding of motor-segment malfunction helps in discovering
the basis of the patient's primary symptomatology, which is usually the
occurrence of pain in its many variations. At this point it is important to
understand that pain is not merely a reaction to the noxious stimuli of
tissue damage. Rather, pain also possesses its own pathological components, which feed back into the affected system, thereby sensitizing the
entire segmental-reflexive complex. Chapter 3 examines the pain syndromes of the motor apparatus, and the pathomechanisms that accompany
every occurrence of pain.

3. The Occurrence of Pain

The original purpose of pain perception is protective.

The emergence of a pain sensation indicates a local irritation of tissue, and can be triggered by any stimulus, regardless of its quality, provided that the stimulus exceeds a predetermined threshold. Remember that a sensation of pain is dependent not only on external stimuli, but also on internal circumstances. The source of pain must be considered when attempts are made to localize and differentiate its occurrence. For example, with regard to the perception of pain "depth," a lucid, clear, sharply defined pain often indicates damage to the outer layers of body tissue, whereas deep, throbbing discomfort usually indicates a damage to deep-lying structures. Both types of pain can occur together, a therapeutically useful fact that was expounded on by Head in the latter half of the 19th century. This fact, however, is only seldom put to practical clinical use, probably because of "a sort of critical integrity of physicians, who cannot adequately explain this effect, and the almost reflexive use of narcotics in the presence of severe pain." (Hoff)

The most frequent and important type of pain in the musculoskeletal motion system is receptor pain.

The effectors of this type of pain are the ubiquitous nociceptors, the so-called free nerve endings. Signals transmitted through thin, myelinated A-delta fibers impose the first inkling of pain with an intensive, sharp, or cutting character. Via thin, slowly transmitting C fibers, increasing irritations release a dull, deep, poorly localized secondary pain. Thus, delta nociceptors concentrate especially in the skin, whereas those of the C fibers adhere in the deeper structures of the motor apparatus and in internal organs.

3.1 NOCICEPTION AND REACTION

Pain is a signal of damage. This holds true even during therapeutic intervention.

The first stop for the afferent nociception of pain lies in the dorsal horn, where all other receptor afferences (mechano-, thermo-, and proprioceptive receptors) also are assembled and integrated. Here, the intensity of the incoming stimulus, together with the inhibiting efferent impulses from higher neurological function centers, determine whether further transmission is to be achieved. Because the pain threshold is slightly higher than the activation threshold of the nociceptors, spatial and temporal summation in the central nervous system (CNS) are required to produce perception of pain. For this reason, then, one should not automatically equate the nociceptor with the oversimplified concept of "pain receptor." If generalization is to be permitted at all, nociceptors serve primarily as the reporters of damage. As the stimulus intensity increases, the frequency of reached action potentials in nociceptors increases in linear fashion, functioning in a sense as an "intensity encoder," until the pain threshold is crossed. In addition, many afferent C fibers correspond to a single dorsal horn neuron, thereby contributing to a summation of the stimulus (the convergence principle). Moreover, the stimulus intensity dampens rather slowly at the spinal level, which correlates well with reports of lingering pain perception. An important therapeutic consideration is that the first inhibitive mechanisms already take place in the dorsal horn, partly through the tracts descending from the periacqueductal gray matter, or the reticular formation, but also partly from the effects of afferent stimulation from the periphery. It is additionally presumed that spinal activity can be stimulated through the peripheral therapeutic stimulation of mechanoreceptors and A-beta fibers, which in turn achieve inhibition of pain through descending signals after these incoming signals reach the periacqueductal gray matter.

In the Gate Control model of pain (a controversial but, nevertheless, not-yet-replaced theory), therapeutic stimulation of thick myelinated fibers can close the "gates of pain" directly in the dorsal horn (see Figure 2). The nociceptive information rising in the CNS, which is switched to the contralateral spinothalamic and spinoreticular tract via the internuncial neurons, reaches the brain stem switching area, either directly or multisynaptically, resulting in affective and emotional reactions. Finally, the nociceptive information reaches the cortical centers, where a conscious pain perception results.

The intensity of perceived pain also depends on its perceived meaning.

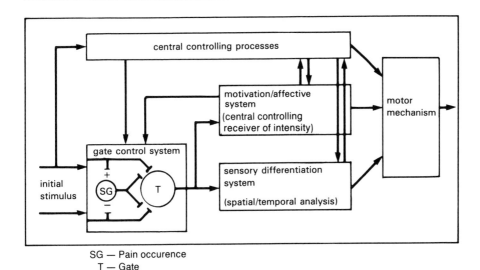

SG — Pain occurence
T — Gate

Figure 2 Circuit diagram of Melzack and Wall's Gate Control Theory. *Source:* H. Tilscher and M. Eder, *Textbook of Reflex Therapy.* Hippocrates Publishing Co., Stuttgart, 1986.

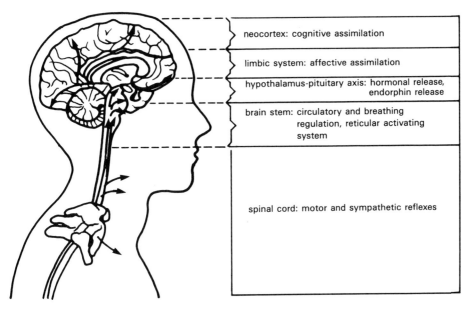

Figure 3 Reactions to occurrences of pain at the different processing levels. *Source:* M. Zimmerman, Physiological mechanisms of pain and pain therapy. *Triangel*, 20 (1981).

The occurrence of pain is differentiated in these higher brain centers into the psychological dimensions of pain, as follows:

• sensory—distinguishing
• motivational—affective
• cognitive weighting

Psychosomatic coupling develops here; this association negatively or positively influences the primary pain occurrence and helps to vary the clinical picture of accompanying vegetative reactions, emotions and psychological cortical reactions (see Figure 3).

> Chronic pain often changes the psychological situation in the direction of depressive conditions.

Essential to the development of clinical symptomatology is the spinal channeling of the nociception to the internuncial neurons of the dorsal horn, which not only opens a direct link to the anterior motor horn, but can also activate the sympathetic ganglia in the lateral horn.

3.2 THE MEANING OF ALGESIC SUBSTANCES

> Algesic (pain-causing) substances substantially influence the intensity of pain.

The spread of an agitating stimulus in all sectors is guided by biochemical reactions. The course and intensity of pain occurrences are dependent on these reactions, and certain therapeutic measures also have an effect. In the area of the nociceptors themselves, the chemical micromileau affects irritability. The increased release of certain endogenous substances, such as potassium chloride, hydrogen ions, serotonin, bradykinin, and prostaglandins, increases irritability and inflammation. In high concentrations, these substances intensify pain; even in lower concentrations, they lower the sensitivity threshold of nociception to mechanical and thermal irritants (see Figure 4). The consequentially pain-determining prostaglandin synthesis can be retarded by nonsteroidal anti-inflammatory drugs (NSAIDs), which are used extensively in medical therapy when the irritating stimulus persists. This type of therapy, however, brings only temporary relief.

3.3 ON PSEUDORADICULAR PAIN (SCLEROTOGENOUS PAIN)

> Pseudoradicular pain is a result of reflexive processing of pain. Its main effector is the muscular system.

As previously mentioned, receptor pain that is felt in its place of origin is a large component of pain in the motor apparatus. Even this local pain, however, exhibits tendencies to radiation, which shows seemingly seg-

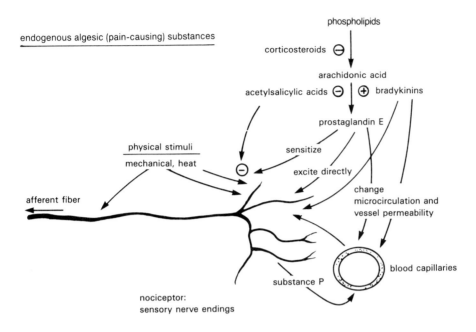

Figure 4 Algesic substances excite and sensitize the nociceptors (Zimmermann)

mental distributions; thus it has often been (and still is) confused with radicular pain mechanisms. As early as 1938, Kellgren began to elucidate the difference between these types of pain when he stated that radiation patterns in seemingly segmental paravertebral structures could be created by injecting hypertonic saline solutions into joints, ligaments, and the muscular system. Kellgren's results were further substantiated by Taillard, who performed similar experiments, using a local anesthetic to block the nerve roots to rule out their responsibility for the radiation. Later, the famous neurosurgeon Cloward made similar observations while performing discographies, which led to a further recognition of sclerotogenous pain. Brugger coined the term *pseudoradicular* in 1967. There are other names, but the term *pseudoradicular* best conveys the general essence of these authors' meaning and is therefore used throughout this text.

> Pseudoradicular syndromes are differentiated from radicular syndromes by the lack of neurological findings.

Pseudoradicular symptoms can represent practically the entire response to the developed nociception in a given case; therefore, these symptoms often appear to be the best representation of the expression of pain and pathomechanics in the motor apparatus.

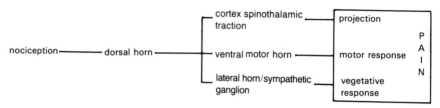

Figure 5 The actual "picture of pain" is the result of variable mixing of individual components (projection, muscular, and vegetative nociceptive reaction)

As previously mentioned, nociception is expressed (after the switching occurs in the dorsal horn) as "nocireaction" in three ways:

- over the anterior lateral tracts to the brain stem and cortex
- via the lateral horns to the sympathetic ganglia
- through direct switching into the anterior motor horn

This direct switching to the motor neurons of the ventral horn stipulates that, after the observation of pain through the cortex, a segmental increase in muscular tonus is the first accompanying reaction of nociception (see Figure 5). With lasting irritations, a feedback mechanism develops with the gamma system, and the increased tonus escalates to hypertonus and tautening, with consequent hypoxia. This hypoxia finally leads to structural damage in the sense of the myotendinopathy. Tied to this development are the efferent impulses from the sympathetic ganglia, which affect the vascular system and capillary permeability, causing chemical changes in the colloid structure and connective tissue environment with resultant symptom exacerbation. The original, segmentally restricted muscular reaction can eventually spread over other myotomes, primarily because of the multisegmental nature of muscular innervation, but also because of the functional kinetic chains existing between the muscles. The resultant spread of hypertonicity and spasm thus begins to develop into an undefined sclerotogenous distribution.

In long-lasting illness, a systemic involvement or even a generalization of symptomatology can develop, a process that should be strongly taken into account in situations of so-called fibromyalgia or generalized myofascitis.

3.4 TRIGGER POINTS

Trigger points are a result of chronic muscular "nocireaction."

The pressure-sensitive points of irritation, with their typical radiation patterns, defined by many different manual therapists as myofascial trigger points, can of course also be attributed to the aforementioned pathomechanisms. According to Travell and Simons (1983), who have extensively explored the problem of trigger points, the resulting radiation of pain beyond the realm of mere pressure sensitivity comes primarily when increasing numbers of muscle fibers become involved in the hyperirritable condition. Further, one needs to differentiate between latent trigger points, which cause pain only when externally stimulated by manual pressure or needle, and active trigger points, which independently radiate into the referral zones because of multiple physiological processes. Important for therapeutic considerations is the fact that trigger points have a certain potential for autonomic facilitation, which means that even after the primary cause of irritation is removed, their symptoms may linger.

3.5 REFERRAL OF PAIN

The exploration of pain referral dates back to the 1898 work of the therapist Head, who first recorded and mapped stereotypical zones of hyperalgesis in connection with specific organic illnesses. An explanation of this phenomenon, which still possesses some validity today, did not come about until many years later with the advent of the field of neurophysiology. This explanation supposes that the common streaming of afferent impulses from different body structures into the dorsal horn and the transmission of nociceptive signals through the spinothalamic tract to the cortex causes a perceptual "deception." This is reinforced by the fact that the skin, which is most often attacked by noxious stimuli, is represented most strongly in the cortical centers. As a result, all "reported" instances of damage are projected back to associated regions in a given segmental arrangement and perceived accordingly. The experiments of Head, which were confined to the connection between organs and skin zones, allowed no clearly recognizable analogous conclusions to be drawn for corresponding monosegmental projections from the motor apparatus, since most organs are innervated by multiple segments. However, if one recalls the origin and perception of irritation and the concept of pain, it becomes clear that embryological somite arrangement and the mono- or pluri-segmentality of nociceptive signals are primarily responsible for the location of pain exit points and the perception of radiation or referral patterns.

True, radicular pain may be similar in principle to localized pain in its ability to be localized and its radiation mechanisms. However, a prerequisite for the appearance of true radicular pain (that is, true neuralgia) is damage to the conductive path between the receptor and synapse. Such occurrences cause true neuralgia in the peripheral nerve area or, when they occur secondary to disc prolapse in an intervertebral foramen, a radicular lesion. Depending on the degree of compression or stretching of the nerve root, either sensory, motor, or combination lesions can result. Long-lasting compression, such as that seen in disc lesions in the intervertebral foramen (IVF), or in carpal tunnel syndrome, leads to fiber degeneration. This degeneration may cause the fibers to assume the qualities of sensory receptors. The resulting transmission block first damages the myelinated fibers evident in the A-delta group, with a resultant loss of touch and pressure sensitivity—and simultaneous increases of the nociceptive afferent stimuli. This combination often causes a particularly unbearable form of pain.

> The characteristics of the true radicular pain syndrome are "deficit symptoms" (hypalgesia, loss of reflexes and paresis).

Simple muscular spasms, which are still being used as an attempted explanation for peripheral nerve irritation, including those that are given as causes of neuralgia (such as the suboccipitals), do not often cause the same kind of damage. Such syndromes are not indicative of true neuralgia. Radicular pain is not felt at the location of compression, but rather in the distal areas the nerve supplies. Even here, misinterpretation of findings is common, often being explained as if the afferent signals were coming from the attached peripheral receptors. In compression of spinal nerves, the pain sensation is exactly oriented according to segmental arrangement. Sensory findings, therefore, will affect only the corresponding dermatome, or the muscle of the myotome, in the case of motor deficit. In diagnostic segmental examination, pin-prick exams of the dermatome can produce distinctly defined dermatomal borders only with respect to hypalgesia, since hypoesthetic zones often have overlapping nerve supply. In addition, dysesthesias are often seen in pseudoradicular syndromes, whereas true hypalgesic zones are found only in cases of true nerve compression (radicular or peripheral compressive lesions).

3.6 VEGETATIVE AUTONOMIC RESPONSE TO PAIN STIMULUS

The inclusion of the vegetative system in the course of pain generation was previously mentioned in connection with pseudoradicular symptoms. However, vegetative reactions are present in most forms of pain and must therefore be given therapeutic consideration. To make these somewhat obscure reactions more understandable, a few anatomical facts are presented here.

From the sympathetic columns of the "intermediolateral" gray column from C8 to L3, sympathetic efferents leave the spinal column (through the ventral roots) as preganglionic fibers and proceed as white rami communicans to the paravertebral ganglia. From here, some of the efferents return to the spinal nerves through the gray rami communicans; others enter ascending or descending postganglionic fibers and eventually become peripheral nerves, which reach the visceral end organs. Some postganglionics also reach the periphery via the adventitia of blood vessels. Though the white rami communicans are responsible for the supply of several segments, the gray rami communicans illustrate a segmentally bound distribution. These fibers, which continue in the dorsal rami, play an important role in the segmental activation of connective tissue and should be diagnostically considered. The accurate observation of sympathetic activity is difficult because the Bell-Magendie law does not apply to the vegetative portion of the nervous system. This is because both afferent and efferent fibers use the ventral and dorsal horns to contact the spinal cord. In other words, the sympathetic fibers by no means reach the sympathetic trunks in their entirety. Moreover, afferent sympathetic fibers are equally capable of transmitting pain perception.

In the peripheral establishment of pain, the primarily responsible C fibers carry not only nociceptive afferent signals, but also sympathetic efferent signals. The sympathetic nervous system is intricately interwoven in all pain mechanisms. The thematically relevant points of attack of the sympathetic efferents are the blood vessel system (i.e., degree of blood perfusion), capillary filtration, and the colloid composition of the affected connective tissue.

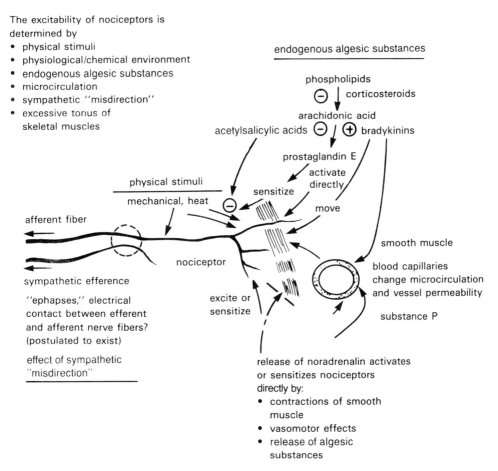

Figure 6 Schematic diagram of an escalation of nocireaction through excessive activation of the sympathetic response. *Source:* M. Zimmerman, Physiological mechanisms of pain and pain therapy.

> The vegetative response to irritation works as a catalyst in the development of pain syndromes.

Reduced to a simple common denominator, the vegetative components of pain formation occur in three phases, as follows:

1. In the first phase, the nociception effects a swelling of the connective tissue in the connected segmental area via the attached sympathetic activation. In addition, C fibers that carry the nociceptive afferents send efferent sympathetic signals to the area of irritation and change the micromileu (chemistry) of this area.
2. The second step of the sympathetic nocireaction is mediated by the freeing of known algesic substances and also through neurotransmitters of the sympathetic system (adrenalin, noradrenalin). This serves as a further stimulation and a reduction of the pain threshold. One such cycle of regulatory changes leads to repeated positive feedback loops, which raise both the intensity and dimensional cognition of the pain. The segmental overlap and quadrant-oriented development of the sympathetic stimulation finally contribute to the blurring and diffusion of the originally segmentally bound pathomechanisms (Figure 6).
3. The third and most intensive step of the accompanying vegetative response to noxious stimuli is reserved for the strongest and most dramatic nociceptions. It is the alarm reaction of the stress adaptation syndrome as described, for example, by Selye.

Chapter 4 explores the disruptive potential of various functional components of the vertebron/arthron.

4. Dysfunction of the Spine

The human spinal column is not frivolously designated as an axial "organ." This terminology seems justified when one defines an organ as the combination of different structures into a functional "community." In cases of functional breakdowns, one or more components of such an alliance may be affected by pathogenesis and the course of disruption to a greater degree than the others, but the organ as a whole suffers in terms of function. The pathogenetic structure of the spinal column includes discogenic, arthrogenic, ligamentous, and muscular syndromes; but functional damage also may occur in neighboring structures. Long-lasting exposures to irritation can produce secondary centers of irritation. Such developments often occur—for example, the intervertebral disc syndrome, which often leads to nerve compression. In this syndrome, discogenic components are primarily involved; and pathologically accompanying mechanisms, tangent to the vertebron at different points, are secondarily involved. Frequently, after laminectomies, persistent—extant or newly emerging—pain complaints that actually represent pseudoradicular mechanisms are reinterpreted as radicular complaints. Based on such misorientation, unnecessary and largely unsuccessful repetitive surgeries are often performed. It must be noted, however, that radicular irritations caused by genuine relapses or previously undetected double prolapses can occur and may, of course, require a second surgery.

All consideration of etiology of pathogenesis in disease states resulting from painful malfunctions of the motor apparatus must be logically explored, and one must not fall prey to causal thought. The following sections, which explain the malfunction potential of the important structures of the vertebral motor units (arthrons), are to be interpreted in this spirit.

The sum of structural symptoms provides the clinical picture.

4.1 THE INTERVERTEBRAL DISC AND ITS POTENTIAL FOR DYSFUNCTION

The human intervertebral disc is a genuine synchondrosis and of distinct significance in determining the potential for movement in the spine. In histological construction, the intervertebral disc falls into the bradytrophic-tissue category, a structural quality that emerges in any tissue subjected to long-standing pressure and dynamic mechanical forces. Because brady-trophic tissue does not have vascular supply, substance exchange is achieved through diffusion, which occurs through a slow pumping mechanism. When pressure is relieved, the fluid content of the discs increases (through imbibition of low molecular weight substances); when pressure increases, the opposite occurs. The discs' lack of vascular supply accounts also for the fact that tissue aging begins almost from the moment of birth and continues uninterrupted until death. This progressive involution provides for a large pathogenic potential in the third and fourth decades of life. Loss of form and elasticity afflict both the nucleus pulposus, the gel-like substance that comprises the core of the intervertebral disc, and the anulus fibrosus, which is composed of sinewy, tightly bound connective tissue and cartilage rings. Degeneration also affects the hyaline cartilage end-plates that attach the disc to the vertebral bodies. In the course of involutional degeneration, functional disrelationships and mechanical overload lead to various pathomorphological changes in the disc. The normal tension force within the healthy intervertebral disc accounts for (together with the simultaneous tightening of the linking ligamentous structures) the maintenance of the constant distance between two vertebral bodies. One could thus speak of healthy discoligamentous stress compensation as an important mechanism for the maintenance of elastic and flexible movement during different spinal column positions. The diminishing height of the intervertebral discs that occurs with aging due to dehydration, leads to a relaxation of the adjacent ligamentous apparatus, which in turn leads to functional imbalance between discs and ligaments.

Further degenerative changes in this area, such as osteochondrosis and spondylosis, actually represent an attempt at self-stabilization through an increase in connecting surfaces and concomitant force dispersal—a concept for which the term "degeneration" alone is not accurate.

> The pathogenic potential for "explosive" disruption of the intervertebral disc is located in its posterior posterolateral portions.

Changes at the anterior borders of the disc give rise to the familiar spurs and extostoses of spondylosis. The degeneration of the disc itself is called chondrosis; additional sclerotic changes of the hyaline end-plates are known as osteochondrosis. Pathogenically more important, however, is the involutional "inner derangement" of the disc, which greatly encumbers the adjacent joint and ligamentous apparatus. This condition, which is most often tied to the clinical concept of intervertebral disc pathology, produces fiber separation in the anulus fibrosus and the extrusion of nuclear material, the so-called intervertebral disc prolapse. In the posterior portion of the disc, the expanding disc material can make direct contact with neural elements and produce clinically relevant irritations.

Prolapses, which make contact with the richly innervated posterior ligaments, appear as "lumbago" in the lumbar spine; in the cervical region, they can even mimic medullary damage. Through dorsolateral movement into the IVF, prolapses can cause nerve compression. This pathomechanism occurs most frequently in spinal regions that are functionally most stressed. The lowest two intervertebral discs, in this case, lead in incidence. Figure 7 shows the frequency distribution of disc prolapses for all spinal levels.

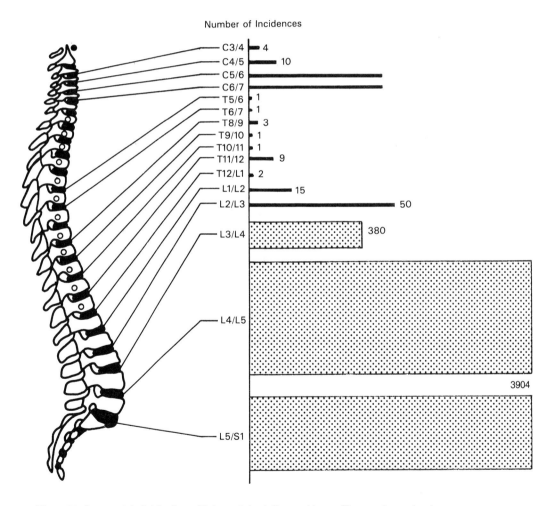

Number of Incidences

Figure 7 Segmental distribution of intervertebral disc problems. The graph emphasizes the relative importance of the two lowest motor segments. *Source:* A. Brügger and Ch. Rhonheimer, *Pseudoradicular Syndromes of the Brain Stem.* Huber, 1967.

U.S. Editor's note: Unlisted segments imply no incidences noted in this study

The strength of the muscular system is perhaps the decisive element leading to an extrusion of the pulposus material and the formation of annular tears. It is no wonder activities disrupting the muscularly secured and protected balance between discs and ligaments provide a significant component in the development of discogenic syndromes. Such negative influence can be brought on by difficult or incorrectly performed physical work or by overexertion in athletics. On the other hand, these negative influences also can result from so-called light duty if it involves long periods of sitting (e.g., handicrafts, writing or typing, driving a car), especially due to increased kyphosis and the consequent imbalances of the regional muscular system. This is particularly true if there is no balancing physical activity, such as an exercise or fitness program.

What are the practical consequences of chiropractic therapy in the case of intervertebral disc pathology? First, one fact needs to be stated.

> It is impossible, through chiropractic therapeutical means, to replace a true disc prolapse.

Anyone who has seen a discotomy performed and has noted how the prolapsed material, sequestered or not, has spread out and how nerve roots were compromised by the need for space in the IVF, will be cured of the supposition that these situations can be reset through manual therapy. If a clinician is ignorant of this condition or misinterprets the etiology of some acute syndromes, chiropractic therapy may actually result in massive exacerbation of the condition through the extrusion of more pulposus material.

The acute nerve root compression syndrome with a painful antalgia (a posture adopted to maximally open the IVF) does not necessarily provide an indication or advantage for manual therapy, especially when no painless position can be found, or if worsening neurological signs exist. What is frequently possible are light, tractional measures (mobilizations) that serve the purpose of finding the most painless position for the patient, as well as postisometric relaxation treatments for influencing any accompanying pseudoradicular (sclerotogenous) symptoms.

After an easing of the acute phase (and in more protracted, chronic cases), it is quite possible for the arthrogenic and muscular problems, which now begin to dominate the clinical picture, to be resolved through concentrated uses of chiropractic therapy[1]. The decision to employ chiropractic therapy responsibly is not one to be taken lightly; and this decision requires, once again, careful differential diagnosis of subtly differing conditions.

---

[1]Cases of discogenic lesion without prolapse are, of course, included here.

4.2 DYSFUNCTION OF THE JOINTS

The determination of malfunctioning arthrons and respective vertebrons is the primary domain of manual medicine's diagnostics.

All joints in the motor apparatus, not only those of the spinal column,
may be approached in similar fashion. The peripheral joints provide relatively little diagnostic difficulty because of their mechanics, functional ability, or clinical manifestation; but the joint apparatus of the spine is much
different. These relationships are among the most difficult to assess because of the unique functions of each spinal column region, and because of the relatively small maneuvering room of each segmental joint.
Corresponding information necessary for diagnosis and therapy of joint
malfunctions in the spine, is illustrated in the following sections. For chiropractic consideration, both the functional anatomical and neurophysiological idiosyncracies of various spinal regions have significance; these idiosyncracies shed light on the function of the joint apparatus as a guiding
organ of proprioception.

In the general study of arthrology, one can find few joint constructions
that correspond, in method of movement, to that of the spinal facet joints.
With the exception of certain upper cervical segments, the spinal facet
joints are arranged in pairs; thus, in lateral flexion and rotation, the joint
partners of opposite sides move divergently. The chief means of motion is,
of course, a gliding of the joint surfaces. The joints' facets in the lumbar
spine, for example, sink down and approximate during extension and separate during flexion (Figure 8).

This gliding motion corresponds to that of a piston; in fact, spinal facets
are termed *piston joints* in some literature. In the lordotic regions, the joint
facets are oriented dorsally, with the motion axis located in the area of the
spinous process; in the kyphotic regions, ventrally, with the motion axis

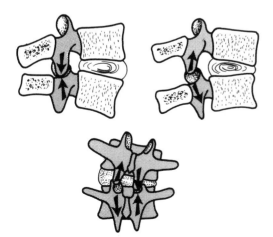

Figure 8 Displacement of the
facet joints during extension,
flexion, and lateral flexion
(convergence-divergence) (Med
and Cihak)

lying in the vertebral body; and in the transitional areas of the spine, flowing from one form to the other in gradual fashion. The almost generally found incongruence of the articulating surfaces makes biomechanical analysis difficult. Only relatively general summary statements can be made about the courses of motion in single regions of the spinal column.

The sacrum, located between the two pelvic halves, functions as the base of the entire spinal column. The sacroiliac joints, in the anatomical sense, must be considered true joints, but actually function as amphiarthroses because the overall tight ligamentous junction and the cartilagenous, uneven joint surfaces leave minimal space for movement. Moreover, there is no single muscle that causes a programmed motion of this joint. Despite this, the sacroiliac joints are important in chiropractic therapy, because malfunctions of the small, but important, compensatory motions in the pelvic bowl can have significant consequences for the spine, especially in the lower lumbar segments. This compensatory motion occurs continually during gait and is termed *nutation* (spiral type of rotation). It pulls the sacral base to the posterior and superior on the side of the leg stepping forward, while the ilium swings forward and slightly lateral. The fifth lumbar vertebra is rotated simultaneously by the iliolumbar ligament on that side.

The sacrum dips anterior and inferior on the side of the stance legs. As soon as the stepping foot is flat against the floor, the same reaction develops contralaterally.

The physiological motion of the sacroiliac joints is nutation.

In the lumbar spine, with its sagittally oriented facets, flexion, extension, and lateral flexion dominate the possible motions. Rotational ability is much less. It should be mentioned here that an exception exists in the L5/S1 segment, in which the articulating facets are again more frontally oriented. This situation gives the fifth vertebra a so-called double construction, wherein its facets with the L4 segment have the sagittal orientation, while those with the sacrum are more frontal.

The greatest lateral flexion in the lumbar spine is in the L4/L5 motor segment; the most distinctive extension in the L5/S1 motor segments.

The joint facets in the thoracic spine also lie in the frontal plane, with a noticeable ventral inclination at their superior end. Because of links with ribs, which always join with two contiguous vertebral bodies, a transverse process and the sternum anteriorly, the overall movement possibilities of the spinal joints in this region are minimal. Movement in the sagittal plane dominates in this region.

Rotation and lateral flexion of the thoracic spine occur primarily in the lower thoracic segments, that is, the thoracolumbar transitional area.

The largest motion in spinal joints occurs in the cervical spine. With the exception of the upper cervical segments, the joint facets face in an anterior-superior to posterior-superior orientation. This slanted position of the facet joints stipulates a shift, during forward- and backward-bending motions, of the cranial on the caudal vertebrae. Rotation and lateral flexion are coupled and so arranged that every lateral flexion is accompanied by an equal degree of rotation. The rotation occurs in the direction of the concavity; that is, a right lateral flexion causes a right rotation, and vice versa. The maximum motion occurs at C2. The degree of segmental lateral flexion increases until C3/C4, and then decreases caudally. The degree of segmental flexion and extension shows a continual rise from C2 to C5.

The cervical spine is the most movable, but also the most fragile portion of the axis organ.

The upper cervical joints require a separate explanation of functional relationship. They are defined as the functional alliance of the occiput-atlas and axis. The entire "universal joint" mechanism found here is based on the existence of a multitude of joints in this sector. The uppermost cervical joint, between the occiput and atlas, consists of two anatomically separated joints wherein the convex, almost half-spherical occipital condyles join their corresponding concave joint partners on the atlas. The atlantoaxial joint consists of three additional joints. A single central joint is formed by the anterior arch of the atlas, and the axis dens (which also carries a "joint surface"). The paired lateral joints, which show a ridge in the frontal plane, provide a further supporting link with the axis. From a mechanical standpoint, this means that, at the uppermost cervical joint, flexion, extension, and lateral flexion are possible, but there is no meaningful rotation. Rotation, on the other hand, is primarily seen at the atlantoaxial joint. Approximately 40° to 50° of the total 180° rotational ability of the cervical spine (chin from shoulder to shoulder) takes place in this joint. That means that approximately 20° to 25° of the total rotation radius to any one side takes place at the atlas. After this point, the more caudal cervical vertebrae begin to participate in rotation. There is relatively little pure lateral flexion capability in the C1/C2 motor segment.

The given anatomical relationships establish a necessary coupling of lateral flexion and accompanying rotation in all spinal regions. The direction of this coupling, however, is different in specific spinal regions.

For example, scoliosis that shows a spinal rotation toward the opposite side of lateral flexion (e.g., a left rotation in the direction of convexity with right lateral flexion of the region) is known as "Lovett positive." This behavior is typical for the lumbar spine, but only when it is lordotically positioned. When flexing (kyphosis) with simultaneous lateral flexion, the result is a rotation of the spinal body toward the flexed side, or the concavity, known as "Lovett negative." The rotational behavior for the cervical spine corresponds to Lovett negative.

Rotation toward the convexity = Lovett positive.
Rotation toward the concavity = Lovett negative.

An understanding of the arthrogenic vertebral symptomatology depends on knowledge of the neural supply to the spinal joints. The superior portion of the motor segments, with their joint and ligamentous apparatus, is innervated by the dorsal ramus of the spinal nerve, which also supplies the posterior skin and the autonomically controlled muscular system. The dorsal ramus also carries vegetative (mostly sympathetic) fibers in a segmental distribution. During irritation of the joint-ligament apparatus, these innervational relationships cause a noticeable segmental symptomatology, which, in addition to local and radiating pain, shows spasm or pressure sensitivity of the paraspinal muscles. In addition, signs of sympathetic reaction and possible segmentally distributed swelling of connective tissue may result (see Figure 9).

The first part of this chapter hinted that not only must biomechanical aspects be investigated, but that the joints also play a steering role in static and dynamic postures. The joint, as a "feeling organ" of proprioception, possesses (aside from the nociceptors that report damage) specialized sensory elements that consist primarily of two types of receptors. One type rapidly adapts and immediately reacts to any stretch impulse, which allows it to quickly perceive angular changes of joint position. The other type is a slowly adapting receptor, which receives input regarding the stabilizing and "erect" end-position of the joint. The fast receptors are quiescent when the joint is in resting position and send signals regarding movement at a frequency corresponding to the speed of the motion. The total picture of the rest-and-motion frequencies, the so-called afferent pattern, is centrally interpreted and functions as a contributing factor in uninterruptedly controlled and adapted proprioception.

The upper cervical joints influence, as peripheral steering centers of proprioception, the tonus of the entire muscular system.

In the steering of proprioception, the upper cervical joints take on a special significance; that is, they have a far-reaching potential for effect. The afferents of the upper cervical joint region are rapidly channeled to central

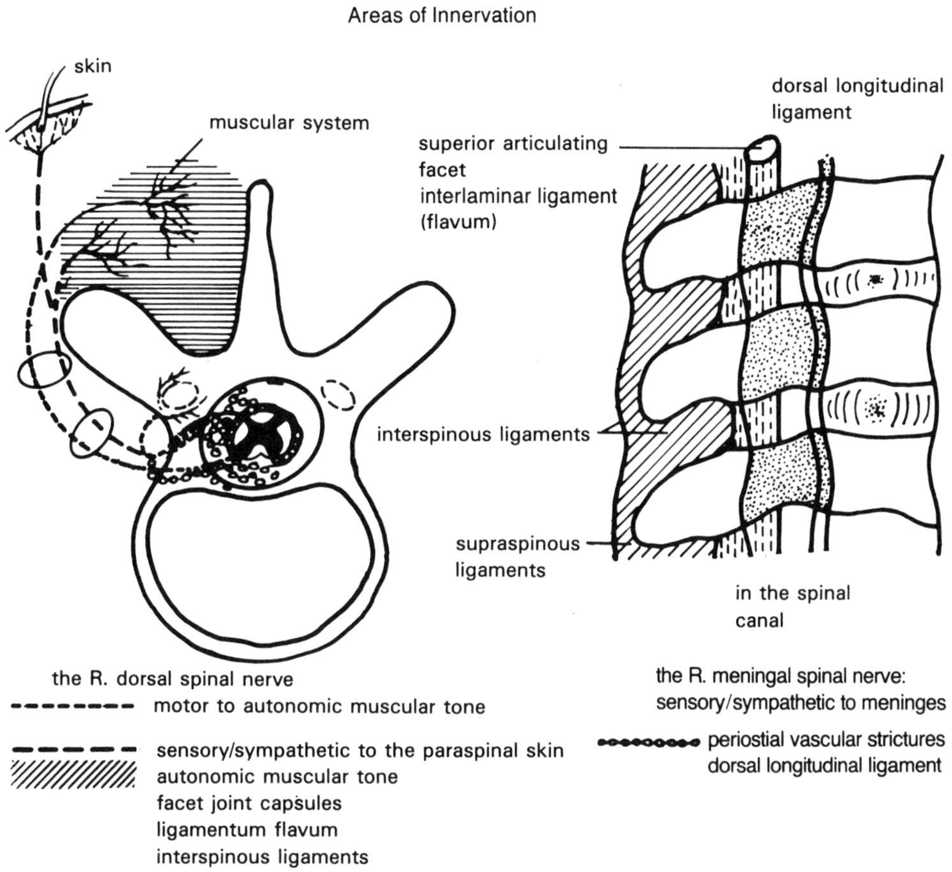

Areas of Innervation

Figure 9 Neurological supply of the motor segment (Delank)

areas of the brain stem and have an active effect in the midbrain and hypothalamus. In this region, these infused afferents can interfere with vital regulatory actions, such as blood pressure, respiration, digestion, and the vomiting center. In this way, the afferents influence the corresponding physical reactions through pathological summation. Moreover, these afferents are carried from the upper cervical joints directly into the vestibular nuclei and the reticular formation. Contacts to the abducens motor neurons could then be possible. Therefore, not only could dysfunction in the upper cervical joint region effect pain reactions, but also far-reaching dysregulations of individual motor stereotypical and vegetative events. These irritations become especially relevant in a clinical sense because these joints constitute a peripheral equilibrium organ that influences balance, along with abducent signals and information coming from the labyrinth. Vertigo and imbalance, in different degrees, often occur even in young people and can be an expression of a relationship and coordination malfunction of the upper cervical joints. In these cases, a targeted manipulative attack can, through elimination of fixations, effect an otherwise unobtainable improvement in health.

> Malfunctions of the joints express themselves as
> 1. minus variants = fixations
> 2. plus variants = hypermobility

The use of the term *fixation* can be regarded as a signal for the use of chiropractic therapy. It must be mentioned, however, that not all malfunctions of the joint gliding mechanism can be characterized as fixations. Equally pathogenic is the emergence of segmental hypermobility. A variance from the normal joint function in a positive direction indicates such hypermobility. If joint function is lessened, there is segmental hypomobility, or fixation. This dual possibility for malfunction is of elementary clinical significance: therapeutic approaches to these two conditions are diametrically opposed. The treatment of hypermobile components with manual mobilizations or manipulations could reinforce the hypermobility and negatively influence the condition. A circumstance that makes initial diagnosis difficult for the practitioner is that the clinical pictures of hypermobility and fixation are similar. Table 1 offers help in finding a single, decisive, differentiating point.

> Only chiropractic diagnosis offers the possibility of distinguishing fixations from hypermobility.

In contrast to hypermobility, where there is a constant exceeding of normal joint mobility (increased joint play), a condition of *instability* exists only when a pathological increase of joint mobility can be tied to degenerative changes.

To test the limit of motion in a joint requires first a characterization of normal function. Normal function is present when both the voluntary and nonvoluntary motion range is completely available. The presence or absence of the nonvoluntary portion is of greatest significance to diagnosis. The necessary testing supports itself on the evidence of:

Table 1 Clinical Findings in Segmental Motion Dysfunction

	Fixation	*Hypermobility*
Pain	pseudoradicular	pseudoradicular
Musculature	spasmed	spasmed
Connective tissue	swollen	swollen
Regional motion	inconclusive	inconclusive
Intersegmental motion	**restricted**	**increased**
Pressure sensitivity	distinct	distinct

• springy—elastic end-feel

which, when expressed, states that when maximum motion of the joint has been achieved, passive overpressure does not stop with a hard impact.

Another criterion for a functionally integrated joint is the presence of intact

• free joint play

which allows itself to be demonstrated by a passive, translational gliding motion (parallel sliding of the joint surfaces).

Finally, a moderate pulling of the joint and obtainable

• tractional movement

through separation and opening between the joint surfaces should be demonstrable.

If joint function is hindered in any one of these three points, a fixation is present. A fixation can be compared with a jammed sliding drawer, in that the free gliding motion is interrupted (Mennell).

When test results exceed the normal amount of expected motion in any one of these criteria, one is justified in assuming an instability of the joint, especially when degenerative changes are present.

Both types of joint dysfunction have in common an alteration of the normal (typical for each joint) afferent pattern of neurological signals. The additional influx of atypical (and thus mostly pathogenic) afferent signals into the dorsal horn complex begins the development of pathomechanics, which can move from subclinical latency to a manifest syndrome. It is not uncommon to find, especially in the spine, both types of lesions adjacent to each other. That is, because of functional linkage, fixations are often bordered by hypermobility and vice versa.

The most problematic irritations and pain syndromes emerge from instability rather than fixation.

> Fixations and instabilities both result from the pathogenic multicausal etiologies emanating from vertebral dysfunction.

In questioning the cause of these joint malfunctions, we can answer only in the sense of the summation of single factors and the knowledge that segmental facilitation of arthromuscular regulatory loops must surely cause an emergence of symptoms. Many factors—static, dynamic, and mechanical—are involved in acute or chronic overloading activities (such as atypical anatomy and work or sports damages). However, other factors also contribute: viscerovertebral segmental sensitization; inflammatory, focal, and metabolic predisposing mechanisms; and psychosomatic factors. In other words, combinations of any of these factors also influence the course of any condition.

In the pathogenesis of pain syndromes of the motion apparatus, multi-causality must be integrated into the planning and performance of diagnostic and therapeutic measures. Failure to observe these connections—that is, to use every mechanistically oriented diagnostic method for such malfunctions—leads invariably to failed therapies, with short-term results at best, and relapses at worst. Here lies a central point to the widely circulated charge that chiropractic therapy is only effective in the short term, and that one "must always return to the chiropractor."

4.3 POTENTIAL FOR MUSCULAR DYSFUNCTION

> The muscular system and joint make up an inseparable functional unit.

Previous chapters elaborated on the eminent regulatory role of arthro-muscular feedback loops. Their irritation is definitely a cardinal factor of those mechanisms, which can lead to painful malfunctions of the spinal column or peripheral joints.

The placement of the muscular system has been too narrowly valued until recently. The current change in trends has allowed the pendulum to swing in the opposite direction, which, of course, has also caused a corresponding change in therapeutic emphasis. An ideological and practical orientation to a "happy medium" would probably be a better goal.

Quantitatively, the muscular system is the largest system in the body; functionally, it is the origin of most sensory afferents and the main effector of all sensorimotor conditions. The muscular system is the binding link, so to speak, between the periphery and cortical, as well as subcortical centers. At the same time, it acts as a necessary guiding element of the body. Considering the muscular system as the guiding organ of static and dynamic motor function, it must be recognized that its essential regulatory component, which passes through the gamma system, is composed of two main elements: (1) the peripheral segmental control (using the gamma loop) and (2) the central guiding system, which emits from the reticular formation and limbic system.

The two controls actually are inseparably coupled through feedback systems and are described separately here only for didactic reasons. The peripheral mechanism serves especially well as an example of a regulatory loop. The central element of this system is the muscle spindle, which serves as the "feeler" by using its integrated sensor, the annulospiral receptor. The spindles, which run parallel to the course of the muscular fibers, register, analogous to their degree of stretch, changes in length of the muscle. Then the spindles send this report, via the dorsal horn, directly to the large alpha motor neurons of the ventral horn, from which the answer returns as a contraction command to the muscle. The muscle assimilates itself through shortening, and thus the muscular spindle is again quieted.

This simple regulatory loop is secured through superimposed tendon receptors, the so-called golgi tendon bodies. These do not step into action until the lengthening of the muscular system has increased overwhelmingly. Their irritation threshold lies far above that of muscle spindles; and their afferents inhibit the alpha motor neurons and lead to a protective relaxation of tension.

Muscle spindles are stretch receptors, and golgi tendon bodies function as tension receptors.

If our muscular system were equipped only with these simple regulators, the same irritation threshold would always be maintained in the muscles and the same tension held. That such a simple regulation does not suffice is evident if one considers the different "settings" necessary for rest, sleep, or high exertional levels.

To achieve a corresponding adaptation, the muscular spindles are themselves changeable in their sensitivity. This change is accomplished through central switching of the annulospiral receptor, which is stretched between two muscle bundles and renders the spindles more or less sensitive to stretch, according to the need. These muscle bundles are known as intrafusal fibers, and their control occurs via afferents of gamma motor neurons in the ventral sector. The common effect of spindle afferents and dictates of tension over the gamma loop adapts the skeletal muscular system to changing conditions and secures economy of function (Figure 10).

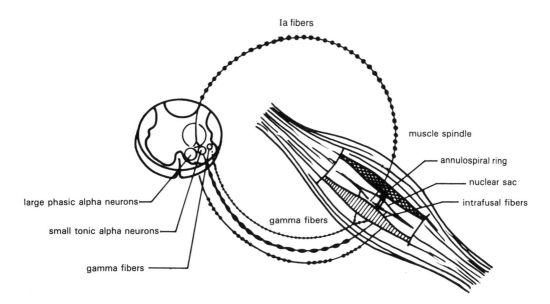

Figure 10 The servomechanism of the gamma loop adapts the sensitivity of the muscle spindle to the prevailing conditions, via the annulospiral receptor and the intrafusal fibers.

> The sensitivity of the muscle spindles is governed by the annulospiral receptor and the gamma loop.

The previously mentioned tension dictated by the gamma loop leaves open the question of location of the exit point of switching information. The answer lies in the central regulatory mechanisms. The switch information emanating from here is not responsible for the presensitization of the aforementioned servomechanism, but rather unites what is known in neurophysiological terms as support and target motorics into an inseparable unit. As the name implies, the support motoric has the task of preparing the basic static situation for the expected dynamic one (target motoric). The responsible centers lie in the reticular formation and over the lateral vestibular nuclei and red nucleus. The combination of the support and target motorics over efferents of the aforementioned centers is achieved through *alpha-gamma coupling,* which means that the influence of both the alpha and gamma neurons occurs through these impulses. Central switching of the gamma system through the reticular formation and limbic system is also made possible by connections between motivating-affective reactions and the tonus situation of the muscles. This gives a path for psychosomatic influence of the motor apparatus.

> Derailments of gamma regulation are the central point of vertebrogenic syndrome construction.

Malfunctional influences not only affect the tonal regulation, but are strengthened because of another characteristic of the muscular system. The classification of muscles, according to histological qualities, into smooth and striated, satisfies a simple illustration of anatomic relationships, but is insufficient for functional explanations.

> The skeletal musculature must be functionally subdivided into
> 1. prevailing tonically reacting muscles
> 2. prevailing phasically reacting muscles

Neurophysiological examinations have shown the need for a further subdivision of the skeletal muscular system and indicate an almost completely divergent relationship of muscles or muscle portions. This relationship correlates well with the ideas of the support and target motorics. This is readily seen in the terminology insofar as muscle parts are arranged according to the task involved, as tonic, postural muscles (which correlate to support) or phasic muscles. The respective response characteristics such as activation speed or irritation threshold already differ by definition, but in some cases are even diametrically opposed.

Tonic, postural muscles tire relatively slowly, are activated easily, and incline toward shortening. They exhibit a lower discharge frequency and a slower transmission speed. The phasic muscular system tires quickly, is slow to activate, and leans toward weakening. Transmission speed and discharge frequency are higher (see Table 2).

Further difficulty in the clear explanation of muscular functions arises because there are no isolated single muscular actions; muscle activity occurs in the form of chain reactions. The originally subcortically governed primitive motions evident in childhood are transformed in the course of development into cortically controlled and anchored motion patterns. Almost reflexively, all constantly repeated movements of daily living are carried out in individually typical, varied form. This preprogramming is vulnerable to inactivity or disruptive influences. All too often, healthy motoric stereotypes can change into malfunctioning stereotypes. One need only think of the numerous loads and overloads, resulting from work, sports, or leisure activities. Continuous and damaging irritative conditions (such as the chronic overexertions previously mentioned) primarily affect the tonic muscular systems, which can carry the most stress. The susceptible phasic muscles, which frequently are functionally antagonistic to tonic muscle groups, experience a corresponding targeted inactivation, according to Sherrington's law. This law states that the antagonist of an irritated (activated) muscle group will experience a relative "relaxation." In normal cases, this principle provides for economy in function. In cases of malfunction, however, the tension build-up in the tonic muscle, which can go into hard spasm, may elicit a weakening of the antagonistically oriented

Table 2 Characteristics of Phasic and Tonic Muscles. Introduction of the Most Important Muscle Groups

Postural Musculature: Tires slowly, is activated easily, inclines toward shortening	*Phasic musculature: Tires quickly, is slow to be activated, inclines toward weakening*
triceps surae	tibialis anterior
rectus femoris	vastus lateralis
tensor fasciae latae	vastus medialis
sartorius	
biceps femoris	gluteus maximus
semitendinosus	
semimembranosus	
short abductors of the upper thigh	long abductors of the upper thigh
	gluteus medius
iliopsoas	
piriformis	
back extensors	straight and oblique abdominal muscles
quadratus lumborum	
pectoralis major (sternal portion)	rhomboideus
	serratus anterior
upper trapezius portion	middle and lower trapezius portions
levator scapulae	scaleni
flexors of the hand	intrinsic hand and foot muscles

phasic muscles. The resulting increase in muscular imbalance is not only a necessarily pathogenic factor in conditions of the motor apparatus, but also, as a consequence, often results in a particularly resistant problem in therapy. To summarize, the following is an outline of the possible pathogenic potential of the muscular system:

- Any incidence of irritation that is greater than the irritational threshold leads to an increase in tension in the affected segmental musculature and to a higher sensitivity to additional irritations. In long-lasting irritation, it can lead to the formation of a hard spasm.
- Muscle actions occur in the form of chain reactions. Pathological occurrences affect the entire chain. Functional antagonists atrophy, and gamma innervations become derailed.
- The ensuing muscular imbalances disturb the joint apparatus.
- The effects on arthromuscular feedback loops are manifested by regulatory catastrophes.
- Syndrome development escalates. (See Figure 11.)

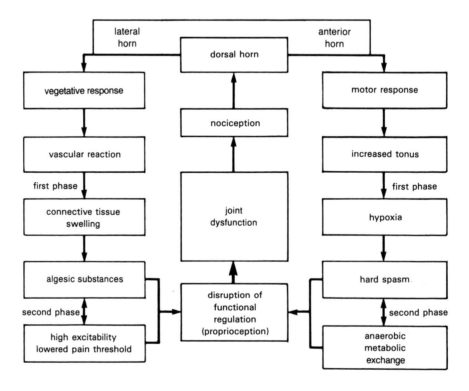

Figure 11 This block diagram indicates motor and vegetative nocireactions seen in joint dysfunction, including the closely associated progressive disruption of functional regulation (proprioception)

4.4 POTENTIAL FOR LIGAMENTOUS DYSFUNCTION

> The ligamentous apparatus of humans is vengeful. It avenges itself for hardship through chronic pain.

Until recently, ligamentous structures, especially those of the spinal column, were more or less neglected. Only in cases of fractures in the extremities was a certain role for torn ligaments in causing pain recognized. With increasing knowledge of the meaning of muscular disturbances and their attendant myotendinopathies, the ligamentous apparatus also has become the focus of clinical interest, mainly because of its similar receptor armament. Above all, the insertions of the ligaments contain a wealth of neural elements, which merely provide a later irritative response than musculotendinous receptors. They therefore usually begin to fire when the muscular system has become fatigued because of continuous overload (i.e., when static holding functions are being carried by ligaments alone).

In general, the ligamentous apparatus is quite resistant to tensile and compressive forces because of its inclusion of elastic fibers, especially in cases where these forces alternate repeatedly. Subjection to sustained forces or acute overload, however, can lead to damage and loosening of the ligamentous structures, especially when corresponding predisposition exists (e.g., constitutional variants, hypermobility, weakening of connective tissue, and CNS disturbances). Long periods of treatment and protection allow the tissue to regenerate in significant percentages, but an increased susceptibility to any new overloads remains.

When such instances are repeated, the results are tearing, scar formation, and lasting ligamentous laxity. If elasticity is lost, the function of the tissues is so far curtailed that even such daily activities as standing, sitting, and bending can elicit pain on short order. In particular areas of weakened or untrained muscles, where the work of providing needed support falls completely on the ligaments, these are susceptible to injury. This imbalance can be called a disturbance of musculoligamentous teamwork; in this respect, one should remember the previously mentioned derailment of the muscular balance between postural and phasic muscle groups, a circumstance that serves to support such developments. Knowledge of the circumstances required for ligamentous breakdown is of paramount importance in chiropractic approaches. Pain syndromes that have developed in this direction must be carefully differentiated from arthrogenic, fixation conditions with similar symptoms.

> The lumbosacral region and upper cervical joints have a predilection for conditions of instability and their disruptions.

The spinal column presents two problem regions: the lumbosacral region and the upper cervical joints. Disturbance of the discoligamentous pressure presents the most significant problem in the lumbar spinal regions (whereby the primary noxious stimulus is most often within the intervertebral disc). The transverse ligament of the atlas and cruciate ligament form the corresponding weak spot in the upper cervicals. This ligamentous combination serves as the dorsal base for rotation for the dens and is most often overloaded when the cervical vertebrae are flexed. The overloading forces can increase when flexion or extension is hindered in the atlantooccipital joints, as seen in a raised atlas (basilar impression). Superior or inferior positioning of the atlas, often due to trauma, can also have this effect. Tissue damage of this region may also develop as a consequence of inflammatory arthritides.

The clinical picture of ligamentous pain is distinguished through specific characteristics, shown in the listing that follows. It should also be noted that females seem to have a somewhat higher predisposition, as do people of middle age, when obesity is more significant as a burdening factor, but also when those active in sports often suddenly end their athletic ambitions and degeneration of the protective muscular system begins. Ligamentous pain is characterized by the following:

- Historical data:
  - Gradual increase in pain, then a chronic pain continuum, often lasting years
  - Morning pain increase with a need for "warming up"
  - Pain with long periods of standing, sitting, or a flexed position (office, cocktail parties, car, domestic work, gardening)
  - Premature fatigue
- Clinical signs:
  - Pressure sensitivity of the ligamentous insertions during pain palpation
  - Pseudoradicular pain distribution
  - No neurological losses
  - Regional, hard muscular spasm
  - Pain provocation with sustained stretches of the elements (differential diagnosis: muscular insertions)

4.5 CONNECTIVE TISSUE DYSFUNCTION

> Pathological changes in connective tissue must not only be considered diagnostically, but also in a direct therapeutic sense.

Although the structural and functional partners of the arthrons (i.e., vertebrons) have roles that are readily recognizable and easily accepted in disruptions of the motor apparatus, the role of the connective tissues does not appear to be as clear. Some have noted a constitutional, characteristic "weakening of connective tissue" as a concomitant element in certain spinal complaints, but have characterized this factor as being insusceptible to change, and have left it at that. The following details will show that this explanation is too superficial.

From a thematically relevant standpoint, not only must the mechanical aspects of fibrous connective tissue structure be noted (i.e., ligaments) in cases of connective tissue weakness, but also the "soft" connective tissue. This key material, which links the entire human organism, consists of a gel-like liquid matrix with embedded cellular elements, capillaries, and lymphatic vessels, as well as free-ending nerve fibers. From a regulatory standpoint, this tissue can be interpreted as an active, metabolite-exchanging colloidal medium. Cells and matrix are in a balanced, dependent relationship, whose constant maintenance is seen as a dominating, biologically basic regulatory system.

Disturbances of this system in sustained irritations can affect the entire organism, given the ubiquity of the substances involved. The response to irritation, therefore, occurs independently of the irritational source in a predetermined series of reactions. This unspecific so-called mesenchymal reaction is thus also effected by mechanical irritation. In fact, the following noxious stimuli all cause an identical mesenchymal reaction:

• mechanical irritations (traumas)
• bacterial infections
• allergic reactions
• hypoxia
• overexertion
• weather influences

The main components of the unspecific mesenchymal reaction lie in changes of the colloid composition, which is dependent on different physical and chemical influences, such as pH values, active membrane components, electrolytes, bioelectrical circumstances, pain, and inflammatory chemical changes. All these changes help to determine the functional condition of the actual colloidal substance (based also, of course, on degree of blood perfusion). These reactions are clinically meaningful because they are not merely quiet background occurrences, but leave behind visible and palpable tracks, which must be considered noteworthy in the development of disease and in choice of therapeutic measures.

> The clinical significance of edemas of the connective tissue is often neglected.

In this connection, the previous discussion of the body's response to nociceptive irritations is relevant, as is the vegetative reaction with its segmentally bound manifestation in connective tissue. Simultaneously, there is a difference in reaction of connective tissue, depending on the disease condition. Acute disruptions in the reflex zones provoke edema of the connective tissue, which can be observed as a soft generalized swelling on gentle palpation. Chronic processes manifest themselves as dehydration and hardening of the connective tissue with a waxlike consistency on palpation. Analogous edema and dehydration hardening also occur in other connective tissues of the motor apparatus, such as ligaments, fascia, joint capsules, and tendons, and influence the function of these structures. If one supposes that an irritation is expressed, for example, as a joint fixation, doubtless the irritation is caused partly by changes of the connective tissue in the joint area and thus is accompanied by functional changes in the surrounding tissues. If the corresponding development goes undetected, it could lead, together with muscular pathomechanisms, to a therapeutically unresolveable, permanent fixation over time. Moreover, chronically changed connective tissue zones frequently provoke a secondary irritation, with a tendency toward autonomization.

From this vantage point, connective tissue changes take on a new meaning for chiropractic therapy. For diagnostic considerations, these changes are palpable indications of the segmental localization of disturbances. In a therapeutic sense, the changes must be carefully watched and treated; not only surface structures, but also deeper tissue layers, obviously can be affected by connective tissue changes or reflex stimulation.

In the practical realm of diagnosis and therapy, knowledge of the specific disruptive potential of various structures is implicitly necessary. Without knowledge of this potential or of the nosologically relevant syndromes, mastery of technical information remains pointless. Disrupted function is the main point of attack in manual therapy, and can be recognized and correctly evaluated only when the normal load-bearing capacity of the examined structures is known. Practical chiropractic therapy has the following concept as a basis:

We test normal function to find malfunction.

---

5. Diagnostic Strategy

Chiropractic diagnosis fills a gap in the clinical examination of the motor apparatus.

Diagnosis of diseases affecting the motor apparatus is a most appealing and rewarding aspect of medicine. Diagnosis makes possible the important contact between the doctor and patient. The spoken word, like touching, feeling, and recognition of disruptions, is accomplished without the use of today's more sophisticated diagnostic technology. Indeed, even though the framework of this diagnostic realm includes radiological and laboratory examinations, the value of this technology does not necessarily exceed that of more personal methods in achieving results. Technology is only used to determine aggravating, pathomorphological changes of an inflammatory, neoplastic, traumatic, or metabolic genesis with greater security.

It is not the intention of the authors to propose that chiropractic diagnostic methods are open only to the elite few. Just the opposite is true. The purpose of this text is to achieve further development of a common, basic knowledge that complements existing methods. In other words, chiropractic diagnosis must become a common and indispensable part of all clinical examinations of irritations in the motor apparatus. The word *indispensable* has been consciously chosen here to describe the significance of chiropractic diagnostic methods and show the necessity for their use. An example of this is the vitally important difference between joint function and hypermobility (with its respective instability), which can present with an almost identical clinical picture and can be differentiated only through chiropractic diagnostic methods. In the following section, patient history criteria and the examination of the motor apparatus are described.

5.1 EXAMINATION OF THE SKELETAL SYSTEM

The ideological assumption is that diagnosis is not an end in itself, but that it is a prerequisite for a well-directed and economic administration of therapy. This has led to the proposal that the process of diagnosis be further subdivided into three points of view, as follows:

• locational diagnosis
• structural diagnosis
• actual diagnosis

Locational diagnosis usually is largely explained by the history. Locational diagnosis determines location, type, and character of the problem and produces the information necessary to plan a logical course of examination—sacral dysfunction, cervical syndrome, shoulder/arm syndrome. Structural diagnosis attempts to designate the pathogenetic structures, such as joints, ligaments, or muscles, involved in the described complaint.

The actual diagnosis considers the total picture. The most significant manifestations are incorporated into the actual diagnosis. These include the pain pattern, restriction of movement, loss of strength, sensory disorders, and accompanying autonomic phenomena, as well as the psychological state. The occurrence of pain, however, assumes priority in the assessment. The conversion of this three-part diagnostic framework into practical procedures is accomplished through the following:

• Taking the history
• Examining the body by means of inspection, palpation, mobility testing, and neurological methods
• Ordering auxiliary tests, such as radiographic and laboratory examinations

In most cases, the first locational diagnosis presents a wealth of differential diagnostic possibilities. A further task is to filter out critical information that allows a systematic reduction of the differential diagnostic data into diagnostic probability.

For example, a patient complains of suddenly emerging lumbar pain with radiation into the leg after physical exertion. A resultant diagnosis of "lumbalgia," however, does not reveal which irritated structure is responsible for the pain. Discogenic radicular pain, pseudoradicular pain through iliosacral lesions, and pain in the hip joint could all be components of this locational diagnosis. Pain emitting laterally into the leg and reaching as far as the big toe, which can be intensified by sneezing and coughing, provides further necessary critical information. Therefore, a "lead" symptom has been elucidated, which points to a disc prolapse. To substantiate the probable discogenic origin, further confirmation must be sought.

In addition, typical radicular manifestations (sensory deficits, reflex affirmation, and paresis), shown by physical examination, serve as other "leading" symptoms. Radiography and laboratory diagnostic criteria must be included in the diagnostic program to eliminate grave pathomorphological tumors or metastasis. The following caution should be noted:

| A "lead" symptom alone is not enough for a definite diagnosis. |

Critical information is thus defined as specific results of the physical examination that lead to a given direction of the diagnostic thought processes, that provide for further discovery of other leading symptoms, and that allow a final diagnosis through the use of such available facts, as well as the pain classification.

The following presents another example:

Shoulder pain	= locational diagnosis
Critical information—painful arc	= insertion tendinopathy
Pain palpation and test provocations	= structural diagnosis
Therapeutic local anesthesia (e.g., ice)	= therapeutic trial
Alleviation of the ailment (e.g., ice, transverse friction)	= confirmation of diagnosis

Though there has been a predominance of disturbed function as pain etiology, it is always necessary to rule out a *destroyed* function as the cause. Although destroyed function carries definite accompanying pathomorphological changes (radiographs and laboratory findings are helpful here), one often enters a hypothetical realm when the diagnosis of a purely functional disturbance is reached. The final acceptance of the diagnosis frequently must wait for the results of a so-called therapeutic trial.

Arriving at an absolute structural diagnosis has a certain amount of academic worth, but the primary practical goal must be to differentiate altered from destroyed functions. This process is crucial for the patient because it helps immediately to establish prognosis and shows whether full rehabilitation is possible or whether symptomatic therapy should be the primary approach. An exact structural diagnosis may be quite difficult to reach in an acute condition with its full complement of possibilities; in these cases, accurate diagnosis may be possible only after control of the acute symptomatology.

5.2 PATIENT HISTORY

| The patient's history provides the first critical facts. |

The practical elements of history taking are presented here—but only those points that have special significance for diseases of the motor apparatus. Again, the symptoms of pain are the center of interest: the duration of the complaint; the method of its emergence; and whether it is continuous, intermittent, a first-time occurrence, or residual. Of course, one must also consider intensity (acute or chronic), daily fluctuations, radiation ten-

dencies, and exacerbating factors (e.g., rest, motion, exertion). Chronic af-
flictions of the spinal column, for example, show such a characteristic clinical picture that vertebral genesis may often be discerned from the history.
The following items point in this direction:

- chronic, intermittent course
- paroxysmal presentation of pain
- changing multifocal manifestations
- dependence on static and dynamic factors
- frequently unilateral complaints
- exacerbation through triggering situations (e.g., overexertion, infections, and weather)

After the historical clarification of the pain, further clarification of the
clinical picture is still necessary. Questioning the patient can rule out the
previously mentioned multicausal possibilities of most pain syndromes of
the motor apparatus. Noxious effects of the work environment, leisure activity, and sport/athletic endeavor are as important as chronic inflammatory processes (focal stresses) or psychosomatic tendencies (depressive
clinical pictures).

The history should clarify the following key factors:

- Types of work stress:
  Sitting, standing, lifting, carrying, bending, monotony, assembly line
  work, typewriter or computer, resulting summary of all stress types
- Types of stress resulting from leisure activity:
  Handicrafts (knitting, sewing), garden work, snow shoveling, other
  damage caused by sitting (inactivity, watching TV)
- Sports stresses:
  Sprint or endurance sports, intensity of training or competition (differentiation of valuation of such activity should correspond to the presenting complaints)
- General stresses:
  Eating and drinking habits, bed design, clothing (tight jeans, height of
  the shoe's instep), medications (sleeping potions, nonindicated pyscho-
  pharmaceuticals, pain medications, birth control pills), sensitivity to
  the weather (overheating or chilling)

In most cases, a total stress package results from this type of questioning. The patient will emphasize those noxious stimuli immediately associated with the onset of pain. These factors, however, usually represent the
initiators of pain, which is an ultimate expression of a previously stressed
motor apparatus. Pain only signifies the final decompensation of a system
stretched to the limits.

It is not enough to depend on information that is based on the patient's
explanation, such as: "I have pulled a muscle in my back by lifting a bag,"
or "My knee gave way when I was walking down the hill." Such minor

events are usually the straw that broke the camel's back. The historical synthesis of encountered stresses (which depend on concepts discussed later in this text) cannot be overemphasized. Without observation of such details, even technically sound and perfectly executed chiropractic therapy may founder.

In summary, the introductory history not only is necessary for the immediate construction of a diagnostic and therapeutic plan, but also provides a point of reference for advice to a patient on necessary rehabilitation.

5.2.1 Physical Examination

A prerequisite for all other examinations is for the patient to disrobe down to the undergarments. Only then can the inspection procedure be thorough enough to get needed information.

5.2.1.1 Inspection

> Inspection means to observe, note, compare, and recognize anomalies.

The patient must be judged as a whole—how he or she walks, stands, sits, and rises; general health characteristics; and body proportion. Muscular and subcutaneous fat distribution, congenital or acquired deformities and defects—anything that is different from the normal—should be noted. A look into the mouth also belongs to the general inspection, to evaluate this most common location of focal infection (teeth, tonsils). In the process of gaining an overview of the patient's total appearance and health, the inspection is essential to all further examinations of the body, including the analysis of motion in the individual regions.

5.2.1.2 Palpation

> Palpation is touching, feeling, and exerting tactile pressure. It involves comparing, questioning, and, above all, understanding results.

Palpation is the reliable support of chiropractic diagnosis; in cases of doubt, palpation can always provide deciding factors. First, soft tissue changes, especially in deep structures, are often not visually apparent. Second, motion analysis has certain anatomical limitations, especially in certain spinal regions (sacral, midthoracic joints), and thus must be augmented by other diagnostic means, such as palpation.

There is a difference between so-called tactile palpation and palpation of pain or tenderness. Tactile palpation primarily aids in structural diagnosis, whereas pain palpation helps determine the actual diagnosis. Palpation provides complex sensations both of a thermal and mechanical nature; through bilateral human contact, the informational yield is broadened, in that the sensation of the examiner, as well as that of the patient, contribute to the end result. The prerequisites for accurate palpation results are found on multiple levels. The basis of palpatory capability is, of course, anatomical knowledge. Only the knowledge of normal consistency, tactile resistance, and tension establishes the possibility of accurate evaluation. Though anatomical knowledge can be learned, the touching and feeling ability must be obtained by experiential training and practice. In an age of unimaginable technological reliability, palpatory findings are often discarded too easily because of unreliability, subjectivity, and lack of reproduceable results. Centuries of medical history, however, teach us that a quintessential element of medical knowledge rests primarily on practice and experience.

The knowledge of the normal condition, in every single case, must be based on individual pressure and pain thresholds.

The following is the core concept of palpation.

> Healthy tissue tolerates much pressure; unhealthy tissue often tolerates no pressure.

To determine the border between pressure and pain sensation, the examiner must also talk with the patient, especially while performing comparable palpation on similar sites (e.g., bilateral comparisons). To obtain technical expertise in palpation, one should follow certain guidelines.

Correct palpation orients itself first to the surface layers (to detect turgor and shifting of skin and subcutaneous regions); then carefully penetrates deeper to determine the tonus of musculature (brisk progress often leads to artificial reflexive spasm); and finally evaluates, in sequence, joints, ligaments, periosteal attachments and tendinous insertions.

> Generally, during palpation, movable elements should be explored with stationary fingers, and resting elements should be explored with the motion of fingers.

What one is able to recognize during palpation can be summarized as follows.

In the skin and subcutaneous regions, evidence of turgid consistency, as well as tissue mobility and sensation of pain and tenderness, can be found. Palpation of the skin can also yield information regarding reflexes, which can point to organic involvement at a primary level. Palpation of the muscular system allows one insights into the general tonus and enables one to recognize spasm of entire muscles or isolated muscle sections, as well as active and latent trigger points; thereby, one gains valuable information in the evaluation of pseudoradicular pain. The deep structures, such as joints, ligaments, periosteal attachments, and the diverse tendinous insertions, yield information based on their sensitivity to pressure and pain during palpation.

Following a well-executed patient history, palpation provides the first direct physical contact with the patient. The trust established during palpation can be vital to establishing rapport between the patient and the doctor. Brusque, groping palpation can utterly destroy any rapport. Sensitive and confident palpation, on the other hand, conveys to the patient the sure knowledge that the examiner is not only "feeling" but "understanding."

5.2.1.3 Motion Analysis

In chiropractic diagnosis, history and palpation differ only slightly from standard medical procedures and can therefore be carried out in a uniform fashion. With the initiation of motion analysis, however, one encounters new diagnostic territory—in particular, where intersegmental mobility is concerned. In motion analysis, the practitioner gleans information that broadens the application of traditional clinical orthopedic diagnostic procedures. Consequently, the examination of motion is organized into multiple steps:

> • Test of general ranges of motion
> • Test of regional mobility and motion
> • Test of intersegmental motion relationships

Some of the perspectives of general motion were previously mentioned under the heading of "Inspection." The most important impression to be gleaned from motion analysis is whether the general motion of the patient corresponds to age-related norms or is indicative of a hypomobile or hypermobile state.

Of course, these perspectives also have validity in the testing of regional mobility. Moreover, motion analysis can be complemented by further subdivision of the examination into passive, active, and resistive motion components.

In testing active motion, the patient is asked to move the particular joint or spinal region to be tested about all axes possible for that joint or area. For regional examination of the spinal column, in particular, four methods of movement must be examined.

> • Anterior flexion (forward bending)
> • Retroflexion (backward bending)
> • Lateral flexion (side bending)
> • Rotation (turning)

Analysis of these motions is also necessary for passive motion assessment, which consists of passive movement carried out by the examiner. The range in degrees of the movement will be evaluated; and in lateral flexion and rotation, bilateral comparison will be made. The examiner, of course, will assess the resultant emergence of pain.

Through passive motion testing, the "end-feel" of the motion must be considered and determined; especially whether the end-feel of movement softly fades away or is abruptly stopped.

During resistance testing, the patient must try to establish an isometric level of resistance against all the motions that were previously tested passively and actively. Resistance testing of the individual muscles gives additional information concerning reproduction of pain. It must be completed by a thorough analysis of any muscular restriction or contracture.

What does motion analysis establish? Three individual test objectives are presented here as reference points.

First, active motion testing not only deals with the structures of the arthrons or vertebrons, but also includes neurological and psychological input.

Second, during passive movement testing, both motor and psychological components can be largely eliminated.

Third, resistance testing evaluates the muscle-tendon apparatus for strength and pain reproduction, while eliminating joint motion.

Conclusions can be derived as follows. If active and passive motions are normal and without pain and restriction, a disruption in the local region is highly unlikely. Hypomobilities or hypermobilities, especially with pain, necessitate further examination in terms of the testing of end-feel and translational gliding motion and tractional mobility. These must also be examined further in the context of intersegmental motion, which is described in more detail in later chapters. Further conclusions are then reached through corroborating or divergent results of local regional examinations. If the painful restriction is oriented in the same direction on active and passive examination, arthrogenic origin of the pain is likely. Conversely, directional divergences between active and passive testing indicate a myogenic disruption.

Resistance testing shows, in the normal case, an ability to perform powerful and painless active motion. Pathological results are interpreted on an incremental basis. For example, if pain emerges on application of considerable force, one can assume a severe but exclusively myogenic lesion. The production of pain when only a minimal force is applied can only indicate a more widely dispersed pathology of muscles. A neurological lesion may be suspected when the test reveals a loss of strength without pain.

5.2.2.4 Muscle Tests

In addition to the general resistance tests to be performed in the course of regional examinations, one also must explore the function of the individual muscles in more detail.

It is necessary here to pay attention to

- tonus; that is, muscle shortening or restriction due to repetitive contraction
- weakness of individual muscles or entire muscle groups
- imbalances, especially of antagonistic muscles

Detailed information pertaining to individual muscle tests is provided in the descriptions of the specific regional examinations. Vital to execution of muscle tests, however, is a knowledge of a grading system for muscle strength. In general, such measurements are divided into six categories (Oxford system), as follows:

Grade 5: Full motion is possible against gravity with strong resistance.

Grade 4: Motion can occur against slight resistance.

Grade 3: Motion only overcomes gravity.

Grade 2: Motion is possible only when the effect of gravity is eliminated (e.g., floating in a whirlpool).

Grade 1: Only light contraction of the muscle occurs, without joint motion.

Grade 0: No muscular activity is evident.

From the standpoint of chiropractic diagnosis, weaknesses from grades 3 to 5 are of the most interest. Weaknesses below grade 3 often point to pathology of a purely neurological nature.

The diagnostic value of muscle tests provides a cornerstone of the examination process; the failure to note muscular defects is often responsible for potential worsening of a given condition.

5.3 RADIOGRAPHIC EVALUATION OF THE SPINAL COLUMN— SPECIAL POSTURAL TECHNIQUES

To aid in the interpretation of static radiographic findings, techniques have been developed specifically for the chiropractic diagnostic evaluation. For the lumbopelvic region and the cervical vertebrae, the following techniques have been used.

The routinely practiced sectional series used for pathologic diagnosis may occasionally have some limitations when it comes to interpreting postural considerations in the lumbopelvic region. For example, the standard 7- × 17-inch format used for anteroposterior (AP) lumbar projections obscures the sacroiliac joints, hip joints, pubic symphysis, and iliac crests, which can yield important postural information. To provide better visualization in toto of these structures, a 14- × 17-inch format is recommended (vertically oriented, unless the patient is significantly overweight). The normal lateral lumbar format does not require modification.

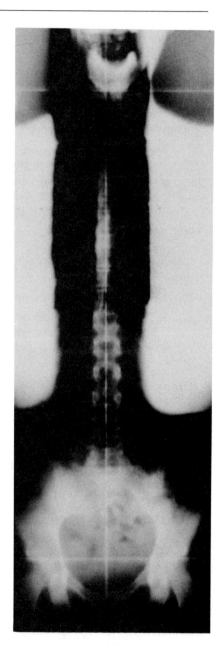

Figure 12 Full-spine radiograph (spinal column with the pelvis and cranium—anterioposterior projection)

U.S. Editor's note: It is highly recommended that the modern-day chiropractor use adequate filtration and collimation techniques during full-spine radiography to maximally reduce excess radiation exposure of the patient.

A further point for discussion: should radiographs be performed in the weight-bearing format or in the usual recumbent format? We see no need for weight-bearing formats, often preferred by purists of chiropractic therapy. Regarding weight-bearing formats as an option is surely the most rational approach, and the guide to their use should take into account the patient's situation, especially the injury mechanism. Whenever it is necessary to identify or rule out significant pathomorphological problems with great accuracy, the usual recumbent techniques must take precedence.

On the other hand, if a functional static postural analysis is advisable (e.g., to verify a genuine difference of length in the legs), a weight-bearing technique should be chosen. To obtain comparative and reproducible results, a full-spine radiographic projection should be taken (Figure 12). This projection, incidentally, requires a special apparatus (14 × 36 cassettes and corresponding bucky), or a combining (overlapping) of the standard lumbopelvic view with sectional thoracocervical views.

5.3.1 Radiographic Positioning for Postural Analysis of the Lumbopelvic Region

Because this radiographic technique is not generally known, it is described here.

For the AP projection, the patient stands exactly in the middle of the cassette. On the top surface of the film bucky holding the centered 14- × 17-inch cassette, a perpendicular gridline is attached to a plexiglass slide, which is centered behind the occiput (e.o.p.), while the bucky is in position behind the head. (See Figure 13a.) The aligned cassette is then brought back down behind the lumbar spine (without any lateral deviation of the body). The central ray is positioned at the umbilicus. Thus the final radiograph's film center will correspond to the actual sacral base center, and the gridline should correspond to the mid-occiput. (In normal posture, the two should correspond to each other.)

For the lateral projection, the patient stands with the ankle malleoli a finger's width behind a line bisecting the foot markings for the AP view (center of *bucky*). With the *bucky* in an elevated position, the sliding gridline is lined up with the external auditory meatus. When the cassette is lowered to the lumbar position (see Figure 13b), the central ray should be positioned at the lumbosacral junction. To prevent distortion, both this and the AP projection should be taken at a film focal distance of at least 72 inches.

5.3.2 Radiographic Positioning for Postural Analysis of the Cervical Region

In the cervical region, there are some peculiarities, as follows.

Although there are relatively few differences in the lateral projections from standard practices, it is better for the AP projection to use a slightly different technique because conventional techniques sometimes neglect the upper cervical area.

A morphologically, as well as functionally, useful depiction of the cervical vertebrae, inclusive of the upper cervical area, is afforded by the use of the Sandberg-Gutmann radiographic technique (Figures 14 and 15).

For AP radiographs, the patient should lie on the middle of the X-ray table (the anal fold directly at the mid-line). By having the patient sit up and lie down several times, a natural position of the spinal column is se-

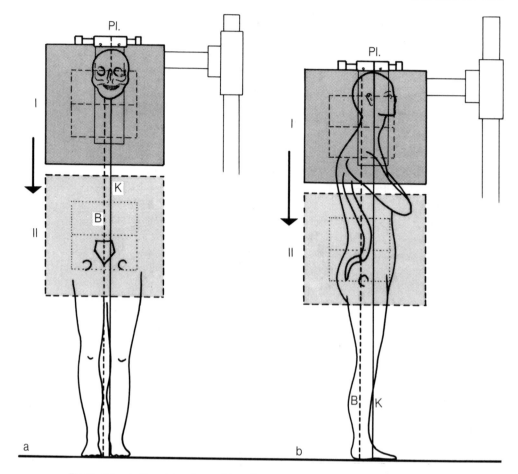

Figure 13 a, b Special radiographic technique for the depiction of the postural relationship, on the sectional views of the lumbopelvic region.

a) B = Sacral Base: Drawn between the center of the support surface between the feet, and corresponding to the middle of the cassette. K = Cephalic perpendicular: Perpendicular placed even with the middle of the occipital region while the cassette is in position. Pl. = movable plexiglass plate, mounted on the upper edge of the bucky with the sunken lead gridline visually focused on the center of the occiput. The bucky will then be lowered from position 1 to position 2.

b) The same procedure is to be used in lateral projection. The cephalic perpendicular will be lined up with the external auditory meatus. The feet will be placed in such a way that the sacral base perpendicular is a good 1/2 inch in front of the middle of the lateral malleoli. The sacral base perpendicular corresponds to the middle of the cassette. The positioning of the head is always the same—looking forward with the maxillae horizontal.
Source: G. Gutmann, *Functional Pathology and Clinical Picture of the Spine,* Vol. I, Pt. 1, I.G. Fischer, 1981.

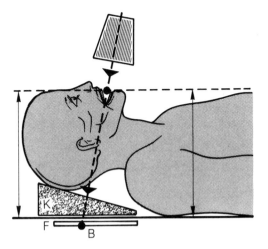

Figure 14 Alignment of the face and head for the anteroposterior (AP) open mouth radiograph of the cervical vertebrae. An imaginary line from the base of the nose to the open lips should be parallel to the film (F). B = Bucky   K = wedge pillow
Source: G. Gutmann, *Functional Pathology and Clinical Picture of the Spine,* Vol. I, Pt. 1, I.G. Fischer, 1981.

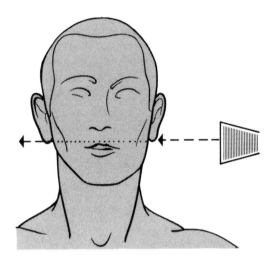

Figure 15 Lateral projection radiographs of the cervical vertebrae are best performed on the seated patient. The central ray is directed to the ear lobes. *Source:* G. Gutmann, *Functional Pathology and Clinical Picture of the Spine,* Vol. I, Pt. 1, I.G. Fischer, 1981.

cured. Finally, the patient should hold the mouth wide open (holding a cork between the teeth may be helpful) so that the forehead and upper lip are in a horizontal line. The central ray should be kept one finger width below the upper first molars and should line up with a point above the palpable occipital base (possible aids are the use of a wedge placed under the head and a plumbline attached to the x-ray tube.) The film focal distance should be exactly 40 inches. For the lateral radiograph, the patient should be in a seated position, with the head positioned horizontally. The patient should look straight ahead and not be allowed to incline to the side (the two mandibles must overlie each other in the radiograph). The central ray is directed onto the tip of the mastoid process; the tube should be at least 72 inches away, to avoid distortion.

These positioning techniques make it possible to posturally analyze the cervical vertebrae, including the upper cervical area. These techniques also promote reproducible comparisons. In some cases, additional conclusions can be made through the use of kinetic radiographs in flexion and extension.

A detailed depiction of nonpostural radiographs of the spinal column, including computerized tomography (CT), myelography, and magnetic resonance imaging (MRI) is available in standard texts.

Section II

6. Principles of Chiropractic Therapy

The structures of the motor apparatus are connected with pressure and tension stimuli in their functional behavior. Chiropractic therapy, therefore, acts as a mechanically oriented method of treatment that uses pressure and tension stimuli already known to the organism. Through the application of different techniques, chiropractic therapy can provide treatment of varying intensities for the given condition. To provide clarity for the understanding of manual therapy, it should be emphasized that such therapy should not be characterized as a mechanically corrective procedure for misaligned vertebrae, but rather that the mechanical impulses serve to resolve lesions that have a reflexive nature. Or, in other words—

> Chiropractic therapy = reflexive therapy

Here, once again, one finds justification for a discussion of the neurophysiological details of joint and muscle function. From hypothetical as well as partly experimentally proven viewpoints, the effects of chiropractic therapy can be explained as follows. The pathological efferent and afferent impulses surrounding functionally incapacitated structures of the motor system can be silenced through the use of manipulative intervention, so that normal impulse patterns may be renewed. The gamma system provides the main focal point through which manipulation can provide for relief of disrupted arthromuscular reflexes.

As previously mentioned, different dosages of intervention may be prescribed by using techniques of varying intensity. A hierarchy of techniques introduces principles of the available forms of manual therapy.

> • Soft-tissue techniques
> • Muscle-relaxation techniques
> • Mobilization
> • Manipulations

The intensity level increases with each methodology, as does the degree of potential efficiency. Other key concepts to remember are as follows.

Findings of the skin indicate therapy of the skin
Findings in the muscular system indicate therapy of the muscular system
Findings in the joint indicate therapy of the joint

6.1 SOFT-TISSUE TECHNIQUES

Soft-tissue techniques of chiropractic therapy resemble the known techniques of massage in many respects. One of the main functions of soft-tissue therapy is to prepare the irritated region for subsequent mobilizations or manipulations. The first step sometimes can be simple, regionally applied massage, which, through segmentally reflexive mediation, can achieve some measure of relaxation. Another possibility for soft-tissue manipulation is a perpendicular pressure of the finger or thumb on the muscle. This ischemic compressive procedure, which also provides neurological inhibition, calls for a one-minute compression of the muscle. The pressure is gradually increased during the first half of the compression, then decreased gradually during the second half.

Before mobilization or manipulation take place, muscle tonicity can also be eased with vibration. The vibration is applied perpendicular to the muscle fibers, with an impulse frequency of eight to ten sinusoidal vibrations per second. The fingertips may be used as a form of impulse mediation. The resulting tonal effect may not immediately be apparent; the average amount of time needed before results can be seen is two to five minutes. Vibration techniques are among the most difficult soft-tissue-treatment methods when applied manually, and they necessitate a high degree of sensitivity to tissue tone. These techniques are therefore very well suited as a training prerequisite for manual therapists.

Another classical soft-tissue technique of chiropractic therapy is a gentle stretching impulse applied to the surface layer of the skin, perpendicular to the course of the muscle fibers (without a gliding or rubbing motion of the therapist's hand).

6.2 MOBILIZATION

The term *mobilization* implies the passive movement of a restricted joint in the direction of restricted motion, through use of the nonvoluntary ranges of motion (joint play). The objective is to reestablish normal motion, at least as closely as possible. Perhaps the least "invasive" method of treatment is to begin within the realm of nonvoluntary motion by using techniques which reestablish long-axis traction and translational glide. One or both of these techniques will be possible in most areas, depending on anatomical considerations.

Beyond passive mobilization, the possibility of mobilizing the voluntary (active) ranges of a joint exists in almost every joint of the spinal column and the periphery. In addition to achieving a full range of motion, mobilization also attempts to regain a smooth and elastic end-feel. Depending upon the existing type of motion restriction, the following ranges of motion are induced: flexion or extension, rotation, lateral flexion, or combinations of all these. The main principle behind all mobilization techniques, including translational and tractioning techniques directed to both nonvoluntary and voluntary motion ranges, lies in fixing one joint partner while moving or establishing motion in the other. (See Figure 16.)

The fixed-joint partner in the thoracic and cervical spine often is the vertebra caudal to the segment being treated. Only in the lumbar spine (below L3/L4) is it the cephalad vertebra, because in this region the legs and pelvis often serve as mobilization levers. In extremities, the bone to fix in mobilization is most often the proximal joint partner.

For successful mobilization, mobilization impulses should start only at the point of motion restriction. It is senseless to apply impulses in the free, active joint-motion range (a common mistake often observed in the novice) and to expend strength and impulse energy that could be more efficiently and economically applied in treating the restricted area. Furthermore, special attention should be given to the tractional component of mobilization. Where anatomical relationships allow traction to accompany mobilization, traction should be used as an integral part of the treatment program. In many cases of pain-induced "failure" of a mobilization technique, that is, when angular or even translational force vectors produce increased pain, pure traction techniques may still be useful. This fact reinforces the concept that traction is one of the least invasive mobilization methods. Integral to its successful application is the use of gentle, rhythmic methodology and the avoidance of any pain provocation. Mobilization treatments should be

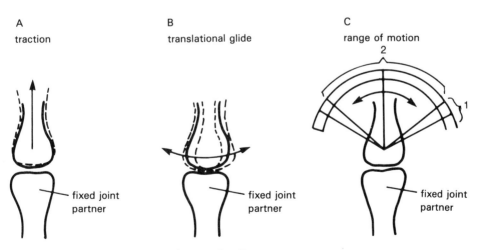

Figure 16 Diagram of joint play and range of motion

1. Nonvoluntary joint motion (joint play).
2. Voluntary motion. *Source:* H. Tilscher and M. Eder, *Textbook of Reflex Therapy.*

used until there is a noticeable improvement in joint mobility and a lessening of existing pain.

6.3 MUSCLE STRETCHING TECHNIQUES

Postisometric Relaxation (PIR)—Muscle Energy Techniques (MET)

In the past few years, these techniques, also known as "isometrics," have taken on increased significance. The focus of these techniques, of course, is the muscular system. In contrast to the methods of Kabat et al., where the muscle is heavily stretched following a maximal isometric contraction, PIR involves only a slight, gentle pressure of the muscle against resistance, followed by relaxation. Equally important, the muscle is only lightly stretched, with use of low force or gravity alone, to the point where restriction or pain is again felt. This process will be repeated using the newly achieved range of movement until the restriction of mobility is reduced, the spasm of the muscle is relieved, and the intensity of the pain can be alleviated. Isometrics can be facilitated through breathing techniques and optokinetic visualization during the treatment.

> Inhaling and holding one's breath, as well as looking in the direction of the resistance, can increase the strain; exhaling and looking in the direction of desired mobilization favors relaxation.

Many useful types of isometrics can be carried out by the patients themselves, after patient education; such isometrics are useful in bridging the intervals between patient visits.

The most commonly used techniques are best subdivided on the basis of their effecting mechanism:

1. Techniques with postisometric inhibition of the agonists:
   (a) Muscle energy techniques (MET), which use only facilitation and gravity during the lengthening phase, with no passive stretching performed by the therapist.
   (b) Postisometric relaxation (PIR), which reinforces the lengthening in the relaxation phase with the application of light force (Figure 17).
   (c) Strongly applied stretching force after strong isometric activity.
2. Techniques with reciprocal inhibition of the antagonists.

The most useful techniques can be placed in the PIR category. A majority of those illustrated later in this text follow this principle.

A modification of the standard procedure occasionally is necessary when increased pain results from the use of these techniques. Reciprocal inhibition of the antagonists can then be used to improve motion.

An example of prescribed techniques follows for a patient in whom left lateral bending of the cervical spine is muscularly restricted.

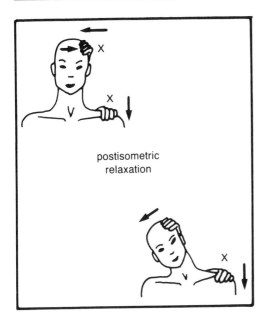

postisometric
relaxation

Figure 17 Principle of postisometric relaxation (PIR) treatment. *Source:* H. Tilscher and M. Eder, *Textbook of Reflex Therapy.*

- The standard program advises:
  - –Patient laterally flexes neck on the left to the point of restriction.
  - –Look to the right—inhale—doctor's counterpressure from the right.
  - –Look to the left—exhale—increase in motion to the left.
- The modified program advises (reciprocal inhibition):
  - –Patient laterally flexes on the left to the point of restriction.
  - –Look to the left—inhale—doctor's counterpressure from the left.
  - –Look to the left—exhale—increase in motion toward the left.

With the introduction of isometrics into chiropractic therapy, the scope of indications for their use undoubtedly has increased. The lack of irritation, as well as the protective gentleness associated with these techniques, allows their use even when chiropractic manipulations might be contraindicated as too forceful. A further advance is that isometrics, on the average, can be effective when psychological factors influence the picture of illness. Considering the benefits of PIR, it is understandable why this technique is being used more frequently.

Because of PIR's low risk, however, there also is a tendency to use this technique when manipulation might be more indicated. One frequently gets the impression that isometrics are also being used as a panacea to camouflage an insufficient knowledge of chiropractic therapeutic skill, especially manipulation skills.

Isometrics are useful, but they have limitations in their efficiency. This is particularly true in the upper cervical and occipital regions.

6.4 MANIPULATION

> Manipulations are methods of treatment that use minimal force to deliver impulses of high speed and small amplitude.

By passively moving a joint beyond its physiological range of motion, avoiding traumatic effect, one arrives at a narrow, therapeutically useful range of joint play (see Figure 16c, No. 1). Within this small field of play lies the realm of chiropractic therapeutic manipulation, which is often characterized by the well-known "cracking" sound. Manipulation can effect the recruitment of afferent patterns of muscle and joint proprioception and, concomitantly, can ease the disturbed arthromuscular regulatory mechanisms. In addition, manipulation can set into motion strong increases in organic regulatory processes. All in all, the stimulus intensity provided by manipulation seems higher than that of other therapeutic methods. It is still possible to quantify the "dosage" of delivered stimulus intensity, however, if one remembers that techniques involving tractional forces are not as intense as those using forced rotations or lateral bending. This principle is particularly applicable to the sensitive cervical spine, where corresponding consideration of all possible motion is necessary.

A prerequisite for successful manipulation—in fact, an essential element—is that the focus of the manipulation acts specifically on the functionally irritated joint. Neighboring joints that are not irritated must be protected from manipulation through joint-locking or manual fixation techniques.

A brief commentary should clarify joint-locking techniques.

In joint locking, one should understand the combination of the different motions in any given section of the spinal column—in a frontal, sagittal, or horizontal plane—that allows the movement of the joints to be "locked." Locking of adjacent segments allows manipulation only of the specific segment to be treated. Other healthy segments are thus spared from unnecessary impulses. The trained hands of the therapist can also be used to "lock" an area (e.g., cervical spine) when the hands are applied in a broad grip around sections adjacent to the irritated motor segment.

We must mention the problems and risks of manipulation. Unfortunately, risks associated with spinal manipulation are often an emotional issue. It is easy, however, to speak to these concerns about manipulation objectively; one simply needs to examine statistics, some of which are offered here to lend credence to an objective analysis.

6.4.1 Incidence of Complication from Spinal Manipulation

Dvorak and Orelli have collected the reports of 203 doctors trained in manipulative medicine in Switzerland. These doctors carried out 2,268,000 manipulations over 33 years, including 1,535,000 within the cervical region alone. In all, 1,408 complications were reported, among them 1,255 cases in the cervical spine. Of the latter, 1,218 were cases of transient dizziness, with no further signs. Only four patients encountered any type of neurological loss, which is an average of one major neurological incident in every 383,750 cervical treatments.

Gutmann questioned 55 manual therapists in the Federal Republic of Germany concerning their complication rate and ascertained that over a 12-year period, 37 doctors reported no complications, whereas 18 doctors reported some complications. In examining 450,000 reported treatments in this group, the following statistic can be calculated: For every 100,000 cervical manipulation treatments, one should expect two cases of marked neurological complication, 15 cases of moderate complications, and eight with light complications (e.g., dizziness). Wolff (1978) reported that at a rate of 2,000,000 manipulative treatments per year, complication rates reported in the literature would yield one major neurological event per 1,000,000 manipulations. Tilscher (1983) reported encountering no substantial complications in 15 years' experience involving 78,000 manipulative treatments reported. Eder, in a period of 28 years, found no substantial complications among 168,000 manipulative treatments.

Because serious instances of complications seem to occur only in connection with manipulations of the cervical region, one needs to take special care when working in this area and adhere to certain precautionary guidelines. For this reason, a special memorandum was completed at the conclusion of the 6th International Congress for Manipulative Medicine in Baden-Baden, West Germany, in 1979.

6.4.2 Memorandum for the Prevention of Complications in Spinal Manipulation

There are ten concepts to consider when one is engaged in specific manual therapy on the spinal column:

1. Cases of death have only been documented for manual therapy in the cervical spine. The primary effect is on the vertebral arteries. This can lead to thrombosis, which can interrupt the flow of blood to the brain. This is a rare occurrence, but it must be watched for constantly.
2. Historical and clinical data often can provide an initial signal of danger: episodes of syncope attacks or dizziness and sharp head and neck pain on movement to the extremes of ranges of the cervical spine can indicate vertebrobasilar arterial insufficiency.
3. Common clinical tests that aid in recognition of problems in vertebrobasilar artery flow include:
   (a) Hautand's test
   (b) de Kleijn's maneuver (Figure 18)
   (c) Underberger's walking test
4. In the manual medicine examination, a cervicocranial pain syndrome should be expected to emanate from the vertebral arteries whenever an atypical clinical picture emerges. In such cases, there is a lack of

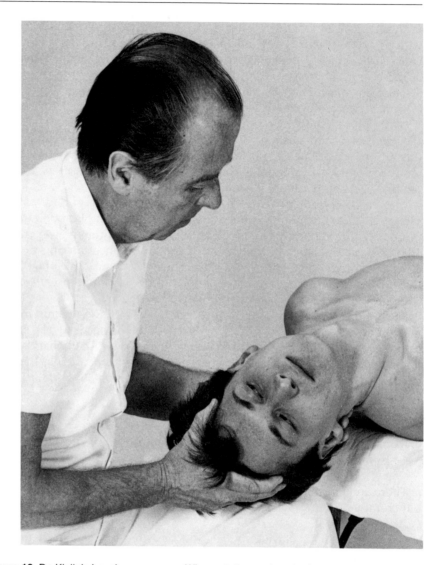

Figure 18 De Kleijn's hanging maneuver. When rotation and marked extension of the cervical spine causes vertigo or dizziness, one should suspect a disruption in bloodflow of the vertebral artery on the side of rotation

motion deficit, end-feel analysis fails to reproduce the complaint, and there are no motor-neurophysiological signs of nociceptive reaction.

5. One should never perform a directed manipulation without precise joint-locking of adjacent segments and a firm stabilizing contact.

6. The manipulative thrust should only be delivered when a "pressure point" has been reached at the end of the passive mobility range, and only when this maneuver has not exacerbated any increase in pain or other symptoms.

7. Only from "jerking" or a "gripping" manipulation through the entire free-motion range does the most serious danger of complications from manual therapy originate.
8. The necessary exact mastery of manual manipulation techniques is possible only through long-lasting practice and instruction, both in coursework and in clinical modes.
9. Proper record keeping and notation of the clinical picture and of specific manipulations performed on a patient are absolutely essential, especially in matters concerning the cervical spine. One cannot be too thorough in this regard.
10. Only when the criteria of sufficient training, careful and exacting diagnostic procedures, and precise applications of specific manipulative techniques have been met, can one apply the principle of "unforeseeable circumstance" to a medicolegal claim arising from a possible accident.

As previously demonstrated by the complication rates, manipulative therapy can be considered as quite low in risk. As with any therapeutic mode, however, these methods also require precise instruction and learning, diligent practice, and an awareness of precautionary measures.

6.4.3 Principles of the Technical Implementation of Manipulation

The practitioner should pay strict attention to the following general criteria of technical implementation.

---

1. The patient must be completely relaxed. This can be facilitated through breathing techniques.
2. The manipulative treatment succeeds when the irritated motor segment is placed in optimal position at the end range of physiological motion, and when precise joint locking of the neighboring segments has been achieved.
3. The line of drive of the manipulation must correspond to the painless range of the joint.
4. The manipulative impulse itself should not cause pain.
5. Failed manipulations should not be immediately repeated using the same technique.
6. After every manipulation, posttreatment testing should be performed to verify results.

6.4.4 Indications and Contraindication for Manipulation

The basic principle is to consider whether manipulation is indicated or contraindicated in a given situation.

> The indication for manipulation is primarily the joint fixation—whenever that is a cause or contributing factor to pain.

For contraindications, the first principle is to be able to differentiate between "lack of indication" and true contraindication.

Lack of indication always corresponds to the *lack of fixation*!

> 1. Contraindication is present whenever there are aggravating pathomorphological changes present along with fixations (e.g., acute inflammation, neoplasm, osteoporotic changes).
> 2. Contraindication is present whenever the fixation causes such acute pain that a full reflexive spasm leaves no pain-free ranges.
> 3. Contraindication may also exist when the conditions described in items 1 and 2, above, accompany a nerve compression syndrome.
> 4. Other contraindications are so-called damp fixations (i.e., those associated with major synovitis), which could occur in systemically febrile or inflammatory arthritic conditions.

A relative contraindication is also present when pain syndromes include hypermobility and its respective instability, along with fixations. Especially important are conditions with marked pelvic ligament weaknesses and hypermobility following the ligamentous damage of hyperextension or hyperflexion trauma of the cervical spine.

In conclusion, we may mention that in some circles, the term *manipulation* is being replaced with the words *mobilization with impulse*. It is not the authors' intention to make unsubstantiated changes in the terminology of the commonly perceived notion of manipulation, which is equated with the therapeutic "invasion" into the paraphysiological motion range. In physics, which is undoubtedly responsible for the mechanics of manual therapy, one can understand the term *impulse* as quantifiable amount of motion, that is, the product of mass times velocity. According to this definition, any motion technique of manual therapy would be a method using impulse. To then expand to a definition of manipulation, one could possibly refer to "mobilization with a quick impulse." Therefore, to avoid confusion, the authors believe that a retention of the term *manipulation* would better serve the purpose of the following material.

6.5 TREATMENT TABLE

Before presenting a detailed explanation of the treatment of the individual spinal regions, we must mention an additional prerequisite of chiropractic therapy. This is the correct positioning or placement of the patient for treatment.

Many types of treatment tables exist for this purpose; available surface area and ease of adjustability seem to be the two most important criteria. A surface of 72 × 25 inches seems to meet most needs. Narrow tables are often unsuitable because of the many changes of position that occur during chiropractic therapy; and elderly patients, especially, feel anxious or insecure on such small surfaces. Such anxiety and its accompanying apprehension and tension can inhibit successful treatment. The height and adjustability of the treatment surface is another important criterion. The table should have a height range of at least 20 to 36 inches. Since the height of treatment is so variable, tables with hydraulic or electrical elevators are recommended. Moreover, the head piece of the table should be adjustable vertically or horizontally; and a cradling section for the face should be built in, so that a neutral head position can be achieved.

A correctly built table offers not only optimal positioning of the patient, but also an economic use of the practitioner's energy. Those who have worked on a treatment table that is contradictory to ergonomic principles can testify to the encumbrance and stress on their own spinal column.

7. From Diagnosis to Treatment

In the concluding part of this volume, details that are directly related to the actual practice of chiropractic therapy are explained according to anatomical region. It should be assumed that of all the possible diagnostic tests, one always would select those most appropriate for a specific patient's complaint and differential diagnosis. If, for example, equally effective techniques could be performed in both sitting and recumbent positions, the reclining position would be chosen if the patient is bedridden or has difficulty when seated.

Furthermore, examination sequences can be coordinated to allow a thorough examination within minutes, allowing for complete analysis even in the busiest practice.

Practitioners must remember that the validity of a single test result is questionable if it is considered alone, without benefit of additional testing and history. Of paramount importance is the fact that one symptom, or one test result alone, is never enough for an accurate diagnosis. There is all the more reason, then, to obtain overlapping findings and information to arrive at a final diagnosis.

In all available textbooks and monographs dealing with manipulative medicine, large numbers of examination and treatment methods are described and illustrated.

This will give the interested reader an overview of the variety of methods available, but may also confuse the physician and make him or her insecure about which methods to use. The missing links in the literature—between examination results and their therapeutic consequences—have inspired the authors to write this book. In addition, this text attempts a more generic depiction of the various techniques available to the practitioner.

This chapter illustrates techniques that have proven effective in the daily treatment of patients. It is often impossible to conveniently separate diagnosis from therapy in a patient, because even the patient's level of interest and expectations become a significant part of the diagnostic and therapeutic process.

To obtain the correct access to pertinent information, one must begin by applying the previously described keys of structural and actual diagnosis of symptomatology. Second, one must combine knowledge of the stimulus intensity of any considered therapy with consideration for the constitution of the patient. It seems clear, for example, that a "Type A" hyperactive personality will be more sensitive to the reflexive stimulus pathways elicited by manipulation than a patient with a more relaxed "Type B" constitution.

Moreover, the acuteness of symptomatology also determines the chosen therapeutic path. The palette of chiropractic therapy offers needed choices, from probing traction to help determine the most comfortable and pain-free positioning of the patient in acute syndromes, to the strong stimulus of actual manipulation of the upper cervical joints in cases of fixation-induced chronic headaches (Table 3).

Next to considerations of acuteness or chronicity, the tissues involved in the condition provide guidance in selecting therapeutic techniques. For example, edema in the connective tissues requires techniques specific to such tissue (such as stripping techniques). Muscular spasm requires inhibition or vibrational modalities or PIR, whereas a restriction of joint mobility requires mobilization or manipulation.

Table 3 Stimulus Intensity of Therapeutic Stimuli Increases from Top to Bottom of the Table

Water Bath Therapy	Heat Therapy	Motion Therapy	Massage	Chiropractic Therapy
Increasing partial baths	Gauze/cotton	Passive motion exercises	Standard massage of body parts	Soft tissue and traction techniques
	Heat lamps	Isometric gymnastics	Lymphatic drainage techniques	
Partial to total alcohol rubdowns	Shortwave and microwaves	Flexibility exercises	Full massage	Muscle-energy techniques
Medicinal baths	Mud baths	Resistance exercises	Intensive manual therapy of connective tissue or trigger points	Mobilizations
Hot spring cures	Hot air		Underwater massage	Manipulation of lower cervical and lumbar vertebrae
	Hot baths			Manipulation of upper cervicals

Source: H. Tilscher and M. Eder, *Textbook of Reflex Therapy.*

Another deciding factor immediately becomes apparent from the diagnostic procedure. This is the vitally necessary determination of the therapeutic direction of movement for any method of treatment applied.

> The principal goal of treatment is the reestablishment of disrupted function. That is, in cases of restriction of movement, treatment is usually in the restricted direction. This rule is applicable only when painless progress is possible, because another principle must be applied, as follows: The best possible method of treatment is that which can be carried out in a pain-free direction, whereby the concept of a free direction not only embraces the affected joint's voluntary movement, but also its attainable passive joint play.

An example of this principle follows. Assume that left rotation and left lateral flexion are restricted and painful in the C2/C3 motor segment, and the regional muscular system is in spasm.

The building of the treatment program could proceed as follows.

Preparatory soft-tissue techniques for loosening of the affected neck muscles proves inefficient because the nociception of the irritated joints is dominant.

Segmental traction is painless and therefore feasible, and translational mobilization also is possible. The ascertained joint restriction has lessened, and the direction of movement is now pain free.

Only now does the corresponding segmental mobilization of the restricted joint first become possible (manual segmental reinforcement of the left rotation and left lateral flexion) and indicates a further improvement.

The concluding manipulation, with almost identical lines of drive, can now be delivered through a high-velocity, reinforcing impulse.

According to principle, all manipulative treatment must be established in such a progressive fashion, inclusive of any regional idiosyncracies in the area of disruption.

> In highly acute situations, every possible direction of motion may be painful; if so, then any manipulative therapy should be avoided. Initial medication might be indicated, as well as rest, or anti-inflammatory physical therapy treatments. Only after these treatments have resulted in pain-free palpation and some pain-free directions of treatment is more aggressive treatment indicated. When this occurs, the correct time has arrived for the use of manipulative therapy techniques.

Despite the observance of those guidelines and principles, successful therapy can be attained only when the patient has been convinced that becoming and remaining healthy is possible only through his or her active cooperation. The multicausal genesis of most pain syndromes of the musculoskeletal system must be considered; without the recognition and exclusion of exacerbating factors (e.g., stress perception from job and sports activity, sedentary life style, obesity) relapses will inevitably occur. Moreover, home treatment, such as exercise or other forms of self-treatment, can be indispensable (e.g., stretching of shortened muscles, strengthening of the weakened muscular system, coordination drills, stabilization exercises in cases of fixation).

The following portrayal of the diagnostic and therapeutic process concentrates specifically on techniques that integrate the path from diagnosis to therapy. In other areas of diagnosis, discussion is limited to a cursory listing of critical details and commentary on important items within the differential diagnosis that can stipulate therapeutic consequences.

7.1 THE LUMBAR-PELVIC-HIP (LPH) REGION

The combination of lumbar spine, pelvis, and hip joints into a single anatomical region occurs here; symptomatology in this region requires a differential diagnostic process involving all these components.

7.1.1 Examining the Standing Patient—Results and Consequences

The examination begins with inspection of the standing patient, according to criteria mentioned in previous chapters. Inspection naturally encompasses the entire spine. This principle of inspecting the entire patient also applies to the evaluation of general mobility. The patient is then instructed to bend as far forward as possible, with the knees extended (Figure 19). With this flexion test, the finger-to-floor distance should also be noted, a concept that needs additional explanation. The basic idea is as follows:

> A large finger-to-floor distance is an uncharacteristic symptom that can have several causes.

The causes of this symptom are as follows:

• General age-related hypomobility
• Shortening of the back musculature
• Shortening of the hamstrings
• Disease of the hip joints
• Disc prolapse with genuine Laseque sign

A normal finger-to-floor distance is present when the fingertips touch the floor on forward flexion. If the patient proudly shows you that he or she can put the palms of the hands flat against the floor, or flexes "in half" like a pocketknife, this is an indication either of excellent flexibility

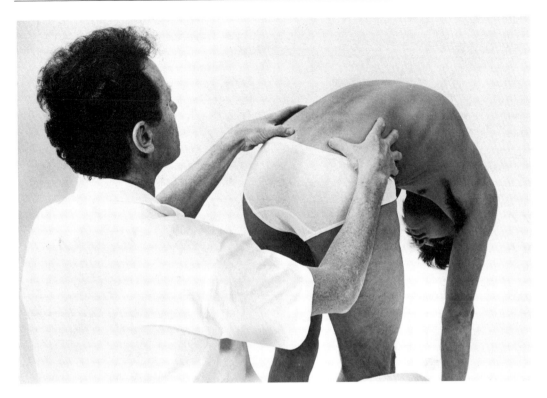

Figure 19 Flexion test—making sure the knees are extended—premature pelvic anteriority?

achieved by exercise and training or of genuine hypermobility. If hypermobility is diagnosed, then the patient must be warned of the potential for injury inherent in instability.

To obtain further information from the forward flexion test, an orientation to the surface anatomy of the LPH region is necessary. The examiner sits on a stool behind the patient and places both hands, thumbs spread over the sacroiliac joints, with the medial side of the index finger across the iliac crests. With this orientation, one may recognize differences in iliac crest height.

Next, the thumbs are placed, keeping the same hand position, against the posterior superior iliac spines (Figure 20).

> Note: The posterior superior iliac spines lie much deeper than one thinks.

When the patient flexes forward, one can note whether both sides rise equally, or whether one side ascends more quickly than the other, or even drops. If there are differences between sides, this is called a "positive-premature anteriority phenomenon," and this is a possible sign of a functionally disrupted sacroiliac joint. Because the appearance of this sign rests on

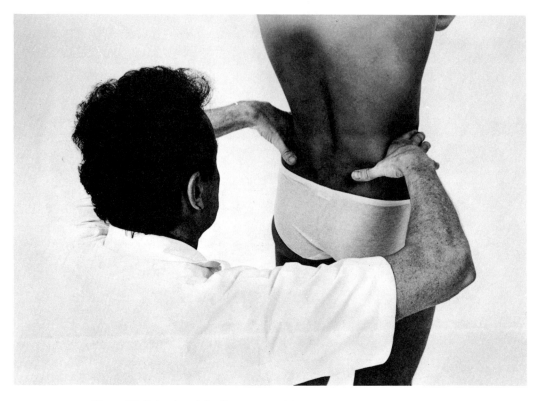

Figure 20 Palpation of the iliac crest and the posterior superior iliac spine

muscular mechanisms, it is often only transiently visible during the patient's movement and must therefore be watched for carefully.

The extension test is next performed. In this test, the harmonic curving of the spine or the appearance of a flattening or plateau is observed. Extension of the lumbar spinal column occurs in greatest proportion at the L5/S1 motor segment, and corresponding fixations, as well as instabilities, frequently manifest themselves at this level (Figure 21).

Once again sitting behind the patient, the examiner now asks the patient to carry out lateral flexion to the left and right, compares the movements bilaterally, and evaluates whether the spinous processes indicate proper coupled motion and curving. Segmental "plateau" formation is an indication of possible fixations. The L4/L5 motor segment is preferentially affected because a majority of lateral flexion range exists at this level (Figure 22). The examination of lateral flexion also can yield information about possible hypermobility, which is assumed whenever a plumb line dropped from the axilla on the side opposite the direction of bending falls past the gluteal crease.

In addition, the anterior superior iliac spines are palpated on the standing patient and compared in height. If both the anterior and superior spines are lower on one side than on the other, one should suspect a probable true leg-length difference (e.g., growth disruption or post-fracture).

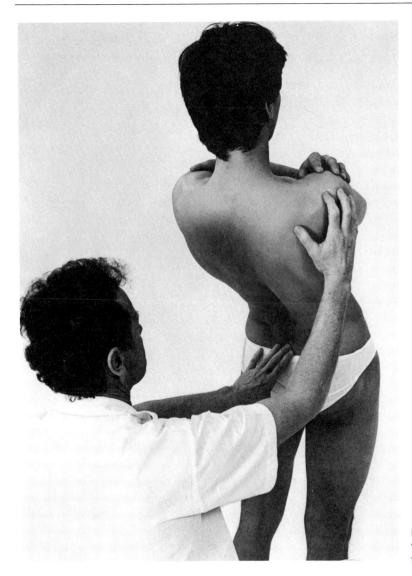

Figure 21 Extension test—harmonic curving of the spine?

Height differences of the anterior and posterior spines on one side, with a mirrored difference on the other, indicate a pelvic torquing, a finding linked with functional disruptions of the sacroiliac joints. Pelvic torquing can cause further problems: posteriority of one ilium causes a functional short leg by raising the acetabulum anteriorly. The differentiation between true and functional leg-length discrepancy is necessary, if only because corrective measures such as heel and sole lifts should be prescribed only for true inequalities.

If one suspects disease of the hip joints or their associated musculature, one should also examine the functional capability of the hip joint abductors (gluteus medius and minimus), which often is decreased in cases of such disruption. The test is simple.

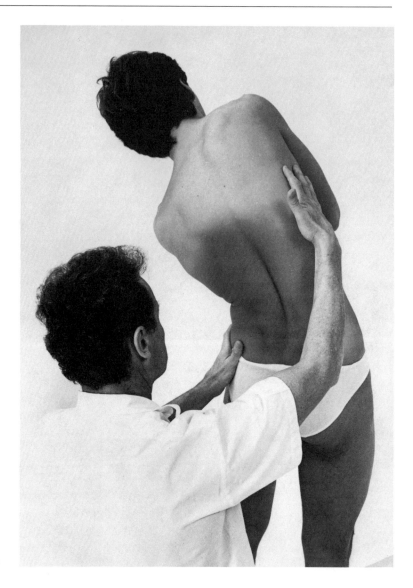

Figure 22 Lateral flexion test—harmonic curving of the spine? Hypermobility?

The patient raises one leg, as if climbing a stair. If the non-weight-bearing side of the pelvis sinks, this is a positive Trendelenburg sign, which indicates muscular dysfunction on the opposite side.

The final examination performed on the standing patient is to test the ability of the patient to walk first on the toes, then on the heels. This is valuable as a neurological "pre-examination" in considering the possibility of motor loss through root compression syndromes. The inability to toe-walk indicates a corresponding motor loss in the area of the S1 root. Inability to heel-walk is typical for L5 lesions.

Which consequences result from these first steps of examination? Thus far, the physician has obtained an orientation to the primary problem; these initial results will call attention to further diagnostic elements. The following are some examples of initial results:

- Enlarged finger to floor distance: determined through which factors?
- Positive premature anteriority: sacroiliac joint? Thoracolumbar transition?
- Curve flattening in extension: L5/S1 fixation?
- Curve flattening in lateral flexion: L4/L5 fixation?
- Pelvic unleveling: Leg lift only for true leg-length discrepancy.
- Trendelenburg positive: Hip joint—capsular pattern?
- Paresis: Further neurological exploration.

7.1.2 Examining the Seated Patient

An examination of the seated patient leads to organization of data previously obtained.

In the seated patient, the lumbar mobility test excludes the influence of the hip joints, as well as that of the hamstring muscles; flexion actually occurs only in the lumbar spine. Further data can be obtained from the evaluation of seated rotation, which, when the pelvis is fixed, occurs primarily in the lower thoracics and the thoracolumbar transitional area.

One should also re-examine the iliac crest heights in the seated patient, using the previously described method. If the discrepancies in height of the anterior and superior iliac spines seen in the standing patient are eliminated when the patient is seated, this may verify the presence of a true leg-length difference. This is especially true if a noted spinal curvature straightens when the patient sits. If the configuration of any discrepancies is similar with both standing and seated positions, one can assume the presence of pelvic torquing.

Pelvic-level differences in the seated patient

- Level anterior and superior iliac spines (though uneven in the standing position) = true leg length difference: anatomically short leg.
- Maintenance or further divergence of the anterior and superior iliac spines = Pelvic torquing: functionally short leg.

7.1.3 Examining the Supine Patient—Results and Consequences

For this examination, the examiner first attempts to raise the patient's straight leg to test for the Laseque sign. To perform this test, the extended leg is passively and slowly raised to the point at which the patient feels pain. A genuinely positive Laseque sign is seen when the indicated pain shoots (like "lightning") into the leg and thereby indicates the corresponding radiation pattern of an irritated nerve root. The patient will often try to evade the pain by raising the pelvis on the painful side or by evading true hip flexion through attempts to abduct the leg. The reachable flexion angle at which pain occurs is estimated and can give an indication of the acuteness of the nerve root irritation. Pain incurred below 45° of flexion is often linked to grave discogenic disruptions (Figure 23).

If pain emerges slowly on the posterior aspect and radiates increasingly to the knee as the leg is raised, one can often assume that the pain results from the stretching hamstrings. This should not be classified as a true Laseque sign. Similarly, the occurrence of pain in the lumbopelvic region brought on by raising the leg indicates irritation of ligaments or joints, and should be designated a pseudo-Laseque sign.

If radiation of pain into the leg occurs, an additional orienting neurological examination must ensue, concentrating on motor loss corresponding to myotomal levels. The inability of the patient to extend the knee against resistance is an indication of lesions of the L3 and L4 nerve roots. Weakening of the anterior tibialis muscle indicates damage of the L4 nerve root and can be recognized if the patient is unable to dorsiflex the foot against resistance. Weakness of the great toe's extension is a typical symptom of L5 nerve root damage. Weakness of resisted plantar flexion or resisted eversion of the foot is an S1 indication.

With respect to deep tendon reflexes, absence or weakness of the Achilles reflex indicates a possible lesion of the S1 nerve root (see Table 4).

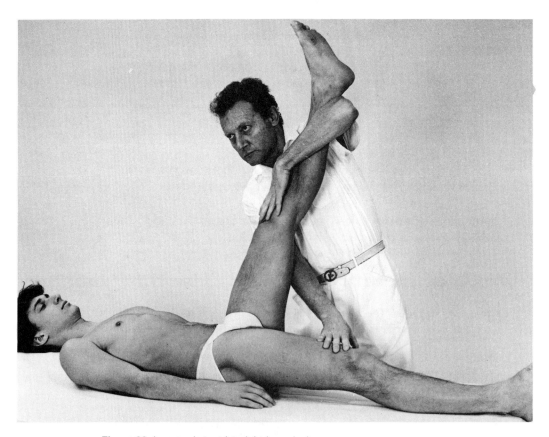

Figure 23 Laseque's test (straight-leg raise)

Table 4 Orientation Table of Radicular Symptoms

Segment	Dermatome	Myotome	Reflex Loss
L3	From the extensor surface to the inner side of the thigh to above the knee.	Paresis of the quadriceps femoris.	Absent patellar reflex.
L4	From the outside of the thigh to the inner lower leg and inner edge of the foot.	Paresis of the quadriceps femoris and tibialis anterior.	Weakening of patellar tendon reflex.
L5	From the outside of the thigh to the big toe.	Paresis of the extension hallucis longus. Heel walking is disrupted.	Loss of the posterior tibialis reflex (not definitive).
S1	The posterior of thigh and lower leg to the 5th toe.	Paresis of the peronei and triceps surae; toe walking is destroyed.	Loss of the Achilles tendon reflex.

Figure 24 Supported supine hook lying arrangement. *Source:* H. Tilscher and M. Eder, *Textbook of Reflex Therapy.*

Absence or weakness of the patellar tendon reflex is found with root damage at the L3 or L4 level.

Acute radicular syndromes often allow simple gentle tractional methods as the only possible initial manipulative treatment. To accomplish this, three-dimensional traction should be attempted with the patient in a supported supine "hooklying" position (Figure 24).

A next step in manipulative therapy may be the attempt to use intersegmental traction mobilization, which is applicable after the initial acute symptoms have abated slightly.

For three-dimensional traction of the lumbar spine, the patient lies on his or her back with the pelvis at the lower edge of the table. The legs are held by the physician, who is standing between them. The lower legs are fixed between the doctor's arms and body, and the doctor grasps the popliteal fossae. The physician can achieve traction through posterior movement of his or her own weight. By three-dimensional variation of the direction of traction, one finds the optimal pain-free position, in which rhythmic traction is then carried out. Bedridden patients with acute lumbar syndromes should be carefully anchored in the pain-free position through the use of cushioning and be positioned squarely in the middle of the treatment surface (Figure 25). If no painless direction of traction can be found in the supine position, a variation in the prone position may be attempted,

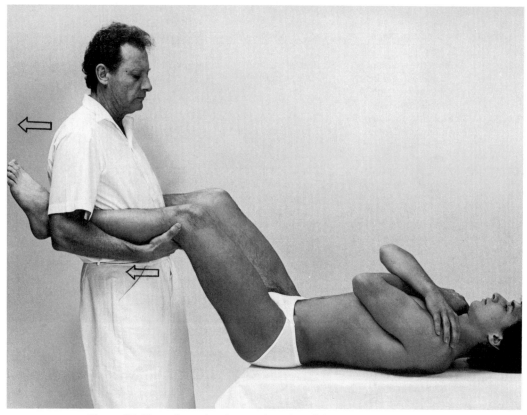

Figure 25 Three-dimensional manual traction of the lumbar spine

in which traction can be facilitated through respiratory-assist mechanisms (Figure 26).

For segmental traction using the side posture (Figure 27), the patient lies on his or her side with the legs drawn up. The physician bends over the patient, the cephalad arm placed over the spinous processes, with the fingertips fixed on the spinous process cephalad to the irritated motor segment. The other hand reaches around the pelvis from a caudal direction and contacts the caudal spinous process. Through rhythmic tractioning on the caudal spine, supported by a caudal pushing of the pelvis with the doctor's upper body in contact with the patient's thigh, segmental traction can be achieved.

If radicular symptoms are absent, the next test to be performed is hyperabduction and assessment of the abductor flexibility in general. Shortening of this musculature can be designated as a positive Patrick sign (Figure 28). The test is performed by having the patient flex, abduct, and externally rotate the leg at the hip, with the sole of the foot contacting the knee of the other (extended) leg. The leg is allowed to fall to the edge of the table and is compared in this maneuver to the opposite side. In a differential diagnostic sense, it remains to be clarified whether abductor cur-

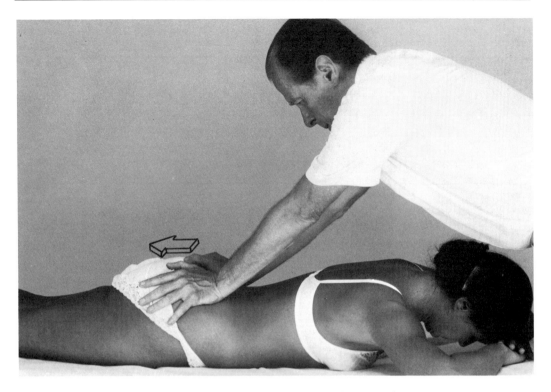

Figure 26 Prone manual traction treatment of the spine, adding respiratory assist. Inhalation—counter pressure; exhalation—push to traction

tailment is reflexively stimulated by a condition of the hip or sacroiliac joints, or whether there is a genuine loss of range of motion at the hip.

Two simple tests that allow clarification of this question are as follows. First is testing of the hip joint (Figure 29): The thigh is flexed to 90°, as is the knee; the hip is then internally rotated by the examiner with both hands. If bilateral observation fails to yield restricted movement or pain, the hip joint can be largely ruled out. Functional disruption of this joint usually expresses itself first as reduced internal rotation, following a capsular pattern of restriction (Cyriax).

The second test is that of the sacroiliac joint, or Spring test (Figure 30a–c): The examiner stands on the contralateral side to the region being examined. With one hand placed on the back of the patient, the examiner pulls the superior leg, which is flexed at the knee and hip, forward, in the direction of an adduction.

The examiner contacts the sacroiliac joint with the free hand, pointing the fingers cranially, exactly in the slight gap that represents the SI joint.

Note: The SI joint often lies further medial than one would surmise.

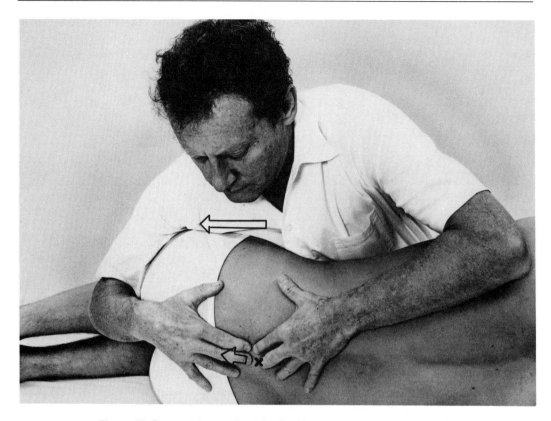

Figure 27 Segmental manual traction in side posture

The pelvis is slowly rocked backward onto the palpating fingers (this lessens the degree of joint-locking adduction), which will be able to detect slight gapping in the joint. The hand contacting the knee performs gentle impulses in a slightly caudal and adductive direction. Typically, a fixation is felt as diminished joint play.

The examination of the recumbent patient is continued with a bilateral palpation of the iliacus and psoas muscles for pain and tenderness. (Figures 31 and 32.)

The iliacus lies in the area above the outer third of the iliotibial band. Thickening and tenderness can signify an accompanying pelvic torquing (often because of sacroiliac joint dysfunction). The psoas may be palpated through the abdominal wall, especially if the extended leg on the side being tested is slightly passively raised by the examiner, thus affording better relaxation of the muscle. After the muscle has been palpated in this relaxed position, the patient is then asked to hold the leg up without assistance. If pain is felt on this maneuver, even without deep palpation, this can indicate a pathological spasm of the psoas.

To conclude examination of this area, the hip joint, pubic symphysis, trochanters, adductor attachments, and the pes anserinus need to be palpated.

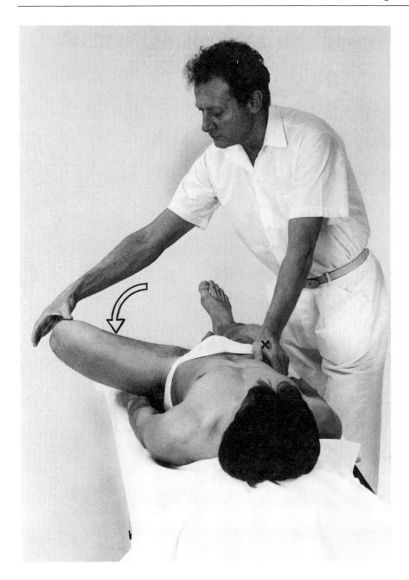

Figure 28 Performing the Patrick sign—hyperabduction test

The examination of the patient in the recumbent position yields the following information:

- Confirmation of a possible radicular syndrome
- Functional condition of the hip joint
- Sacroiliac joint function (Patrick signs, Spring test)
- Determination of muscular irritations (e.g., iliopsoas).

7.1.4 Examining the Prone Patient—Results and Consequences

At the beginning of the examination, one should obtain an impression of the general skin turgor and mobility. This can be done either by a gentle

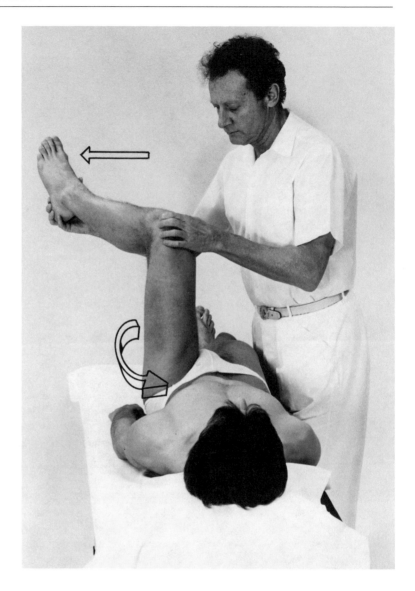

Figure 29 Testing of the hip joint—internal rotation?

palpation and moving of skinfolds (Kibler, 1955), (Figure 33): or by performing a "diagnostic stroke" of the connective tissue (Figure 34). As previously mentioned, segmentally reflexive involvement may be indicated by the presence of edema or changes in turgor. Repetitive execution of this diagnostic palpation may begin to stimulate effective treatment of such connective tissue edema.

Palpation further enables one to recognize regional surface and deep muscular spasms, which also can provide data corresponding to a segmentally facilitated lesion. It is possible to treat these zones through inhibition or vibration to determine whether they will release or whether they continue to exist as an expression of an overriding reflexive stimulus.

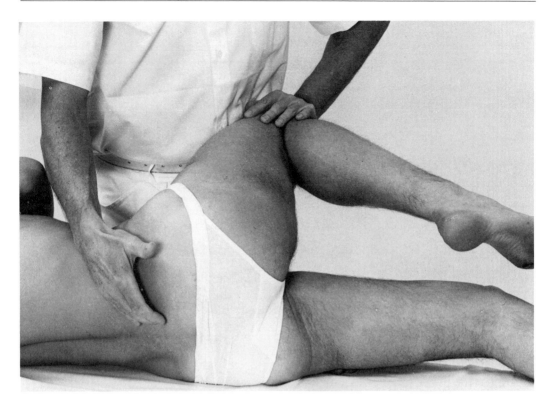

Figure 30a Spring test of the sacroiliac joint from the contralateral side

Common muscular trigger points are further to be found on the medial insertion of the gluteus medius (Hackett's D-point), over the piriformis, as well as on the muscular insertions on the ischium.

When palpating for painful areas, one must also consider the sacroiliac joint, the iliolumbar ligamentous attachments (checking for ligamentous insufficiencies), the interspinous ligaments, and the tip of the coccyx (coccydinia).

To complement the Spring test of the sacroiliac joint (with the patient in the supine position), the so-called shaking test can aid in confirming a diagnosis. In this test, the patient's anterior pelvic crest is ventrally grasped and shaken with small, dorsally directed impulses. The fingers of the other hand, lying over the sacroiliac joint, sense the elasticity or fixation of the joint (Figure 35). An additional test of the sacroiliac joint uses posterior-to-anterior pressure over the lower third of the ilium, while the fingers of the other hand note the response at the sacroiliac joint (Figure 36).

Also valuable is the so-called three-phase test. In phase 1, one hand of the examiner encircles the patient's extended leg and guides it into extension while the other hand applies counterpressure on the outer pelvis. If pain emerges at the hip joint, this indicates a disruption in the hip. In phase 2, the counterpressure is applied over the sacrum; if extension evokes pain, the sacroiliac joint should be considered. In phase 3, the

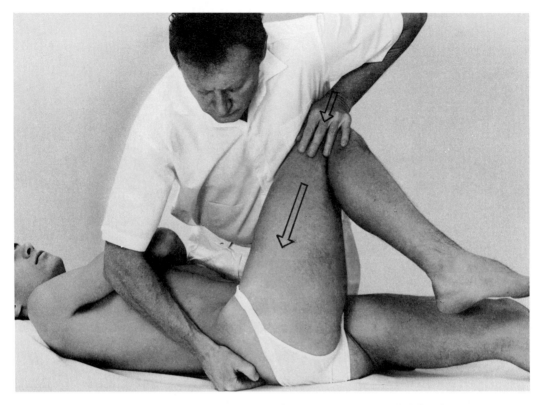

Figure 30b Spring test of the sacroiliac joint from the contralateral direction

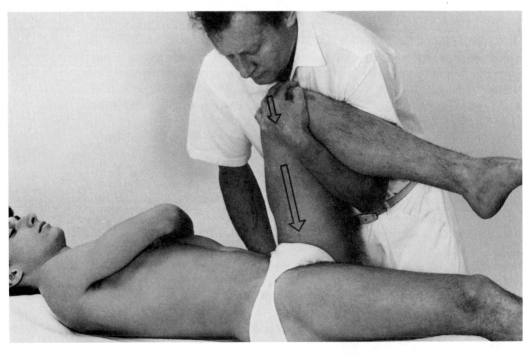

Figure 30c Spring test of the sacroiliac joint from the homolateral direction

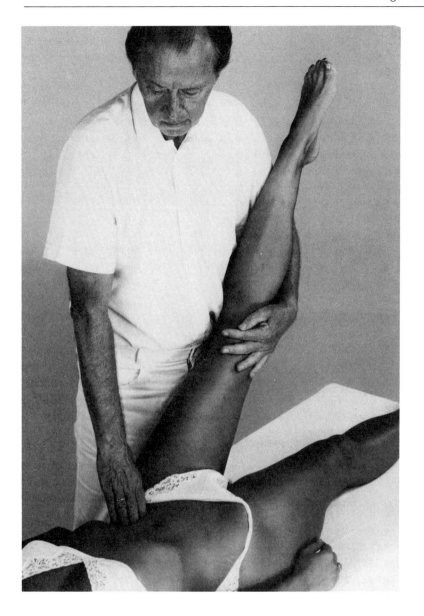

Figure 31 Palpation of the psoas

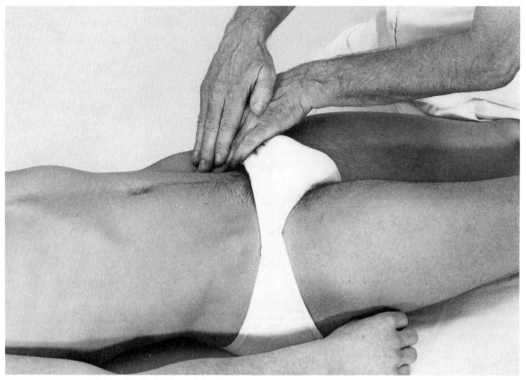

Figure 32 Palpation of the iliacus

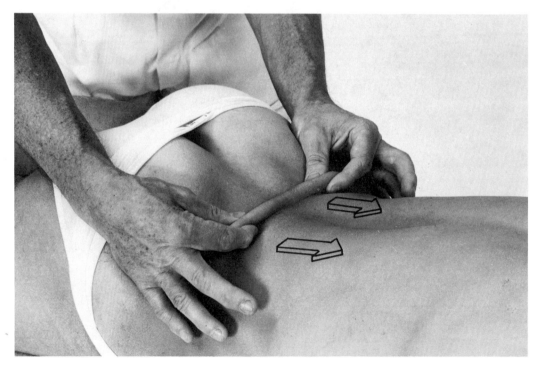

Figure 33 Kibler-type skinfolds

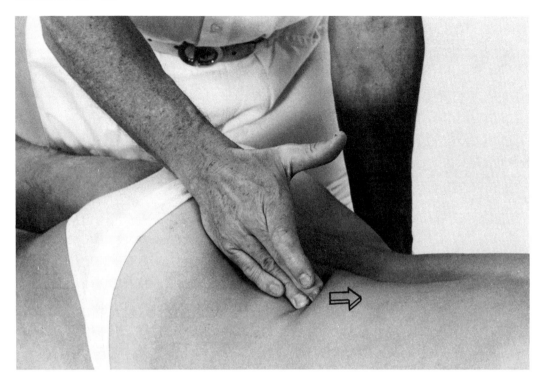

Figure 34 The "diagnostic stroke" of connective tissue

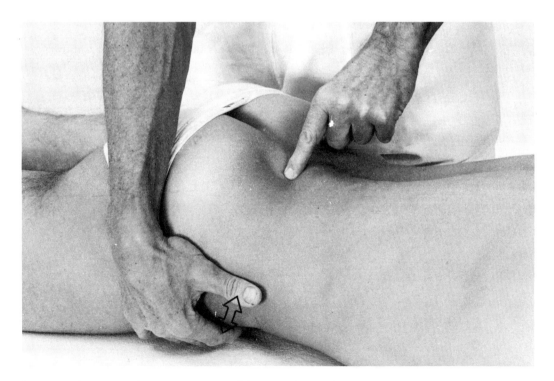

Figure 35 Shaking test for the examination of the sacroiliac joint function

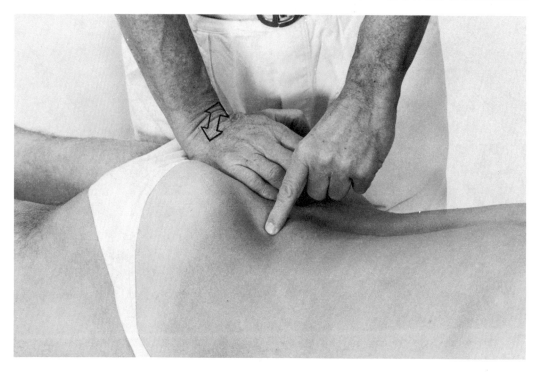

Figure 36 Testing of the sacroiliac joint—posterior to anterior pressure on the lower third of the sacroiliac joint

counterpressure is applied over the fifth lumbar vertebra; if additional extension causes an increase in pain, then one should suspect a lumbosacral lesion.

The examination in the prone position complements the examination regarding:
- the segmental connective tissue quality as well as the tonus situation of the muscular system
- the functional condition of the sacroiliac joints
- possible coccydinia
- ligamentous irritation or instability

Thus far, we have discussed several different methods of examination for the sacroiliac joints. No single method is absolutely reliable in diagnosing functional disruptions. Therefore, one must extract corresponding conclusions from multiple procedures, which possibly will yield overlapping information.

The general theme of sacroiliac joint disruption has developed into an ideological playing field for theorists of manipulative therapy. Furthermore, the sacroiliac joint has been stylized into a hypothetical complex that often may exceed its actual clinical significance.

To orient the examiner to findings that can be indicative of a possible disruption of the pelvis and its joints, the following should primarily be considered. Disruptions of the sacroiliac joint function are assumed when these findings are present.

- Pain exists in this area.
- Pseudoradicular, dull emissions emanate into the dorsolateral leg region or the groin region.
- The sacroiliac joint painfully reacts to pressure.
- Muscular pain syndromes or imbalance is present.
- A pseudo-Laseque sign is observed (see previous description).
- Spring and jolting tests are positive at the sacroiliac (SI) joint.
- The second phase of the three-phase test is positive.
- Premature anteriority occurs upon forward flexion.
- Function disruptions are noted in the thoracolumbar transition.
- The iliacus is thickened and appears sensitive to pressure.
- A psoas spasm or shortening exists.
- A Patrick sign produces SI pain.

The frequent presence of psoas spasm represents an important pathogenic factor in disruptions of the sacroiliac joint function. The origin of the muscle, from T12 to L5, and its insertion into the lesser trochanter, as well as its course over the upper branch of the pubic bone (akin to violin strings over the bridge), can cause a tilting of the homolateral pelvic bowl in cases of spasm or contracture. In such cases, the ilium rotates dorsally so that the posterior superior iliac spine may stand lower than the anterior superior spine. This distortion of pelvic geometry (the acetabulum moves anteriorly and cranially) often causes a functional homolateral leg deficiency, as well as forming the cause for the previously described premature anteriority during forward flexion. The resulting functional disturbance also causes simultaneous countermotion of the sacrum (in the sense of inferiorly oriented nutation). In this sense, an overlap arises between pelvic torquing and sacroiliac joint fixation, because this sacral positioning is seen most frequently in fixations of this joint.

Let us summarize those consequences that result from the diagnostic—and therapeutic—procedures surrounding such disruptions.

1. Sacroiliac subluxation and its pelvic torquing and sacroiliac joint fixation, despite being distinct and separate entities, are often clinically inseparable.
2. While the prevailing mechanism is thought to be mechanical for the sacroiliac fixation, reflexive mechanisms are seen as being the main culprit in actual sacroiliac subluxation. Disruptions in the thoracolum-

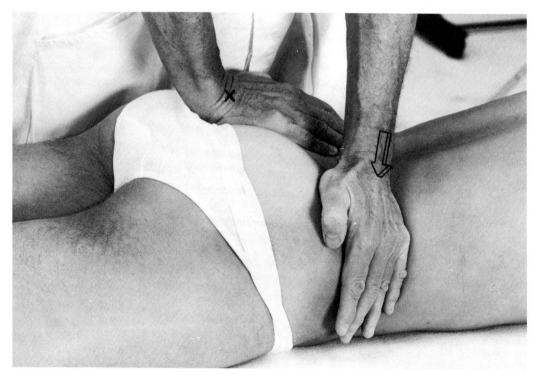

Figure 37 Setting up for mobilization and manipulation of sacroiliac joint fixation

bar transitional area and the hip joints, as well as discopathies and viscerosomatic reflex paths, should be considered.

3. The symptoms listed in this chapter, which point to a disruption in the pertinent sense, are seldom present in their totality. Demonstrable single symptoms and signs serve as indicators for the relevant diagnosis.

From a chirotherapeutic perspective, the following considerations will help lead to a beginning of therapy. Direct mobilization and manipulation of the sacroiliac joint is the first choice, if the symptoms of fixation prevail (determined by the Spring test, Patrick sign, and pressure sensitivity of the sacroiliac joint area).

The treatment must be carried out in a more complex arrangement of multiple layers if signs of pelvic torquing dominate. These include premature anteriority during forward flexion, functional leg length differences, divergence of iliac spines, psoas tension, and thoracolumbar fixation. Next to the release of the thoracolumbar motion restriction and a possible necessary stretching of the psoas, corrective mobilizations or manipulations have their application here. The required techniques, however, may lead away from direct SI joint manipulation and concentrate instead on pelvic motion and mechanisms, using the previously discussed principle of inducing motion in an unrestricted direction.

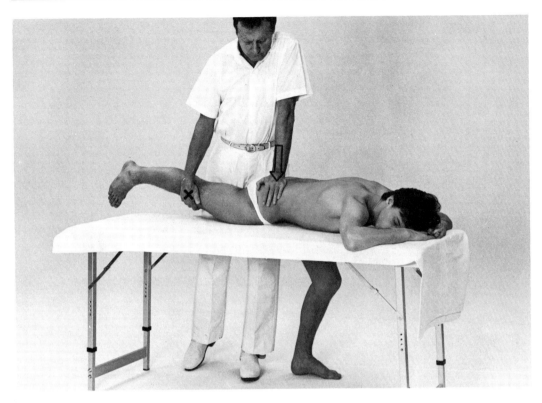

Figure 38 Technique variations for mobilization of the sacroiliac joint

The most universal possibility of both mobilization and manipulation of the sacroiliac joint is probably seen in the prone position of the patient. This technique is especially indicated when, as in most cases, the sacroiliac joint fixation finds the sacrum locked anteriorly and the ilium in a dorsally rotated position.

The practitioner stands on the contralateral side of the joint to be treated. With the practitioner's hands crossed over one another, the sacrum is fixed homolaterally and contact is made contralaterally on the dorsal sector of the pelvic crest. The contact hand can give a rhythmic pressure impulse in a posterior-to-anterior direction (mobilization). A manipulation can be achieved through a short, high-velocity, low-amplitude impulse on the ilium, which must be preceded by elimination of tissue lag (Figure 37).

A variation in techniques can be used in cases of unsatisfactory completion of this manipulation. The patient moves toward the edge of the table and flexes the leg at the hip and knee so that the foot moves toward the floor. This eliminates the lumbar lordosis and locks the joints of the sensitive lumbosacral transition. The extended leg on the side to be treated is now grasped by the practitioner (standing to the contralateral side), raised, and brought to total extension to stretch the hip joint, preventing the treatment impulse from affecting this joint. The heel of the other hand provides the impulse, as in the original method (Figure 38). The frequent finding of a caudal sacrum can be treated by an attempt made according to Sell's modification. The patient position remains the same, except that the patient moves toward the lower edge of the table, far enough so that the leg on the side to be treated can be held in a scissors hold between the practitioner's legs, and slightly extended. The ulnar edge of the practitioner's hand then makes contact one finger's width to the side of the tip of the sacrum. After increasing tissue tension through pulling the leg into extension with the scissors hold, the practitioner carries out the cranially directed manipulative impulse with a simultaneous, impulse-like increase in traction through the scissors hold (Figure 39).

A similar therapeutic goal is seen in the so-called sacral tip impulse, which can be used when the patient is lying on the side. The inferior leg lies extended, the upper leg is flexed. The therapist stands facing the patient. The therapist grasps the upper thigh with the cranially positioned hand to avoid locking the sacroiliac joint. The other hand's ulnar edge makes contact on the contralateral side of the sacral tip and gives a cranially directed impulse (Figure 40). A variation of this is also possible with the patient lying prone (Figure 41).

A technique of mobilization that possibly can direct the ilium ventral/posterior also can be performed with the patient in the side position, but with the lower leg flexed (by bending). The iliac crest is moved ventrally with the therapist's upper hand, and the caudally situated hand encircles the upper thigh and delivers a lightly abducting pressure, so that a locking

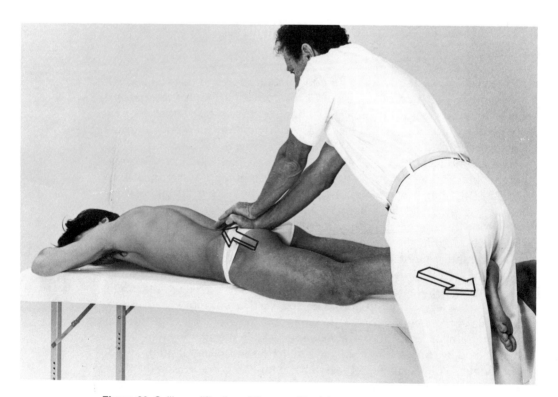

Figure 39 Sell's modification of the sacroiliac joint treatment

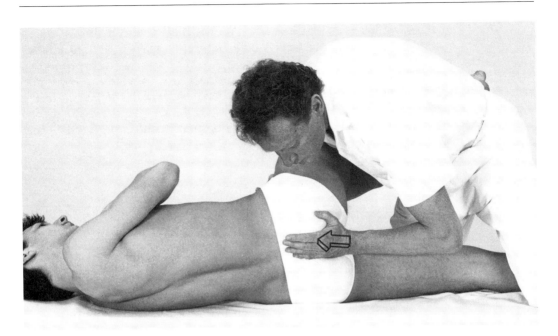

Figure 40 Sacral tip impulse with the patient lying on the side

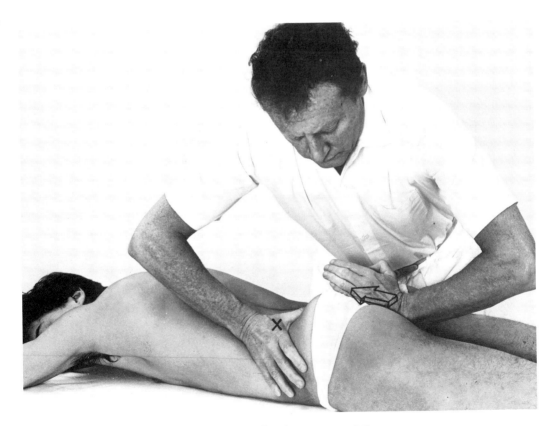

Figure 41 Manipulating the sacrum in the cranial direction—prone variation

of the sacroiliac joint during adduction is avoided. The therapist's hand makes contact with the ischial tuberosity and delivers a cranial/dorsal impulse (Figure 42).

If the ilium is ventrally inferior with the sacrum superior, a more rare occurrence, the following technique can be used. With the patient in the side position, the upper leg is flexed and the lower leg is extended. The therapist's caudal hand presses the buttock curve ventrally, and the other hand presses the iliac crest dorsally (Figures 43 a and b).

The following therapeutic consequences also emerge from the information collected thus far:

• Anatomically short leg	— elevation of the sole or heel
• Hip joint disease	— orthopedic therapy, mobilization
• Radicular syndromes	— three-dimensional traction, positional rest, segmental traction mobilization
• Sacroiliac joint fixation	— manipulations and mobilizations in the prone position
• Sacroiliac joint subluxation	— mobilization corresponding to the adjustment (e.g., sacrum ventral—ilium dorsal)
• Connective tissue edema	— connective tissue massage
• Muscle spasm or contraction	— stretching treatments

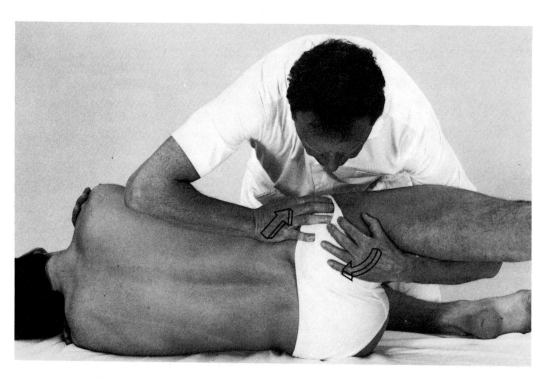

Figure 42 Mobilizing the ilium in the ventral direction

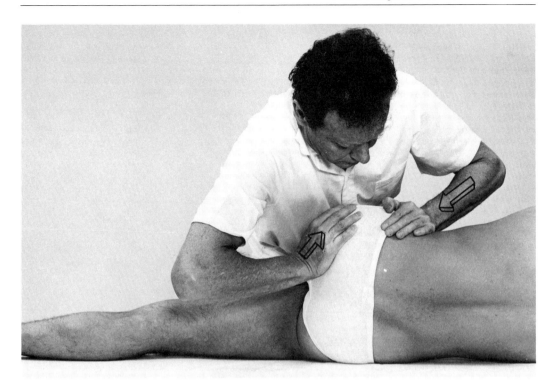

Figure 43a Mobilizing the ilium in the dorsal direction

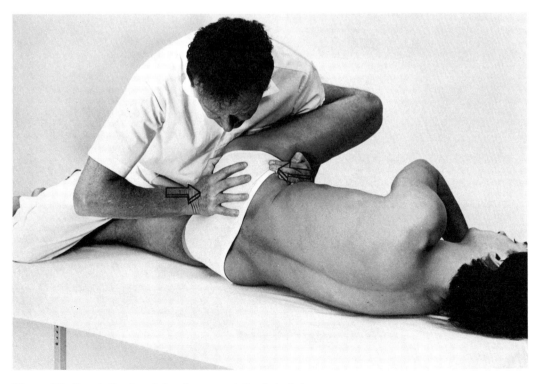

Figure 43b Ilium in the dorsal direction—a variation in technique

7.1.5 Continuing Examination of the Lumbar Spine—Results and Consequences

The so-called lumbar springing test is an important contribution to the localization of disruption in the lumbar spine (Figure 44). In this test, one places the second and third fingers of one hand parallel to the lumbar spinous processes (keeping the spinous process free of contact) and seeks contact with the laminae of each successive caudally lying vertebrae. The

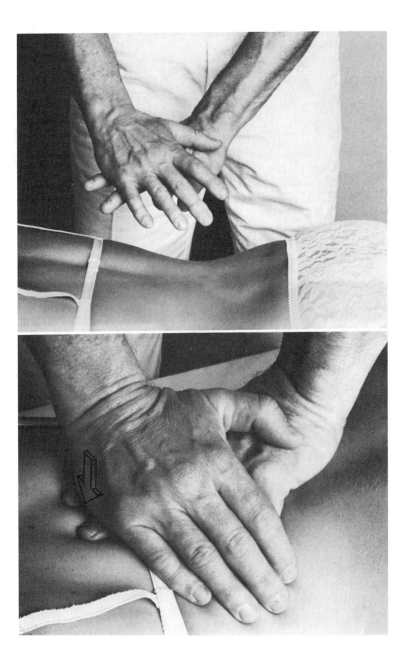

Figure 44 The lumbar springing test

ulnar edge of the other hand should lie flat over the palpation fingers, and evoke a slow, responsive, and intensive pressure into the palpation fingers as they lie over the laminae. The following items can be evaluated:

1. A springy tension in the laminar area as an expression of intact joint function
2. The absence of springiness as a sign of a fixation
3. A patient's indication of a segmentally sensitive increase in pain, which is frequently an expression of irritation of the dorsal ligaments in dorsal disc protrusion
4. A similar increase in pain, indicative of a segmental instability (i.e., facet syndrome)

A necessary complementary test for the recognition of frequently observed hypermobility is the instability test of the lumbosacral transition. With the patient lying on the side, the examiner places the fingers of both hands over one another on the fifth lumbar vertebra to fix it in place. The legs of the patient are bent at the knee in a 120° angle. Axially rhythmic impulses are carried out by the examiner on the sacrum of the patient, using the examiner's upper thigh, which is in contact with the knee and femur of the patient. If such impulses allow movement of the sacrum dorsally under the fifth pelvic vertebra (with the receptor of motion being the resistance-bearing hands), an instability of the lumbosacral junction can be assumed (Figure 45).

This examination tests translational gliding in principle: exaggerated gliding shows instability, and the absence of gliding indicates fixation. Absence of translational movement also indicates fixation in the remaining lumbar vertebral segments and may be tested in a similar manner.

While the patient is in the side position, the therapist can check the relation of movement of each individual lumbar motor segment. Flexion, extension, and lateral flexion can be tested progressively, segment by segment, to the level of L1.

For the segmental analysis of flexion, the patient should lie on the side; the legs are bent at the knee and the hips are repeatedly angled over the pelvis by the examiner. The examiner's fingers are placed between the spinous processes, and they feel the accompanying spreading of the spinouses or lack thereof, in the presence of a fixated segment (Figure 46).

The extension test is carried out in an analogical fashion, with the patient's legs being moved dorsally repeatedly. The pelvis tilts ventrally, the lumbar lordosis is increased by extension, and the examiner's palpation fingers sense the approximation of the spinuous processes (Figure 47).

For the segmental lateral flexion test, the patient's pelvis is raised to the side over the legs, which are bent perpendicularly at the knee and hip. The examiner's fingers are placed between the spinous processes, and the resulting lateral flexion of the lumbar vertebrae can then be segmentally tested (Figure 48). In all three of these individual tests, the observation of the end-feel is of particular importance.

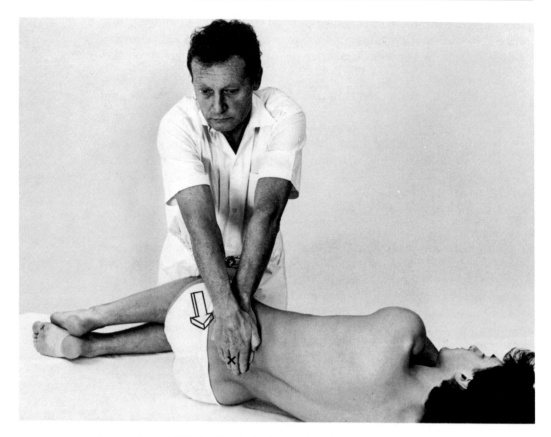

Figure 45 Instability test for the lumbosacral junction

Through the use of the lumbar springing test, the instability examination of the lumbosacral junction, and segmental mobility tests in
the side position, one can differentiate between fixation and hypermobility.

If movement restrictions are found during the aforementioned tests, a
mobilization treatment or even PIR relaxation can immediately be implemented, without changing the position of either therapist or patient. The
single difference lies in the action of the testing hand, which is fixed on
the cranial spinous process of the disrupted segment in cases of mobilization (Figure 49).

Some manipulation treatments that often are necessary toward the end
of the patient's therapy can also be performed with the patient lying on the
side.

Of the many types of manipulation techniques for the LPH region, several others are particularly useful. They are described as follows.

The segmental rotation manipulation is perhaps the most widely used
technique, although most often it seems to be applied in a rather nonspe-

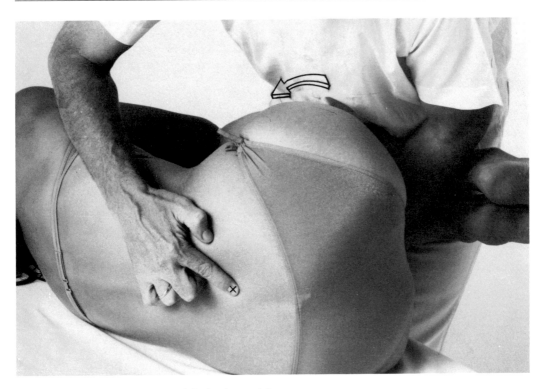

Figure 46 Segmental flexion test of the lumbar vertebrae

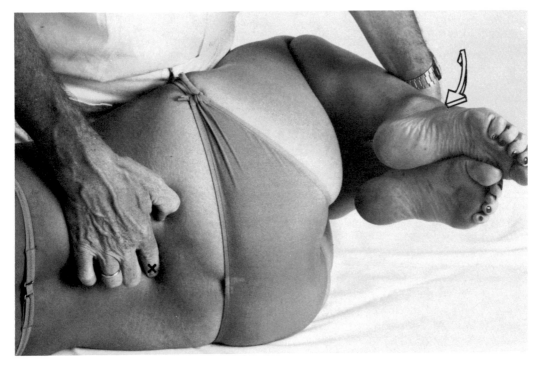

Figure 47 Segmental extension test of the lumbar vertebrae

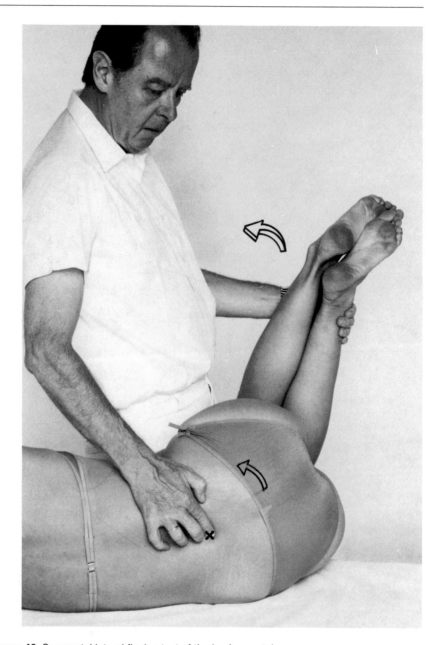

Figure 48 Segmental lateral flexion test of the lumbar vertebrae

cific way. To arrive at a methodology that is directed exactly to the disrupted segment, many factors must coincide. The patient lies on the side, and the lower shoulder is pulled toward the edge of the table, to prevent an extension of the lumbar vertebrae during the ensuing upper body rotation. The lower leg lies slightly flexed, the upper leg is noticeably bent, and the foot is hooked over the middle of the calf of the lower leg. (This is the position for the L5/S1 motor segment.)

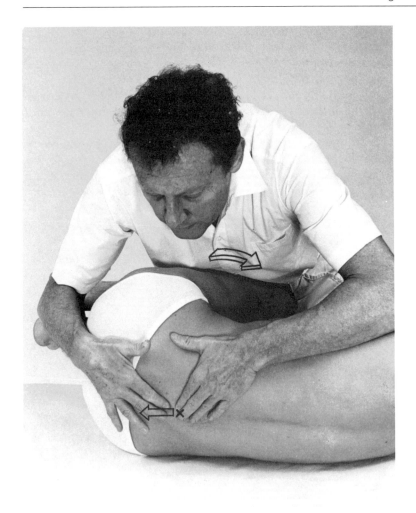

Figure 49 Segmental mobilization—the cranial spinous process is fixed

For motor segments lying above (e.g., L4/L5, L3/L4), the upper leg must be more noticeably bent and must hook closer to the knee of the lower leg. The increasing kyphosis caudal to the treated motor segment aids the necessary locking of adjacent joints by tightening the ligaments. Through additional downward, counterrotating pressure, with both forearms of the therapist on the shoulder and pelvis of the patient, the locking of all segments and the desired potential of the single motor segment can be achieved. The thumb of the cranially positioned hand makes contact on the lateral portion of the lateral spinous process of the superior vertebra and thus fixes it. The second and third fingers of the caudal hand pull the spine from below in the direction of torsion. After achieving perfect joint locking and optimal potential, the manipulation impulse effects a high-velocity, low-amplitude rotational increase with the lower contact hand and the underarm. The rotational effect can be increased by the body pressure of the examiner on the bent leg of the patient (Figures 50–52 and 53 a and b).

The treatment of the upper lumbar vertebrae (superior to L3/L4) is similar, but placement of the impulse is now achieved through the fixation of the caudal motor segment and impulse from the upper contact hand (Figures 54 and 55). With tough and extremely fixed segments, a pretreatment of isometrics can be used. This procedure corresponds to that previously described for manipulation up to the point of achieving total joint locking and potential. Instead of effecting a manipulation impulse, the patient con-

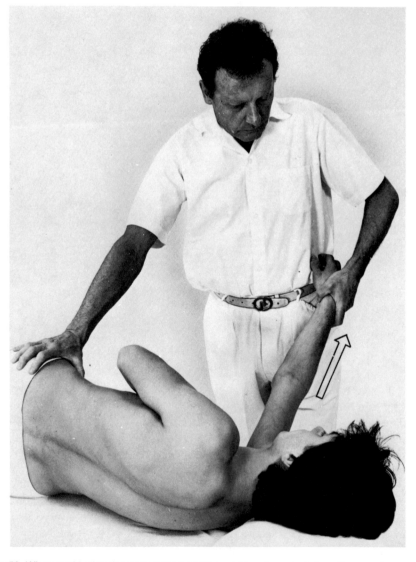

Figure 50 When positioning the patient for a lumbar rotational manipulation, the examiner pulls the patient's lower shoulder to the edge of the table

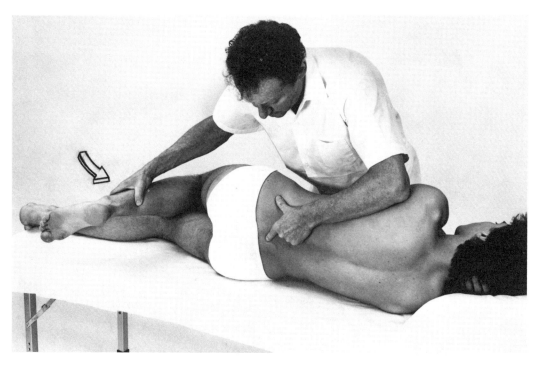

Figure 51 The patient's upper leg is bent and the foot is placed on the middle of the calf of the other leg for the treatment of the lower lumbar motor segments

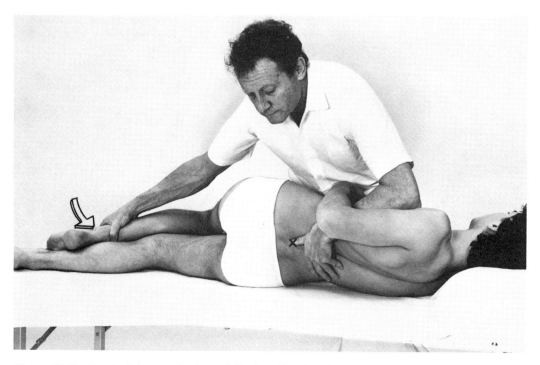

Figure 52 The thumb of the examiner's cranially placed hand applies pressure on the upper spinous process of the fixed motor unit; the elbow rests on the upper thorax and increases the rotation of the trunk

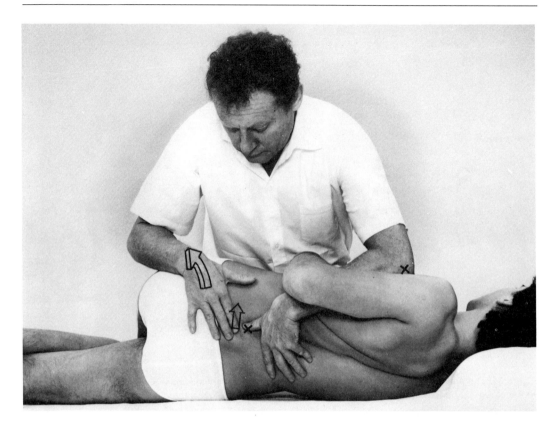

Figure 53a The second and third fingers of the examiner's lower hand make contact with the lower spinous process (on the side close to the table). The actual manipulation occurs in this final position

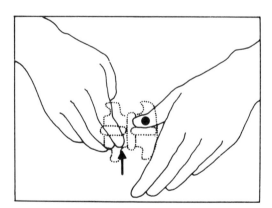

Figure 53b Schematic of finger and thumb contacts on the motor segment. *Source:* H. Tilscher and M. Eder, *Textbook of Reflex Therapy.*

tracts isometrically against the positioned torsion. The direction of contraction, of course, is dependent on the level of the treated segment; and contraction is achieved either through outward pressure of the bent leg against the practitioner, or through a corresponding counterpressure of the shoulder. In the relaxation phase, the original positioning is increased by the practitioner. After a few repetitions, there is usually a significant reduction

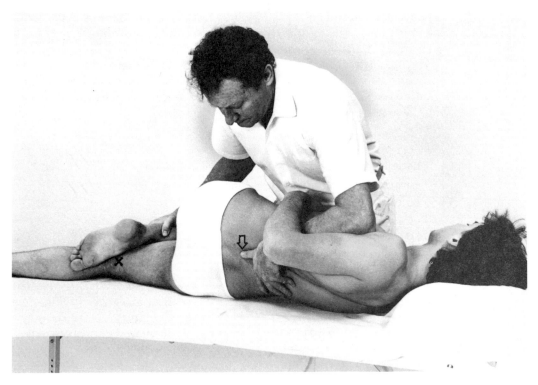

Figure 54 For treatment of the upper lumbar vertebrae, the foot of the patient's upper leg is placed close to the knee of the lower leg

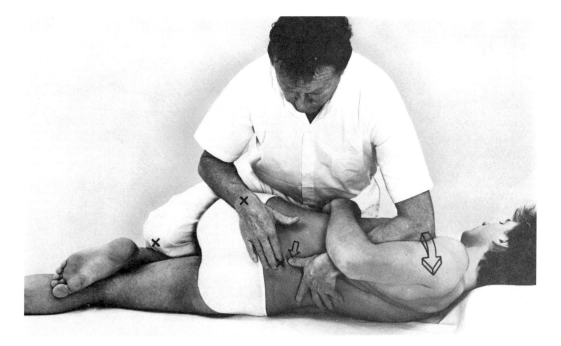

Figure 55 The thumb of the practitioner's cranially placed hand (turned toward the table) provides the impulse of the manipulation, and the rotation of the trunk is increased through simultaneous elbow pressure

of muscular spasm and tension, which leads to the success of subsequent manipulations. The potential disruption of musculature must be considered an additional important pathogenic factor.

The stability of the lumbar spine is ultimately dependent on the trunk musculature. Imbalances in this area are significant because they can contribute to constant relapses of many lumbar syndromes. The following five muscle groups need special attention:

- back extensors
- entire abdominal muscular system
- buttock muscles
- iliopsoas
- ischiocrural (hamstring) muscular system

Spasms and relative contractures of the back extensors often are revealed at the initial inspection because of their visible protrusion. In addition, during range-of-motion testing they restrict flexion ability.

The phasic abdominal muscles, antagonistically placed to the back extensors, traditionally illustrate an opposite problem. In cases of disruption, weakness is by far the predominant finding, often to a remarkable degree.

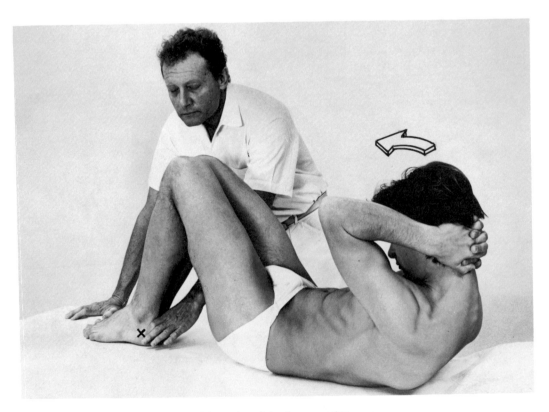

Figure 56 Testing of the rectus abdominus muscles

Testing is performed by asking the patient to perform a slow trunk curl with bent knees. The bent knees are absolutely necessary so that the iliopsoas is not significantly affected by the curling motion and the strength of the abdominal muscles can be evaluated in relative isolation (Figure 56).

Similarly, the buttock muscles, in particular the gluteus maximus, medius, and minimus, tend to show weakening rather than spasm. A weakening gluteus medius and minimus can be determined through the previously described Trendelenburg phenomenon. The strength of the gluteus maximus is evaluated when the patient is lying prone. The patient's leg on the examination side is flexed at the knee. One of the therapist's hands is fixed to the pelvis, and the other hand lies on the upper thigh and provides resistance against the patient's leg extension (Figure 57).

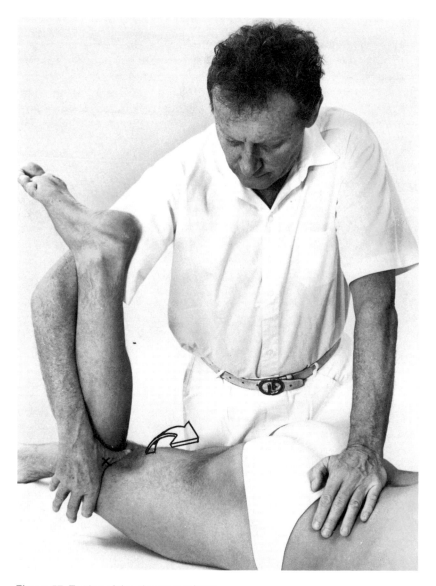

Figure 57 Testing of the gluteus maximus

For the testing of the iliopsoas, the patient is positioned supine at the end of the table. With the patient holding one leg bent to the chest, the thigh and leg on the side being tested are hanging freely over the edge of the table. This leg is then observed to see how far it sinks. A slight extension position should be possible, and the lower leg should hang at a right angle to the floor. If a slight flexion in the hip joint or a sinking of the lower leg fails to occur, it must be further differentiated whether the iliopsoas alone is restricted or whether the rectus femoris is also in spasm. The differentiation is simple. If the hip flexion increases through further passive flexing of the same leg at the knee, then there is a restriction of the rectus femoris. If the position of the hip joint remains the same, this indicates the sole restriction of the iliopsoas (Figure 58). A shortening or spasm of the ischiocrural (hamstring) muscle system, on the other hand, is indicated by a positive pseudo-Laseque sign.

The following principle is of primary importance (see the previous explanation of antagonistic mechanisms in the section on the disruptive potential of muscular tissue): Shortened or spasmed muscles must first be stretched—only then can weakened muscles be strengthened.

Stretching of the back is performed with the patient supine, using resistance of the flexed knees, against a slight isometric caudal pressure and followed by passive pressing of the knee toward the chest (Figures 59 and 60).

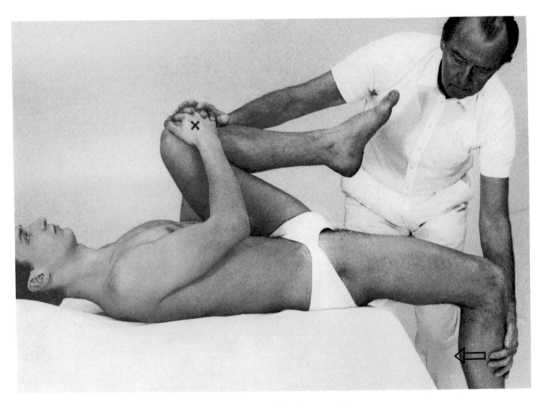

Figure 58 Testing of the iliopsoas and rectus femoris

Figure 59 Stretching of the back extensors, using postisometric relaxation (PIR)—knee to chest

For spasm of the back extensors and quadratus lumborum, which limits both flexion and lateral flexion, traction and massage perpendicular to the extensors has been shown to be quite effective. The patient lies on the side with arms and legs slightly bent. The practitioner, facing the patient, supports himself or herself by placing the elbows on the patient's shoulders and pelvis. With the fingers of both hands, the therapist then stretches the paravertebral muscle bulges laterally away from the spinal column (cross-fiber or transverse massage). The therapist then augments the stretching by a lengthwise traction, which is produced by the simultaneous pushing of the elbows against the patient's shoulder and pelvis. This is rhythmically repeated until the spasm lessens (Figures 61 a and b). Figures 62a and 62b show methods of self-treatment by the use of muscle energy techniques (MET).

To stretch the iliopsoas, one uses the patient position previously described for testing this muscle. The stretching treatment is effected by a flexion against resistance on the lower thigh, followed by reinforcement of the stretch (Figure 63).

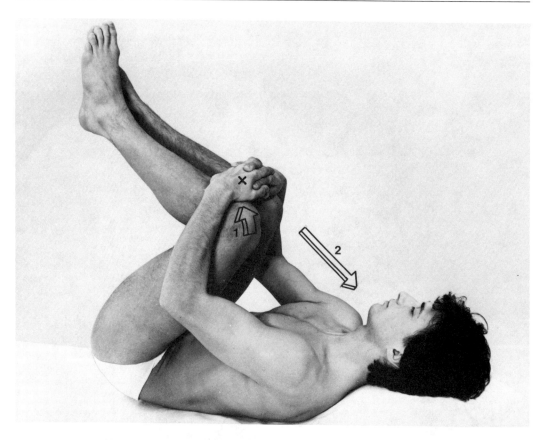

Figure 60 Self-treatment of restricted back extensors through postisometric relaxation (PIR)

Self-treatment also can be performed with MET (Figures 64 a and b) or through active stretching (Figure 65).

In cases of coccydinia, the gluteus maximus will be stretched with the patient prone. After passive pressing apart of the buttocks, these muscles are activated by having the patient pinch together the buttocks against the resistance of the practitioner's hands. The buttocks halves are pushed further laterally in the relaxation phase (Figures 66 and 67).

Stretching of the gluteus medius is best carried out with the patient supine, with the leg on the unaffected side flexed at the knee and hip, and crossed over the other leg, which lies extended on the table. The extended leg is then pushed into maximal adduction by the practitioner, and contracted isometrically in this position. It is stretched by adduction in the relaxation phase (Figure 68).

For isometrics of the piriformis, the patient should be prone, the leg on the side to be treated flexed at a right angle. The practitioner now guides the hip joint of this leg into maximal internal rotation. The externally rotating piriformis is brought into the position of greatest length, from whence it is isometrically contracted. Stretching is effected in the relaxation

Figure 61a Cross-fiber (transverse) massage with traction, for spasm of the back extensors and the quadratus lumborum (step 1)

phase through an increase in internal rotation. The therapist's other hand should fix the pelvis to keep it from being lifted in this phase (Figure 69).

The treatment of the ischiocrural (hamstring) muscles corresponds to the position of the Laseque sign. At its highest point of elevation, the leg will be isometrically extended against the fixed hands of the practitioner and stretched through further increases in elevation during the relaxation phase.

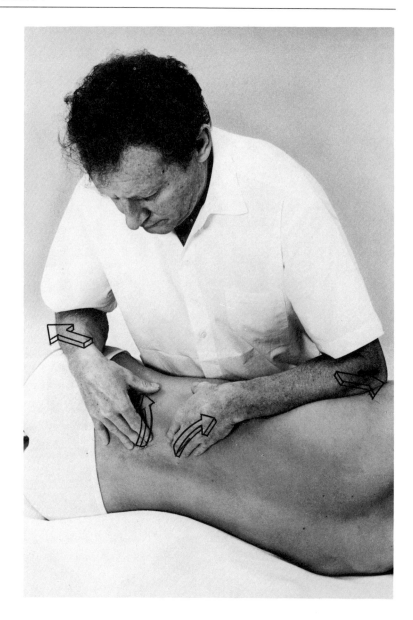

Figure 61b Cross-fiber massage with traction for spasm of the back extensors and the quadratus lumborum (step 2)

The indications for treatment of muscular disruptions are as follows:
1. palpation of pain or spasm
2. indications of restriction or contraction
3. resistance testing with pain provocation

7.2 THE THORACIC REGION

In the previous discussion of examinations of the lumbar vertebrae with the patient in the standing position, the thoracic spinal column was also

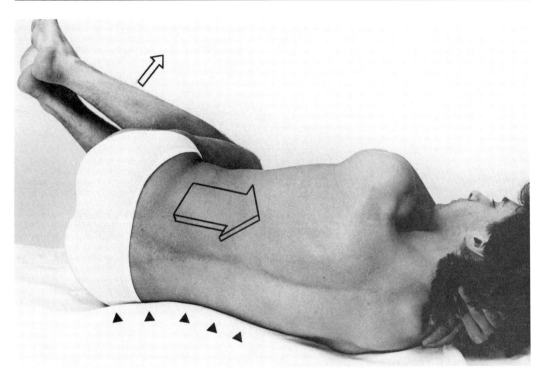

Figure 62a Self-treatment of spasm of the quadratus lumborum through muscle energy technique (MET)

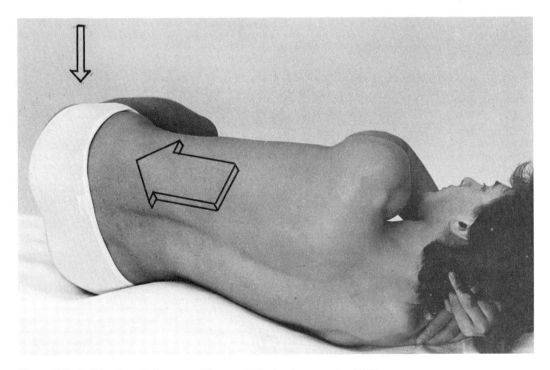

Figure 62b Self-treatment of spasm of the quadratus lumborum using MET

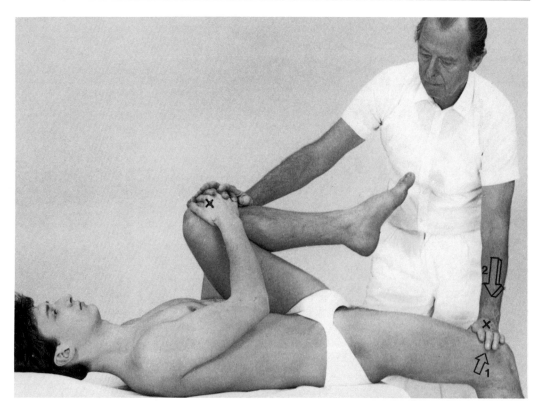

Figure 63 PIR of the iliopsoas

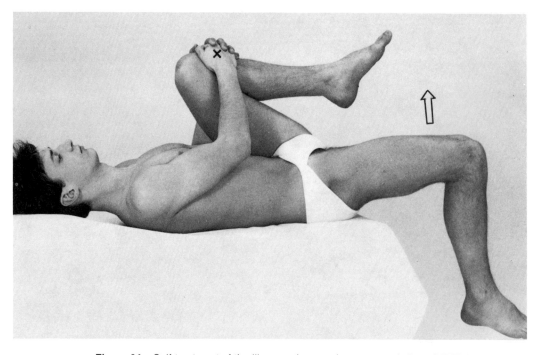

Figure 64a Self-treatment of the iliopsoas by muscle energy technique (MET) (step 1)

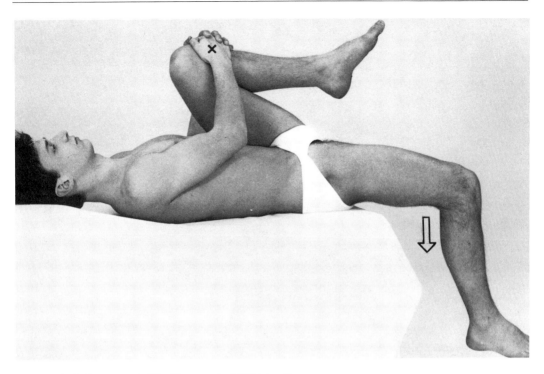

Figure 64b Self-treatment of the iliopsoas by MET (step 2)

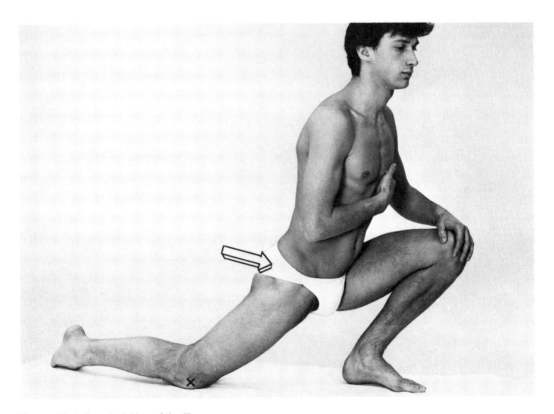

Figure 65 Active stretching of the iliopsoas

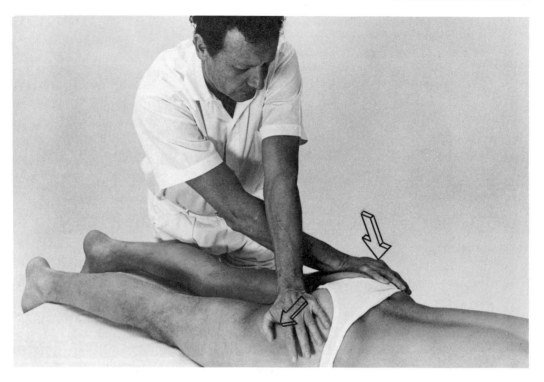

Figure 66 Postisometric relaxation (PIR) of the gluteus maximus in coccydinia

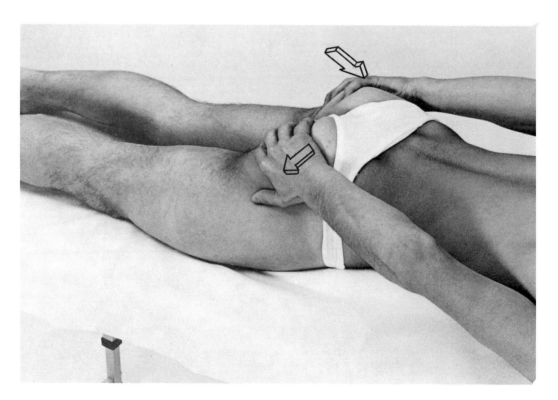

Figure 67 Self-treatment of the gluteus maximus

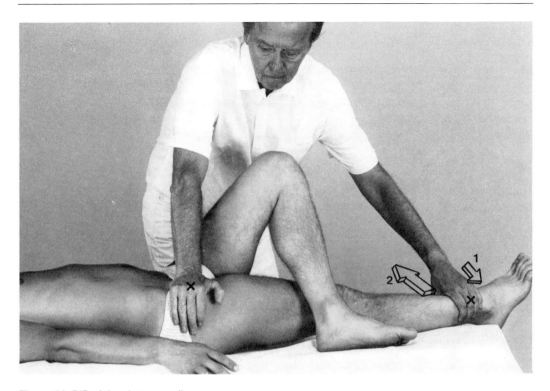

Figure 68 PIR of the gluteus medius

considered in part. For further exploration of this region, we recommend that the patient be positioned straddling the examination table, to fix the pelvis during subsequent portions of the examination. Initial palpation will yield better results when it is repeated and compared when the patient is in the prone position because many structures are better palpated in one position than in another.

With the patient seated, all structures that optimally present themselves should be explored, especially when the patient crosses the arms in front of the chest and grabs the shoulders, thus exaggerating the thoracic ky-phosis. In this position (named the *Pharaoh's position* by the authors), the thoracic vertebrae separate, the scapulae move apart laterally, and the ribs are much more easily palpated (Figure 70).

The Pharaoh's position is useful because the fibers of the iliocostalis cervicalis, which inserts on the costal angle of the upper ribs (2nd to 5th), are prone to tendinosis at this location—a condition more easily observed in this position. The pressure sensitivity of the interspinous ligaments is also better elucidated in this position. Although the thoracic region provides only superficial access to many structures, pressure sensitivity can still provide information regarding disrupted motor segments.

The thoracolumbar junction deserves special attention.

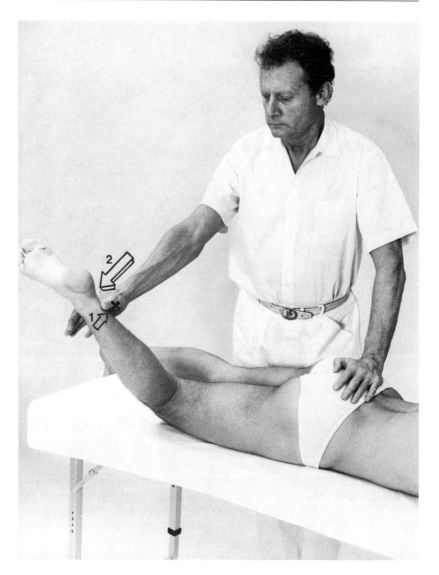

Figure 69 PIR of the piriformis

The area of transition from the thoracic to lumbar spine is another sensitive area. This is true because of not only local biomechanics (greater lateral flexion and rotational ability) but also the degree to which segmental reflexes of a viscerosomatic nature influence this area. Fixations or irritations, therefore, must be analyzed from all aspects. A first step in this direction is testing mobility of this region.

7.2.1 Mobility Testing—Results and Consequences

For mobility testing, the patient clasps the hands on the neck and brings the elbows together in front of the face. This position allows clear observation of the back.

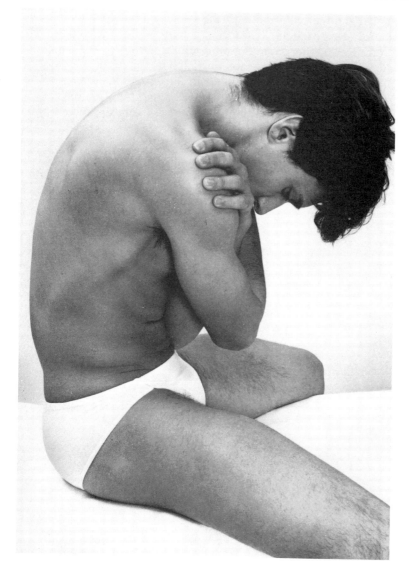

Figure 70 "Pharoah's position"

Active motion testing consists of flexion and extension, as well as lateral flexion and rotation, which are, of course, compared bilaterally.

For additional passive testing, the patient's upper body is encircled by the practitioner's arm from the front and is guided by the practitioner's elbow or shoulder into the desired direction. It must be cautioned that the lumbar vertebrae should remain as motionless as possible, which is best achieved through support of this area by the practitioner's free hand.

Passive mobility testing can be augmented by resistance testing. If, for example, passive left rotation is restricted and painful, the principal etiologies for the disruption are either arthrogenic or muscular. When the end range of passive rotation is reached and the patient's attempt to resist further rotation exacerbates the pain, one can assume that a muscular irritation exists in the right-sided rotators. If the pain does not change with this resisted motion, an arthrogenic disruption is more likely, and can be verified in the course of further examination (Figure 71).

Segmental mobility tests serve as the next step in the verification of joint lesions. This testing can be implemented in all four directions of movement. The basic position of the patient is once again with hands clasped behind the neck and the elbows brought in front of the face. The examiner grasps the elbows or the distal upper arms from one side to guide the upper body. The index finger of the hand touching the patient's back palpates between the spinous processes. From this position, spreading and approximation of the spinous processes can be set in motion through flexion or extension, and the relative degree of motion can be evaluated. It

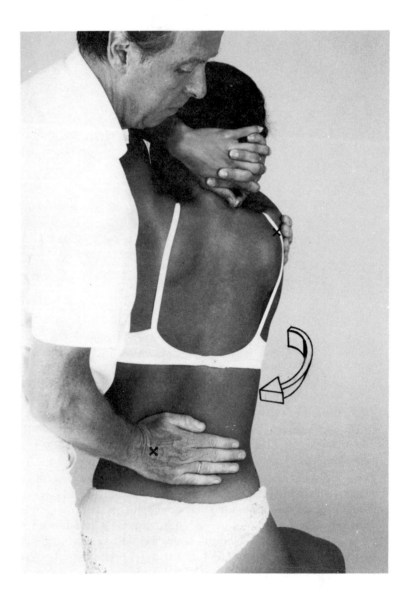

Figure 71 Resistance testing of the right rotators

must be cautioned that every motor segment from T1 to T12 should be checked and none skipped. Testing of segmental lateral flexion and rotation begins the same way; the only difference is that the practitioner's hand guides the upper body from the front, with an assist from his or her contralateral shoulder (Figures 72–75).

With these sequences of examination, one may decide whether disruptions are mainly arthrogenic or muscular. In addition, these tests pinpoint the segmental localization of the existing pathomechanics and the points to which chiropractic therapy can be applied. If restrictions are found during segmental function testing, a mobilization treatment can be implemented without changing patient position. The palpating hand merely moves from the interspinous area, and the thumb fixes the caudal spinous process of the disrupted motor segment. The guiding hand leads the thorax in the restricted direction and, after reaching the disrupted region, repeats the rhythmic mobilizations (Figures 76 and 77).

For regional (nonspecific) mobilization of restricted extension, the patient sits and leans his or her forearms, crossed over the head, onto the shoulders of the therapist, who is standing in front of the patient. The therapist encircles the patient with both arms and places the fingers of both hands on the fixated spinal region. Through rhythmic, backwards, perpendicular movements of the upper body—coupled with simultaneous anteriocranial pulling of the upper body—an extension (back-bending) mobilization effect can be achieved (Figure 78).

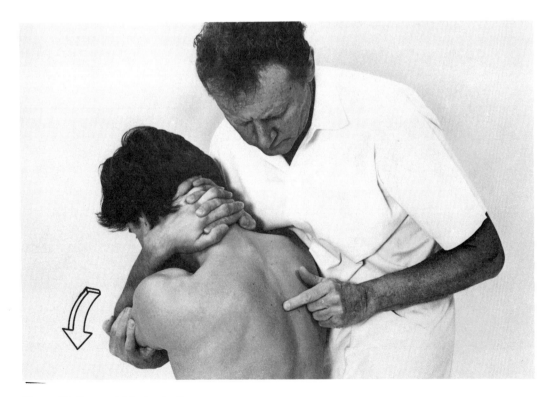

Figure 72 Segmental flexion testing

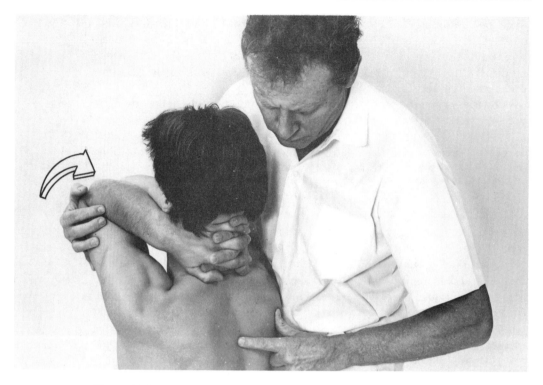

Figure 73 Segmental extension testing.

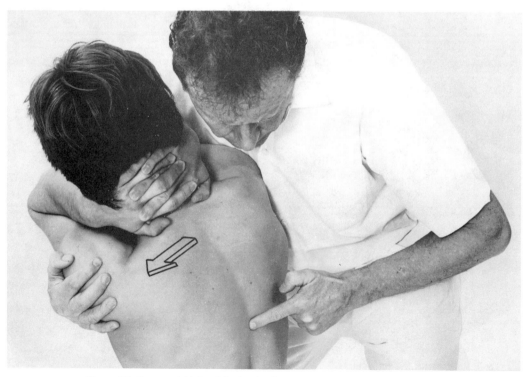

Figure 74 Segmental lateral flexion testing.

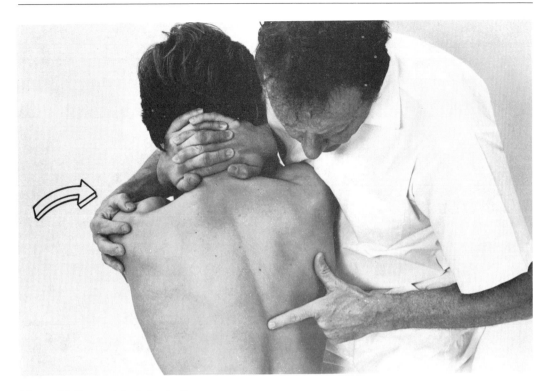

Figure 75 Segmental rotation testing

A common and generalized tractional mobilization of the thoracic spine can be achieved with the patient in the standing position. The therapist steps behind the patient, grasping the patient's arms (which are crossed on the chest and placed on the patient's shoulders) by the elbows, pulling the patient toward the therapist and pushing him or her away, guiding the traction by repeated back-and-forth motions of the therapist's upper body (Figure 79). This treatment is also possible with the patient sitting on the table.

Specific manipulations can be carried out with the patient seated or recumbent. For the lower thoracics (the thoracolumbar transition), the recommended manipulation techniques are those with the patient seated in the Pharaoh's position. The therapist encircles the patient from the front, grasps the opposite shoulders, and brings the disrupted thoracic sector into flexion, rotation, and opposite lateral flexion inclinations (e.g., rotating to the right, laterally flexing to the left) as far as possible until the necessary tension on the disrupted segment is achieved. With the thumb of the other hand on the side of the caudal spinous process opposite the side to which the patient is rotated, the therapist achieves a manipulation effect through an impulse-like increase of rotation of the shoulder and upper body, while the spinous process of the caudal segment is resisted (Figure 80).

With the patient in a similar position, the therapist can give the upper vertebra an impulse-like increase in rotation while extending the trunk

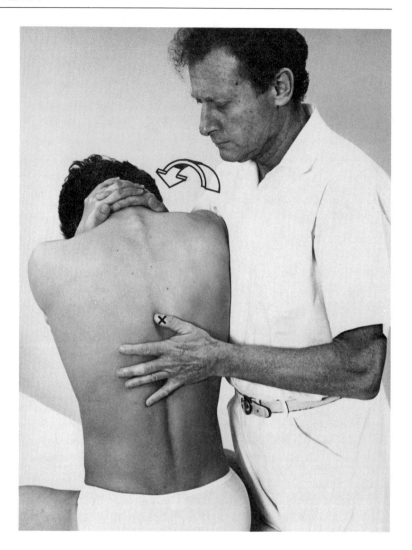

Figure 76 Segmental mobilization—the therapist's thumb fixes the caudal spinous process

with rotation and lateral flexion to the same side. This manipulation is accompanied by a pisiform contact on the transverse process of the cranial vertebra of the disrupted motor segment (Figure 81).

For the thoracolumbar transition, the therapist may use mobilization or manipulation techniques that were previously described for the upper lumbar vertebral levels.

For manipulation of middle and upper thoracics, we recommend that the patient be in a reclining position.

7.2.2 Examining the Thoracic Spine—Results and Consequences

Once again, the first procedure is palpation of the prone patient. The turgor and elasticity of the skin, as well as the tonus of both the superficial

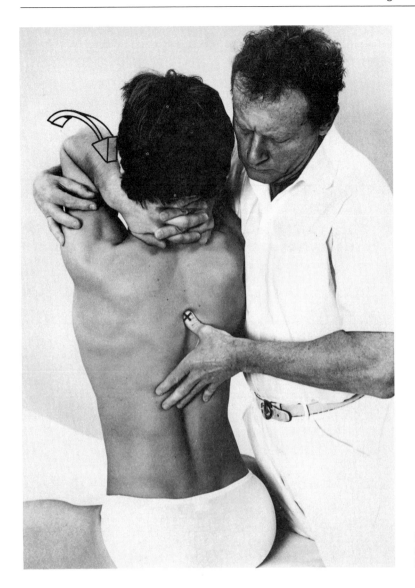

Figure 77 Mobilization of a segmental flexion fixation

and deep-lying paravertebral muscles, should be considered. Pressure and pain palpation of this region should include not only tendon attachments and the interspinous spaces, but also the facet joints and costovertebral joints.

As described in the section on the lumbar spine, the springing test can be applied in the thoracic region; this test will orient the physician, partly by elicitation of pain, to the spinal level of any disruption.

When muscular spasm is noted, one can begin the treatment with soft-tissue techniques. In the lumbosacral transitional area, the therapist can apply cross-fiber (transverse) massage, as in the method introduced for the lumbar spine (Figures 62 a and b). For therapy of the superficial muscles, a purely perpendicular massage is best. The therapist stands contralateral

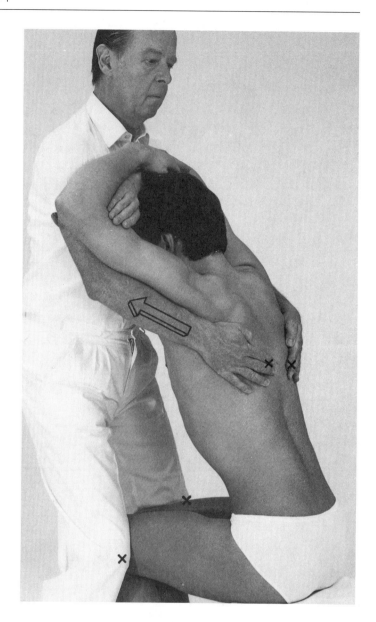

Figure 78 Regional (nonspecific) mobilization of restricted extension

to the side of treatment and places an extended thumb immediately adjacent to the patient's spinous processes and parallel to the erector spinae bulge. With the heel of the other hand, the therapist reinforces the laterally massaging thumb (Figures 82 a and b). Use of a pisiform contact is recommended for the deeper muscle layers; additional pressure may be obtained by placing one hand on the wrist of the massaging hand (Figure 83).

Primary (specific) muscular disruptions also must be therapeutically considered, especially those that involve the pectoralis and interscapular muscular systems. Especially in cases of increased kyphosis, drooped

Figure 79 Tractional mobilization of the thoracic spine

shoulders, or anteriorly rotated shoulders, the pectoralis is frequently hypertonic and necessitates the stretching treatment described as follows.

The treatment of the spasmodic or contracted pectoralis is initiated with the patient in a supine position. The patient's outstretched arm hangs off the table edge in the direction of muscle fiber orientation. The pectoralis muscle, which should be extended to its maximum length, can be isometrically activated against slight resistance of the practitioner's hand and

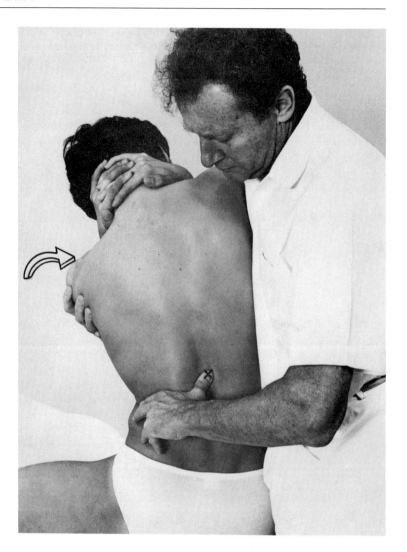

Figure 80 Rotation manipulation in the thoracic spine—"resistive technique"

should be gently stretched in the relaxation phase (again in the direction of the muscle fiber). With the other hand, the practitioner fixes on the contralateral side of the upper thorax to prevent the chest cage from lifting during stretching. Depending on whether the sternal or clavicular pectoralis sector is being stretched, the abduction of the arm must be modified (Figures 84 and 85 a and b).

Isometrics for the spasmodic or contracted interscapular muscular system can be better carried out with the patient seated. In this position, the arm on the side of spasm and pain is maximally adducted (the elbow is guided toward the opposite shoulder) and is stopped or fixed at the point of end-feel by the practitioner's grasp on the patient's elbow. Raising or lowering the elbow allows isometric activation in the exact direction of the muscle fiber spasm; thus, contraction is achieved through the patient's ab-

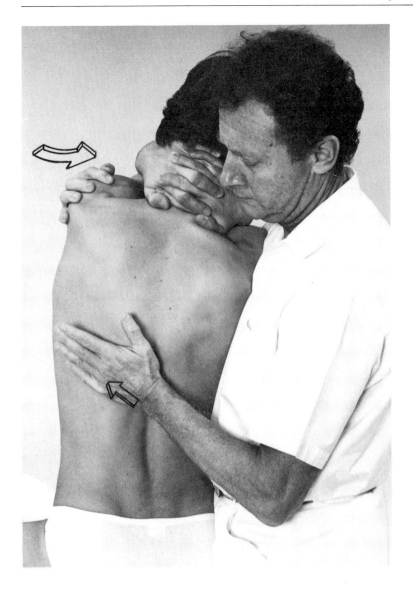

Figure 81 Rotation manipulation of the dorsal spinal column—the "passive technique"

duction against slight resistance (Figures 86 and 87). One indication for this stretching is seen when the described technique provokes interscapular pain when applied in a testing fashion.

In addition to manipulation techniques on the seated patient, which primarily are useful in the upper thoracic spine, another method is universally applicable to all types of fixations in the middle and upper thoracics. The patient is in the side posture, with his or her hands clasped behind the neck, with the elbows over the chest. The therapist approaches the patient from the front and positions the contact hand so that the thumb and index finger form a "V" and the third through fifth fingers are bent at the middle and distal phalanges. The position of this hand on the caudal

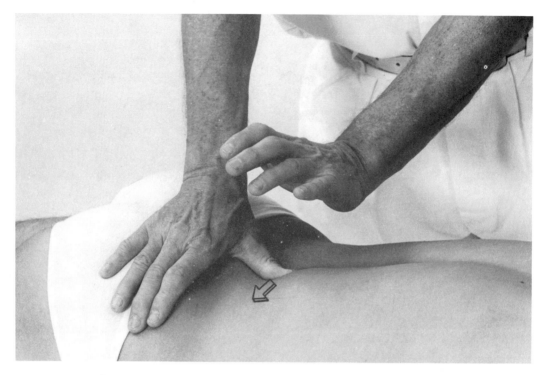

Figure 82a Cross-fiber (transverse) massage of the superficial back muscles in the lumbar and thoracic regions (step 1)

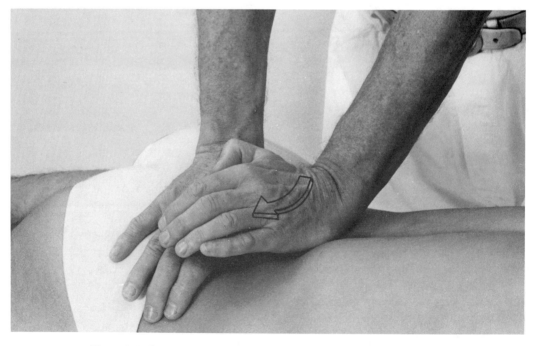

Figure 82b Cross-fiber massage of the superficial back muscles in the lumbar and thoracic regions (step 2)

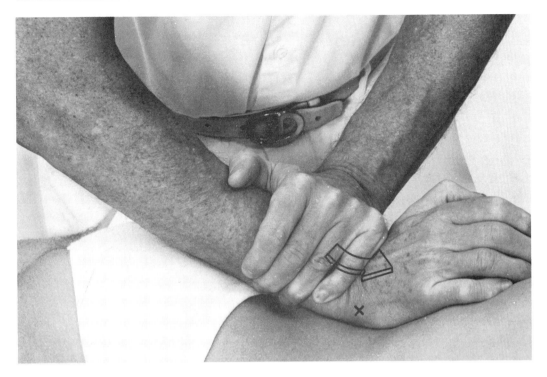

Figure 83 Massage of the deep muscle layers with a pisiform contact

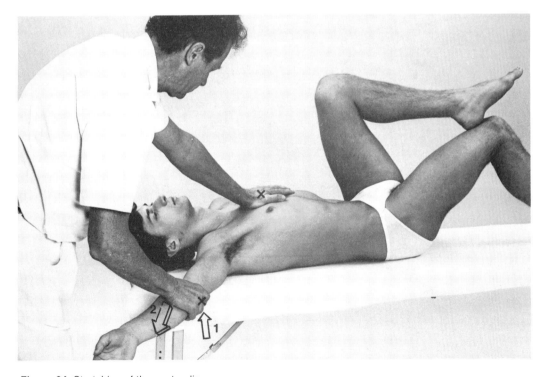

Figure 84 Stretching of the pectoralis

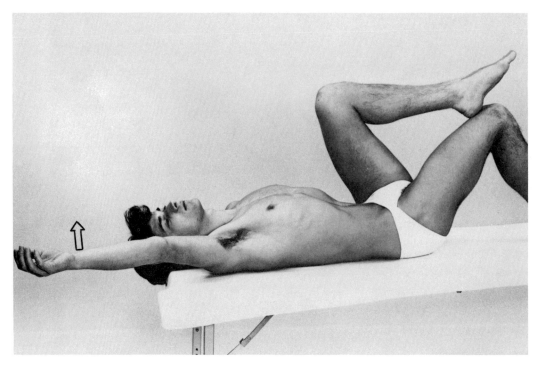

Figure 85a Stretching of the pectoralis—self–treatment using gravity and MET (step 1)

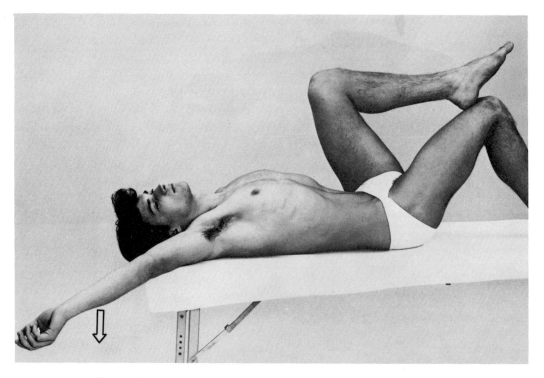

Figure 85b Stretching of the pectoralis—self–treatment using gravity and MET (step 2)

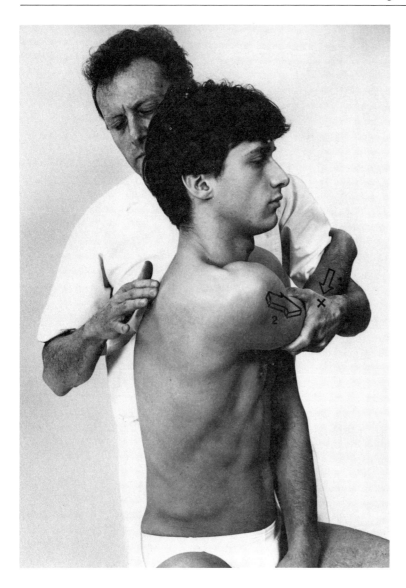

Figure 86 Postisometric relaxation (PIR) treatment for the interscapular muscular system

vertebra of the segment to be manipulated can now be varied in accordance with the type of fixation.

1. The most universally effective technique seems to be "manipulation into extension." The patient's arms are first grasped with the cephalad hand of the practitioner and used to slightly rotate the patient to the side. The practitioner's contact hand is placed on the caudal vertebra of the motor segment, with the middle finger's middle joint and the thumb's metacarpophalangeal joint on the transverse processes. The practitioner then rolls the patient slowly onto his or her back and onto the practitioner's contact hand, and reinforces the tension on the motor segment with the weight of the practitioner's upper body. The

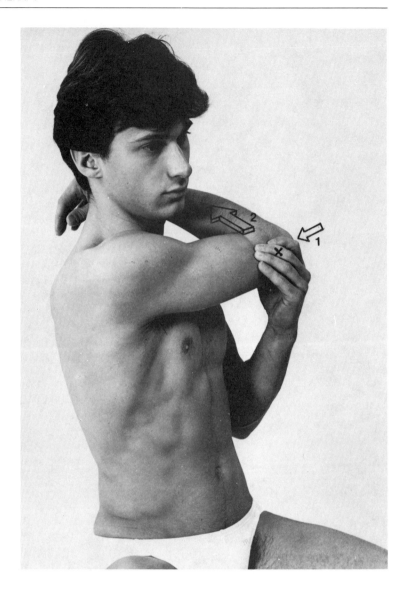

Figure 87 Self-treatment for spasm of the interscapular muscular system

manipulation impulse consists of a pressure of the upper body on the crossed arms of the patient (Figures 88–93).

2. To achieve manipulation into flexion with this technique, the therapist should perform the manipulation impulse with a more caudally oriented line of drive (Figure 93).

3. To obtain an additional rotational effect (which is controversial), the therapist may allow the contact hand to deviate in an ulnar direction. The thumb's metacarpophalangeal joint and the middle finger's middle joint lie on the upper and lower transverse processes of both vertebrae, respectively. The manipulation impulse is against the contact hand and increases rotation of the cephalad vertebral segment toward the practitioner. For example, for a left rotational restriction, the practitioner stands to the left of the patient (Figure 91).

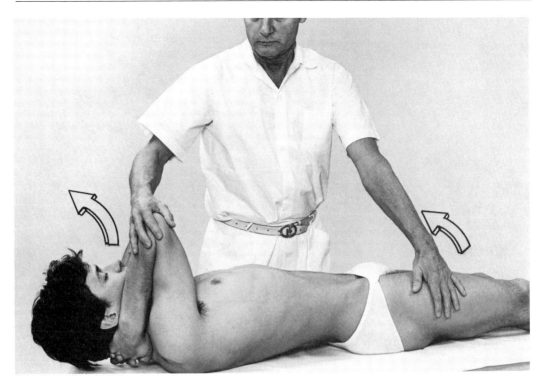

Figure 88 Universal manipulation technique for the thoracic spine. Phase 1: From the supine position, with hands clasped behind the neck, the patient is turned into the side position

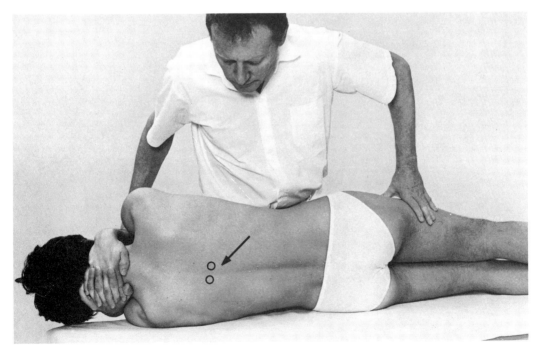

Figure 89 Phase 2: With the patient on the side, the disrupted segment is ready to be contacted

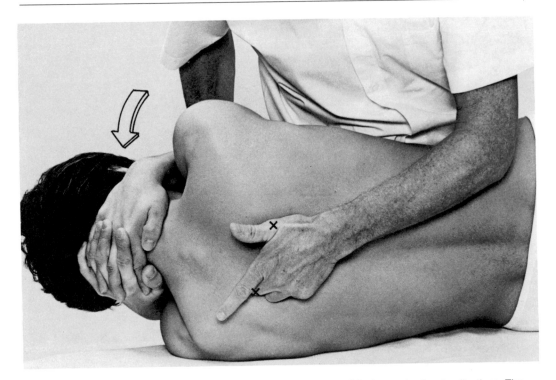

Figure 90 Achieving contact for the manipulation of flexion and extension fixations. The patient subsequently will be rotated onto the back (Phase 3)

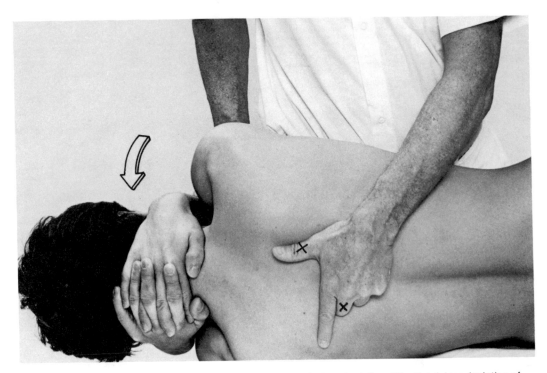

Figure 91 Achieving contact for the manipulation of rotational fixation (ulnar deviation of the wrist joint). The patient will then be rotated onto the back

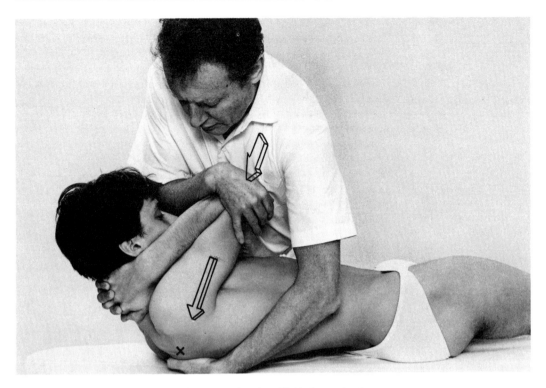

Figure 92 Rolling the patient onto the contact hand and initiating a simultaneous manipulation impulse

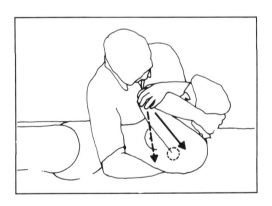

Figure 93 The direction of the manipulation impulse for flexion and extension fixation. *Source:* H. Tilscher and M. Eder, *Textbook of Reflex Therapy*

7.2.3 Costovertebral Joint Dysfunction

Disruptions in the area of the costovertebral joints and sternochondral junctions contribute more to thoracic pain syndromes than one might think. These disruptions often are implicated in mechanically induced dyspnea. Corresponding diagnosis of such syndromes is reached by exclusionary means, which, again, can result only from a thorough, differentially diagnostic examination. If such a corresponding symptomatology exists, disruptions of rib mobility often can be elucidated during examination of the thoracic spine with the patient in a seated position.

Hint: A painful xyphoid process may indicate a functionally disrupted seventh rib.

7.2.3.1 Costovertebral Examination and Treatment Techniques on the Seated Patient

For the costovertebral examination, the practitioner steps to the contralateral side of the suspected disruption and grasps the patient's arm (whose

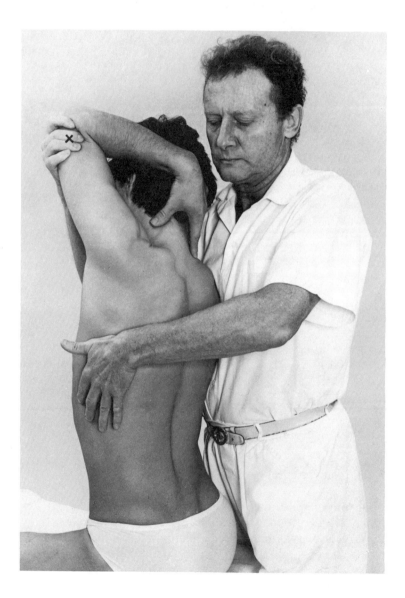

Figure 94 Terrier's harp: Testing of the middle and lower posterior ribs

hand is lying on the back of the neck) from just below the elbow. With one or two palpation fingers of the other hand, which are lying flat on the posterior axillar line of the intercostal areas to be tested, the examiner can discern the degree and synchronicity of rib motion. This test is more sensitive when the patient's elbow is pulled toward the examiner, achieving separation of the ribs. The positions of patient and doctor can be likened to the picture of a harp player; this examination technique is known (after its originator's name) as Terrier's harp. The technique is especially suitable for evaluation of the middle and lower portion of the posterior ribs (Figure 94).

From the same position, one can test the upper costovertebral joints. The palpation fingers lie paravertebrally over the joints for evaluation of joint play, and the examiner's guiding hand makes contact with the patient's elbow, pushing in a posterior direction (Figure 95).

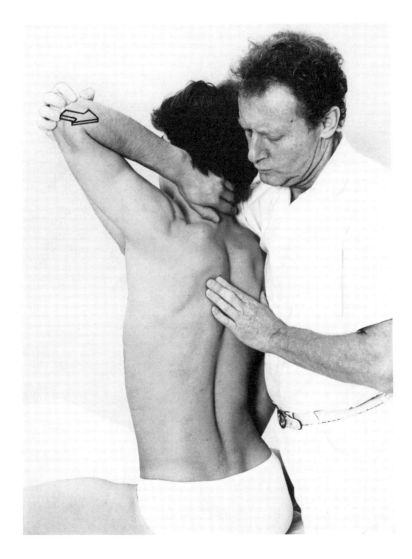

Figure 95 Testing the upper costovertebral joints

Functional disruptions of the first (and possibly down to the fifth) rib should be considered as pathogenic factors of shoulder-arm pain syndromes and of chronic headaches.

For testing the first rib, which has a unique anatomical orientation, two complementary methods are used. In the first, the patient's head is rotated 45° away from the side to be tested and then laterally fixed, perpendicular to the sagittal plane. The lateral index edge of the examiner's other hand acts as a fixing fulcrum in the area of the first rib. The elastic end-feel, as well as degree of motion (glide), are evaluated and compared bilaterally (Figure 96).

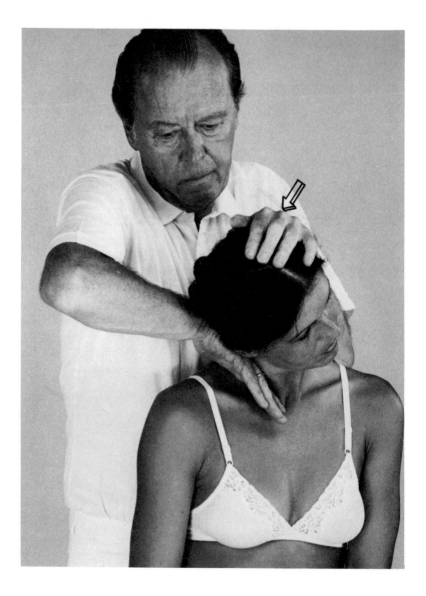

Figure 96 Testing the first rib

In the second method, the head is rotated 45° toward the side being tested. The physician's lower arm and hand secure this position. The curled lateral index finger of the examiner's impulse hand makes contact with the first rib and checks the functional relationship of the first rib through rhythmic pressure directed from anterior/superior to posterior/inferior (Figure 97).

As in previously described examinations, this test variation leads directly into a possible therapeutic maneuver. Repeated implementation of the test movement produces a mobilization effect. In cases of mild fixation, specific manipulation of the first rib can be accomplished, in an analogous sense, with a quick, impulse-like increase in pressure of the mobilization movement.

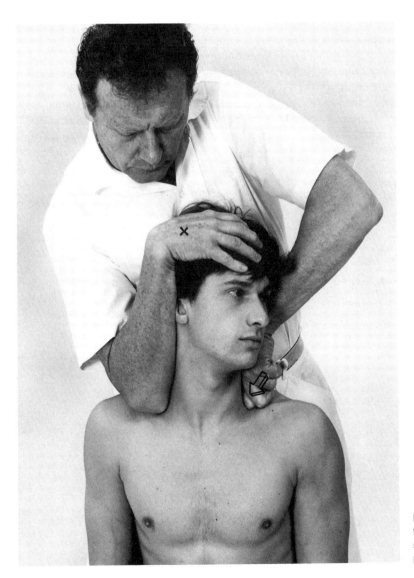

Figure 97 Testing the first rib—modification and simultaneous starting position for mobilization

7.2.3.2 Costovertebral Examination and Treatment Techniques in the Supine Patient

Mobilization of the first rib also is possible when the patient is supine. The therapist stands at the patient's head, holding the head and neck with one hand. The other hand makes caudally directed contact on the first rib with the radial side of the index finger. The forearm of this hand is perpendicular to the rib and is stabilized by the practitioner's elbow, which is supported by his or her own hip. The mobilization is effected when the practitioner pushes this hip-elbow support forward. The impulse passes through the forearm and on to the contact finger (Figure 98). In addition, an isometric variation can be performed from this position. The patient isometrically contracts the neck toward the side of disruption and against the resistance of the practitioner's hand on the back of the head, with further pressure in the direction of mobilization during the relaxation phase (Figure 98).

While the patient is supine, the functions of the second through the fifth ribs also can be evaluated. The examiner makes bilateral comparisons of a contact in the intercostal spaces at the midclavicular line, which evaluates synchronous rib movement during respiration (Figures 99 and 100).

The upper anterior ribs can be treated similarly by using resistance and reinforcement of respiratory movements in both inspiration and expiration. The recommended means of providing resistance is the use of flat

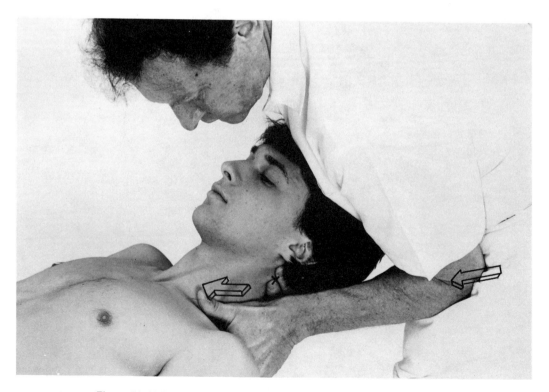

Figure 98 Mobilization of the first rib, with the patient lying supine

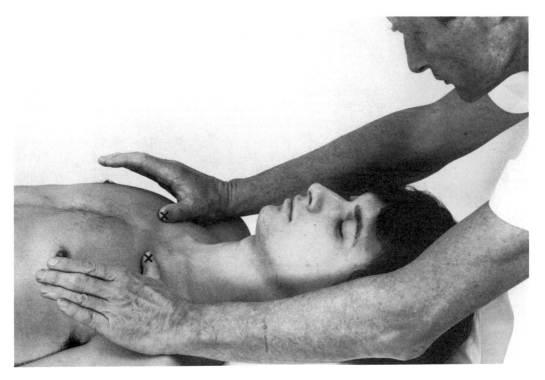

Figure 99 Testing of rib mobility (the second through fifth ribs)—initial position for mobilization

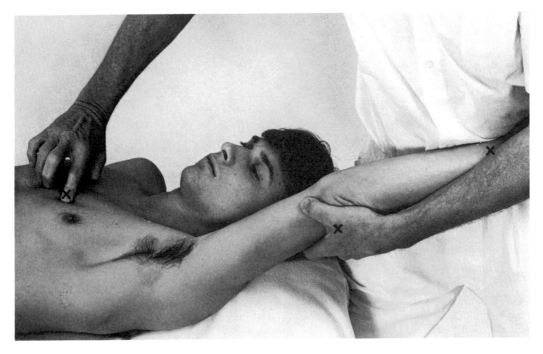

Figure 100 Additional examination of the upper anterior ribs. The intercostally located palpating fingers feel the respiratory movement of the ribs

thumbs in the intercostal spaces. Depending on whether expiratory and inspiratory phases of movement are restricted, either the caudal or cranial ribs are fixed during the opposite breathing phase (Figure 99).

With the patient now in the side posture (the side being tested facing up), the patient's arm is extended overhead. The therapist grasps the upper arm and pulls it slightly in a cranial direction. The therapist's palpating fingers lie in the intercostal spaces at the midaxillary line. With no additional traction of the patient's arm, the therapist may observe respiratory separation and approximation of the ribs. This method is recommended especially for the evaluation of the lateral lower rib sections (Figures 100 and 101). For treatment, this position can be used as a starting point for mobilization or specific manipulation.

To conclude, the end-feel of rib motion of both sides can be tested on the prone patient during other parts of the thoracic exam. The examiner stands at the head of the table and places the hands flat on the patient's thorax—with the fingers pointing anterior and inferior—and directs short pressure-like impulses onto the ribs (Figure 102).

If carried out on one side only, such a test can be used to evaluate the end-feel of motion of individual ribs. In this case, the contralateral side of the thorax is excluded from accompanying movement by a paravertebrally supporting hand, and slight impulses are carried out only on those indi-

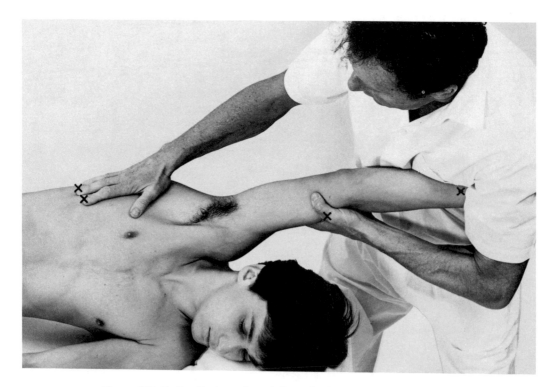

Figure 101 Testing the lower lateral rib sections

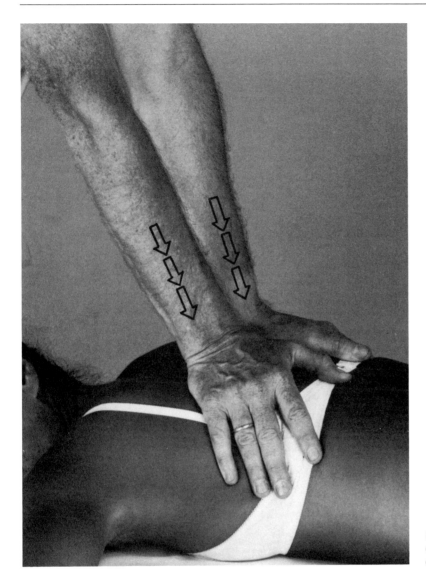

Figure 102 "Elasticity" of the ribs—bilateral comparison

vidual ribs to be examined. Costovertebral fixations can also be mobilized in this manner (Figures 102 and 103).

Using this concluding mobilization position, the therapist can implement PIR without changing hand position. The rib is challenged during the point of greatest excursion during expiration, fixed or resisted with the angle of the hand during inspiration, and then further challenged on the next expirational phase. Multiple repetitions are necessary.

For manipulative treatment of costovertebral joint fixations, the previously described, universal anterior-to-posterior technique can also be used. The only variation is that the maximally bent thumb serves as joint contact and is applied to find an anchor on the costal tubercle (Figures 104 a-c).

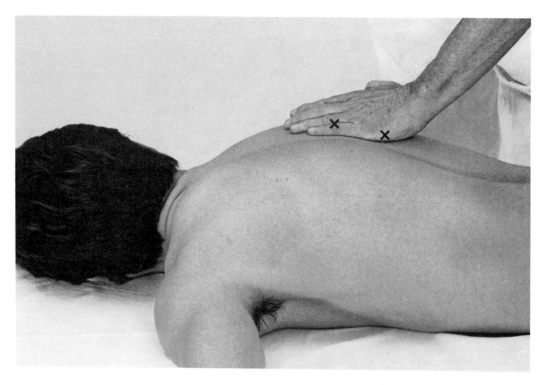

Figure 103a Unilateral elasticity of individual ribs—testing and mobilization (step 1)

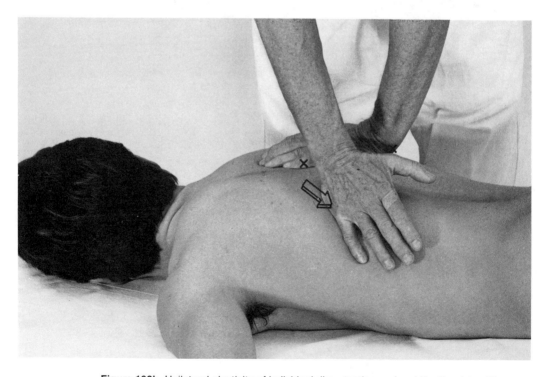

Figure 103b Unilateral elasticity of individual ribs—testing and mobilization (step 2)

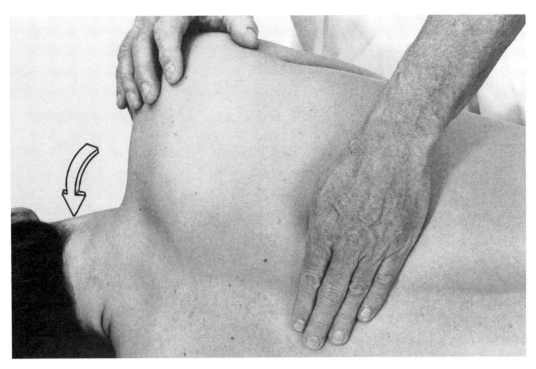

Figure 104a Manipulation of the costovertebral joint with the universal anterior-to-posterior technique. The therapist's bent thumb contacts the costal tubercle

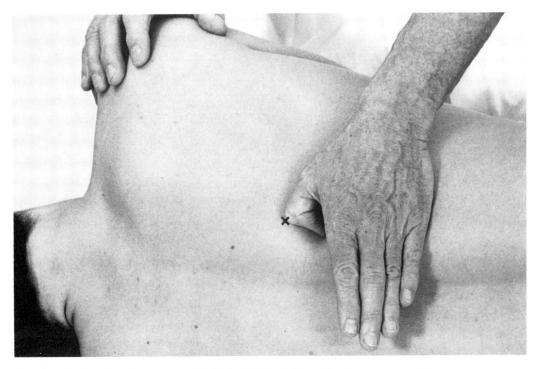

Figure 104b Covering the contact point with the flat hand. The patient is now returned to the supine position

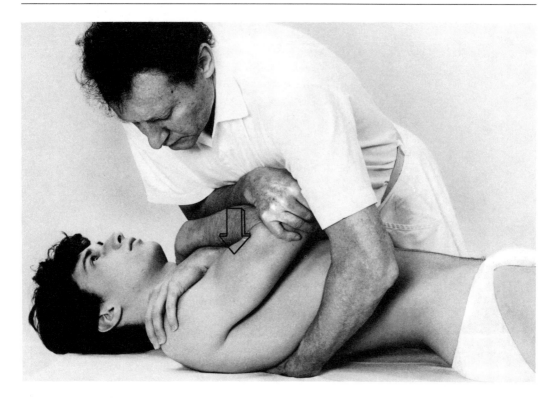

Figure 104c The manipulation impulse

7.3 THE CERVICOTHORACIC TRANSITION

The observation of individual spinal regions, strictly speaking, should never be seen as a solitary and regionally confined procedure. On one hand, the spinal column is an entire functional unit; on the other hand, the biomechanical idiosyncracies of individual spinal regions very much determine the functional and mechanical factors of neighboring regions. This point is especially valid when considering the upper thoracic and lower cervical vertebrae, a sector designated as the *cervicothoracic transition* and consisting of the C6 to T3 segments.

> Transitional areas are highly susceptible to disruptions.

To an even larger extent than in the thoracic spine, segmentally reflexive interactions between the spine and visceral organs should be considered as potential factors in functional disruptions of the cervicothoracic transition. For example, in the cardiovertebral syndromes, the primary irritation can be organically as well as vertebrally induced.

7.3.1 Examination and Treatment of the Cervicothoracic Transition

Because active and passive range of motion testing is an integral part of the examination of both the thoracic and cervical spine, the main interest here is confined to the intersegmental mobility test.

The therapist's hand on top of the patient's head guides the head and cervical spine into normal motion ranges against a palpation finger placed between the spinous processes. The therapist then evaluates the degree of movement and end-feel.

A better glimpse into the functional efficiency of the joint apparatus of this region can be obtained through evaluation of translational glide. The patient's cervical spine, in a "wrap grip" (Figure 105), is pushed slightly posterior in a parallel fashion so that each successive cephalad vertebra glides gently on its caudal partner. The therapist places a finger of the other hand on the interspinous spaces and evaluates this gliding motion, lack of which is an expression of a segmental functional disruption (Figure 106).

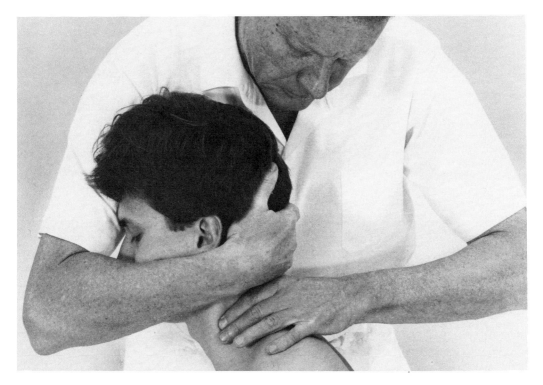

Figure 105 The "wrap grip"

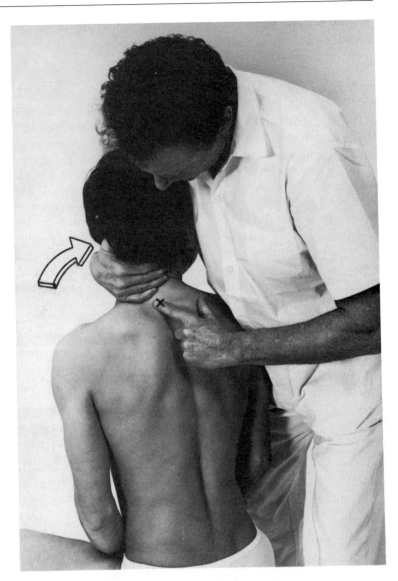

Figure 106 Testing of mobility and translational glide in the seated patient. In the illustration: testing rotation to the right

The "wrap grip" is the most effective method for treatment and support of the cervical spine. It replaces or complements the so-called joint locking of the segments cranial to the treatment area. The head is encircled so that the patient's face is in the crook of the practitioner's elbow, with the practitioner's lower arm and wrist covering the jaw as well as the ear; the ulnar angle of the hand fixes on the cranial vertebra of the given motor segment.

Translational glide testing can be used in both sagittal and frontal planes, thus testing transverse impulses. To accomplish this testing, the patient's head is held in the wrap grip so that the therapist's hand contacts the back of the head and the ulnar edge of the fifth digit is fixed on C1 (atlas). The fixation of the caudal segment is provided by a forked grip (thumb and index finger) of the other hand. The examiner then transversely pulls the cranial vertebra of the motor segment forward and simultaneously applies traction; the examiner can then evaluate the glide of the given motor segment.

These tests can also be carried out with the patient in the side posture. The examiner places the patient's head on the examiner's forearm. The rest of the execution corresponds exactly to the previous examination. These tractional tests can be applied in a similar manner in the remaining cervical vertebral segments (Figure 107). In both examination positions, effective mobilizations can be performed with no change in hand position. By applying traction to the cranial vertebra of the motor segment, the therapist can mobilize the vertebra in all axes of motion against the fixed (locked) caudal segment (Figure 108).

For the manipulative treatment of the more thoracic levels of this area, the previously described techniques of thoracic vertebral manipulation, with the patient in the supine positions, are quite effective (Figures 88–93).

With the patient seated and with his or her arms clasped around the neck, the so-called double nelson manipulation can also be applied. This designation comes from wrestling terminology. The practitioner grasps the

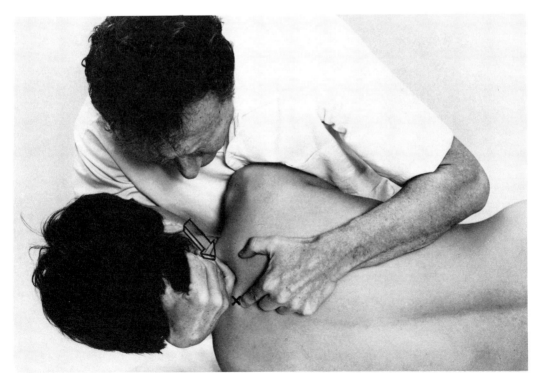

Figure 107 Testing translational glide with the patient in the side posture

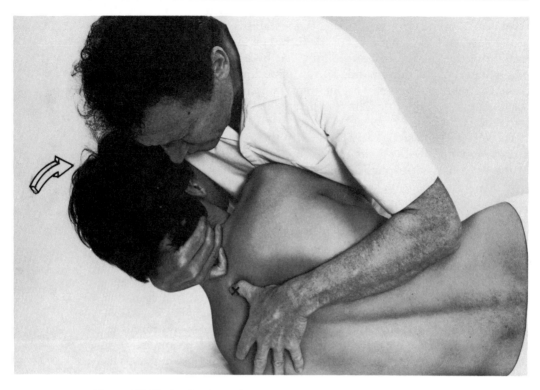

Figure 108 Flexion fixation mobilization in the cervicothoracic transitional area

patient's lower arms from behind, asking the patient to clasp his or her hands behind the occiput and flex the head forward. The practitioner's hands accompany this motion and the second and third fingers of both hands are fixed on the spinous process of the upper cervicals. The necessary tissue tension is achieved as the patient passively leans back. A cranially directed impulse effects the manipulation through the practitioner's fingers (Figure 109).

Lateral flexion and rotational restrictions also can be alleviated in this area through specific segmental impulse manipulations.

The practitioner may put his or her foot on the table, contralateral to the side of treatment; the patient then places an arm over the physician's bent knee and upper thigh to support the axilla.

The practitioner then pulls the patient's trunk toward the practitioner's leg and asks the patient to lean in relaxed fashion on the leg. With one hand, the head is now laterally fixed toward the treatment side and rotated away from the contact hand. In this position, the cervical vertebrae lying cranial to the disrupted segment can be securely locked. It is alternately possible for the patient to simply lean back, relaxed, against the practitioner, who then brings the cervical vertebrae into proper position for treatment. As the practitioner's other hand makes contact, the thumb is on the side of the spinous process of the caudal vertebra. The entire position should be constructed so that the manipulation impulse can work directly on the exact segment at the cervical concavity created by the lateral flexion.

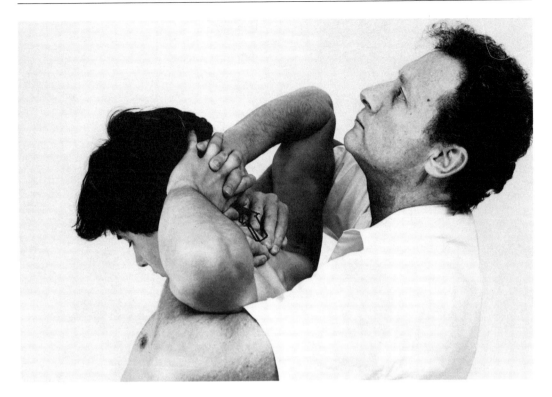

Figure 109 The "double nelson" manipulation

The impulse itself is against the side of the spinous process. The thumb must form a line diagonally down toward the contralateral side and in line with the practitioner's forearm, so that the upper vertebra can be rotated in the direction of treatment. The total relaxation of the patient is important for the success of this manipulation. In particular, the shoulder girdle and the arm must hang relaxed on the treatment side. The manipulative push is produced through a simultaneous, slight increase of the lateral flexion of the spine (Figures 110 a–c).

Another cervicothoracic manipulation technique, which is useful not only for the cervical portion of the cervicothoracic junction, but also for the upper cervical vertebrae, also can be accomplished in the seated patient. The therapist stands in front of the patient and to the side in which the rotation is restricted. One hand encircles the patient's head and makes a forked contact with the caudal vertebra of the disrupted motor segment. The other arm encircles the head from the opposite side and makes contact with its ulnar edge and fifth digit on the dorsal portion of the cranial vertebra. The head is now turned in the direction of the restricted rotation until the end range of physiological rotation of the upper vertebra is reached. Simultaneously, the head is placed laterally as far as possible, so that segments that lie cranial to the lesion are locked. The manipulative impulse consists of rotation and increased traction and is especially effective when this maneuver is coupled with a simultaneous relaxation of the

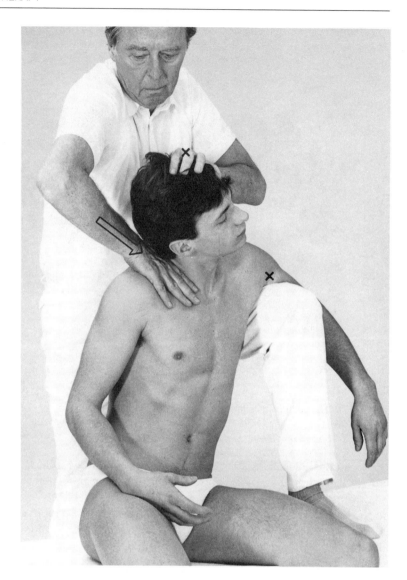

Figure 110a Specific manipulation in the cervicothoracic junction. The contralateral axilla is supported over the practitioner's knee

patient ("he allows himself to sink in the direction of the practitioner") (Figure 111).

7.4 THE CERVICAL REGION

General information concerning the cervical vertebrae is probably evident from the first contact with the patient. Some things to watch for are the shape of the neck, head position and carriage, shoulder carriage, and the height of the hairline on the neck. A short neck with a low hairline possibly indicates existing deformities. High shoulders with a convex tra-

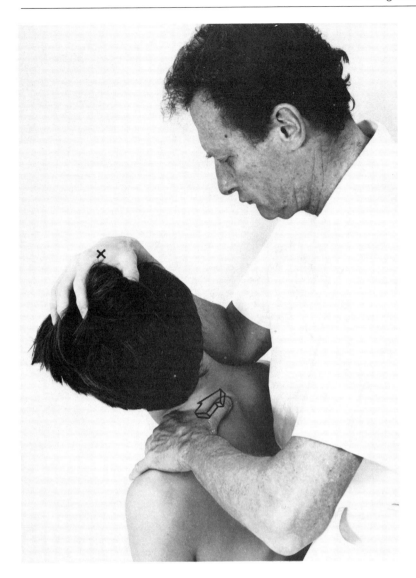

Figure 110b The standard progression of manipulation in the cervicothoracic junction

pezius edge are a sign of spasm of the trapezius. Neck rotation and a tilted position of the head can be an expression of an acute disruption or a spastic torticollis. In addition, the inspection can provide further differentiation because the head and cervical spine will rotate away from a radicular irritation (to open the intervertebral foramen), while the head will be rotated and laterally flexed toward the side of lesion in cases of spastic torticollis.

> The inspection provides important signs to aid in evaluation of the cervical spine.

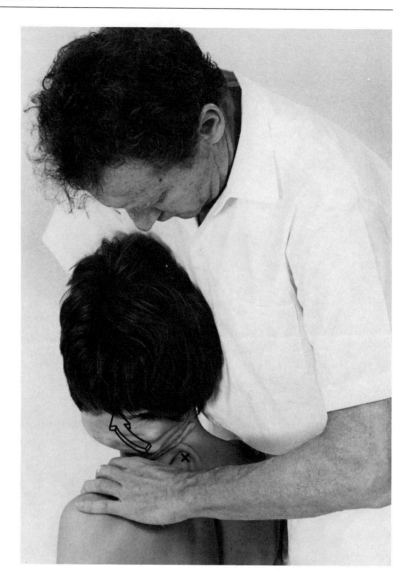

Figure 110c
Implementation of the
"wrap grip" with
additional traction

7.4.1 Examining the Cervical Vertebrae in the Seated Patient—Results and Consequences

During range-of-motion testing, one should pay special attention to possible restrictions. The ranges of motion should be evaluated according to the criteria mentioned in Section II; without knowledge of these details, a functional diagnosis of the cervical spine is impossible. As in previous exam sequences the range-of-motion testing is obtained actively, passively, and in resistance.

In passive testing, the head and cervical spine are guided by the examiner's hand, placed on top of the patient's head. The examiner moves the head and neck through the individual planes of movement, being careful

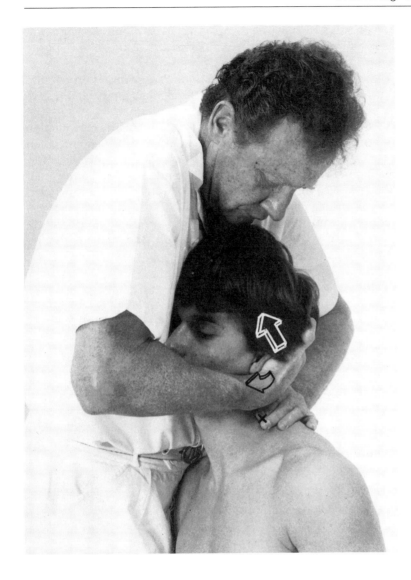

Figure 111 Manipulation using rotation and increased traction—fork-like fixation of the lower joint partner

to compare rotation and lateral flexion bilaterally. The examiner should also note the end-feel of the motion ranges through gentle overpressure, which is often quite difficult in functional disruptions.

Rotation is first tested in a neutral position, which primarily tests summative function from C1 to T3. To perform further differentiation, one then tests rotation with the neck in flexion. In this position, the sectors below C2 are locked, and the noted area of rotation allows inferences regarding the function of the upper cervical joints. When the head is in maximum extension, the upper cervical joints are locked; the rotation takes place primarily in the caudally lying segments.

In resistance testing of the cervicals, the results of resisted rotation are of special interest. To perform this test, the patient attempts to move his or her head isometrically to the opposite side, after having the neck fixed in maximal compression with the wrap grip. If pain emerges or is increased, this is an indication of muscular disruption in the area opposite the side to which the head is rotated.

The next step of the examination is palpation. Using precautions similar to those for the other spinal areas, both superficial and deep palpations are carried out.

One must maintain an awareness of the desired goal of any examination while performing it. For palpation, one must obtain information about structure and vertebral level of involvement, as well as invaluable information about the patient's pain threshold. The findings must be regarded as only partly objective, and must be expanded through further functional examinations. To understand the special relationships within the cervical region, the therapist must systematically probe the most frequent localizations of pain. A list was developed by H.D. Wolff and contains the following sequence of points:

- temporomandibular joint
- lateral mass of the atlas
- Hackett's ABC points on the superior nuchal line (Figure 112)
- tender points in the paralaminar spine
- insertions of the levator scapulae
- interscapular pressure points
- supraspinatus and infraspinatus
- acromioclavicular joint
- greater or lesser tubercle of the humerus
- coracoid process
- sternoclavicular joints
- sternocostal junctions
- medial and lateral humeral epicondyle
- styloid process of the radius

This checklist is useful in further differentiation between arthrogenic and muscular pathomechanics, and it becomes a guide for further examinations and treatments.

Should there be signs of muscular problems during resistance testing or palpation, all corresponding consequences should be examined, especially to discover whether the muscular system is the primary pathological factor.

The following muscles should be especially attended to:

- trapezius
- paravertebral cervical muscles
- levator scapulae
- sternocleidomastoideus
- the Scalenus group

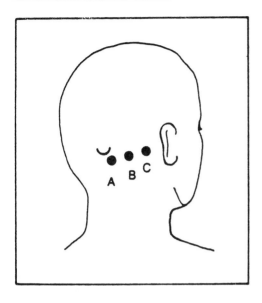

Figure 112 Hackett's ABC points. *Source:* H. Tilscher and M. Eder, *Textbook of Reflex Therapy*

Spasms of the trapezius are expressed posturally through shoulders' being held high on the neck and through a convex-shaped silhouette of the upper muscle edge, as well as through palpation and testing.

Massaging of the muscle edge is recommended as the first step in treatment of this area. The patient must assume a position in which the muscle is relaxed, either prone or seated, with clasped arms supporting the head. The practitioner treats the free dorsal muscle edge with a kneading massage.

For the trapezius, PIR can best be applied with the patient supine. With one hand, the practitioner stabilizes the patient's shoulder; with the other, the practitioner laterally flexes the head as far as possible toward the opposite side and turns the face slightly toward the stabilized shoulder. At the end range of possible motion the patient contracts the muscle isometrically by bending the head against resistance, and the angle of lateral flexion is increased in the relaxation phase. A variation is also possible in which the head is fixed while the isometric contraction stretching is performed by the shoulder (the shoulder is pressed caudally) (Figures 113 and 114).

For stretching of spasm of the levator scapulae, the patient can also be in the supine position. The head lies exactly even with the upper edge of the table, the arm on the painful side is flexed, and the elbow is cranially directed to contact the practitioner's body. The practitioner then uses this contact to direct force through the elbow onto the scapula in a caudal direction and thus achieves a pre-stretch of the levator scapulae. With the hand supporting the back of the patient's skull, the head is then pushed toward the opposite side. At the end point of possible lateral motion, the patient provides isometric resistance. In the relaxation phase, the head should be slightly raised and rotated further to the opposite side. Instead of resisting motion of the head, it is also possible to achieve isometric activation by a cranially directed pressure of the patient's elbow against the body of the practitioner. The direction of treatment in PIR remains the

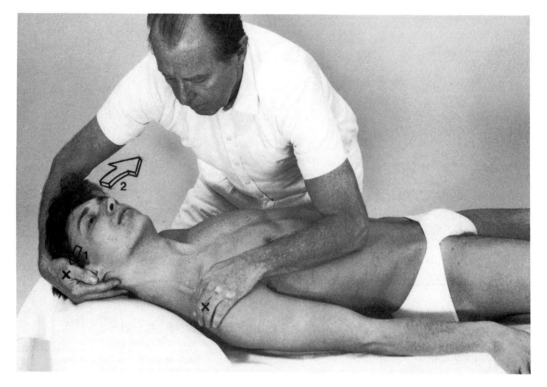

Figure 113 PIR of the trapezius

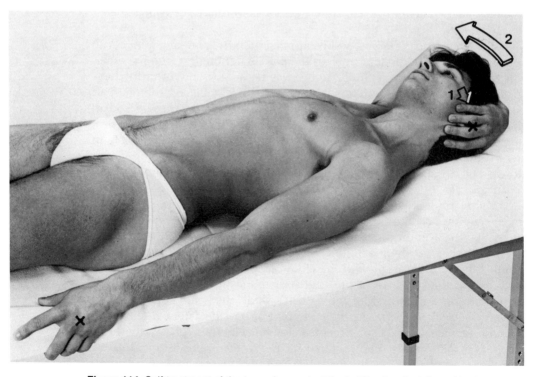

Figure 114 Self-treatment of the trapezius against the holding hand—followed by increase of lateral flexion. The head is slightly rotated toward the direction of stretch

same. Both methods can be interchangeably used in the course of mobilization (Figures 115 and 116).

To relax the sternocleidomastoideus postisometrically, the patient remains supine. The head hangs freely in extension over the edge of the table. The muscle is stretched through rotation to the opposite side. Resistance against the chin builds the pre-stretch. During relaxation, the head should be further extended and rotated, that is, supported and guided. After a few repetitions, the typical pain pressure point located at the clavicular insertion of the muscle declines if treatment is successful (Figure 117).

The common pains and deficiencies caused by dysfunction of the scalene muscles, such as dysesthesias into the arm, impingement sensations, and headaches, can be successfully treated through isometrics for these muscles. This treatment should be performed on the seated patient. The head is extended and rotated to the side opposite the spasm. One hand fixes on the cheek and lower jaw and the other fixes on the upper half of the thorax, with a subclavicular contact. After isometric activation against the fixed hands, the scalene group can be stretched in the relaxation phase by an increase in extension and rotation (Figures 118 and 119).

As seen in the accompanying illustrations, the proposed isometrics, varied in intensity, can be used by the patient for self-treatment.

Spasms of the paravertebral neck musculature respond well to kneading massage, and this method is also useful in preparation for mobilizations and manipulations. The implementation is best on the supine patient.

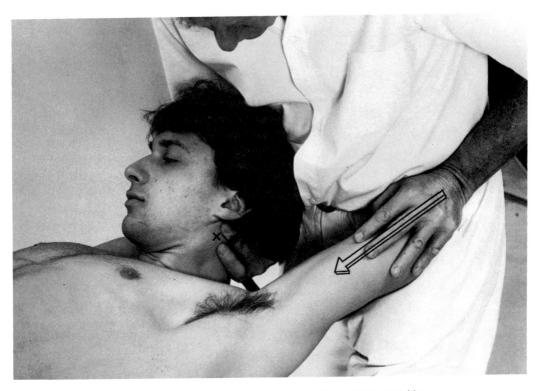

Figure 115 PIR of the levator scapulae—after resistance against the occiput, stretching results through caudal pressure of the upper arm with elbow contact

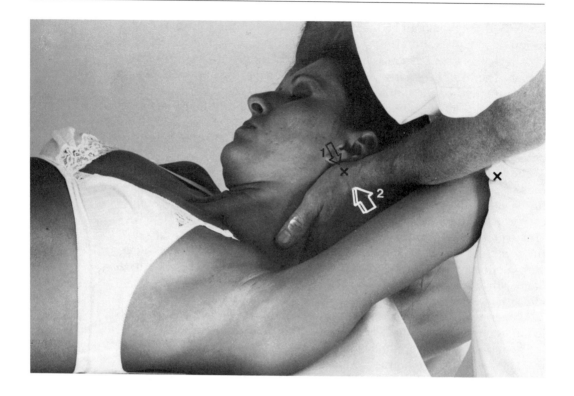

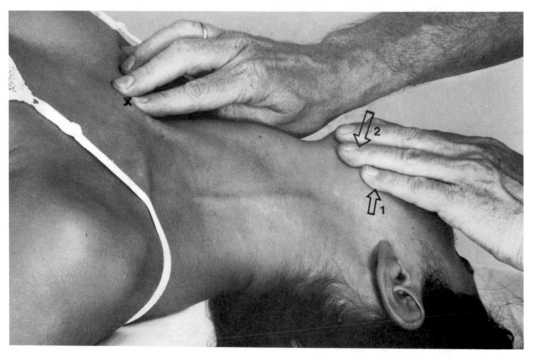

Figure 117 Postisometric relaxation (PIR) of the sternocleidomastoideus. A self-treatment is also possible (the patient's hands fix the chin)

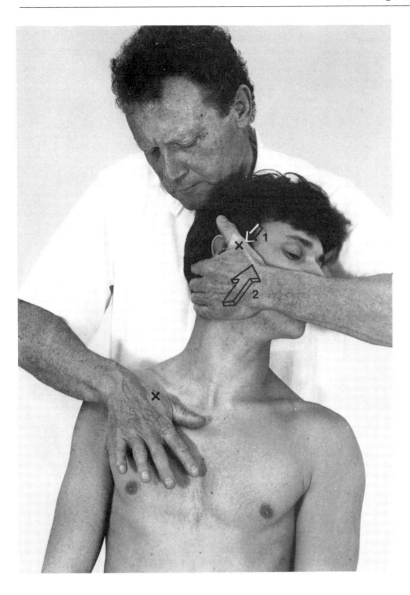

Figure 118 PIR for the scalenus muscle group

For treatment of the superficial muscles, the practitioner stands at the head of the table and grasps the patient's neck from the front so that the second through fourth fingers reach the right and left paravertebral muscle bulges and the fingers can stroke laterally and ventrally. The muscular system is pressed, loosened, and stretched away from the spinous processes (Figure 120).

For further treatment of the neck musculature the practitioner moves to the side of the patient's head. To stretch the muscles on the left side, the practitioner stands to the right, places the left hand flat on the patient's forehead and reaches around the front of the neck with the right hand as far as possible so that the fingers reach the muscles on the left side. The right hand then pulls the muscles toward the practitioner while the left hand simultaneously rotates the head (via the forehead contact) in the op-

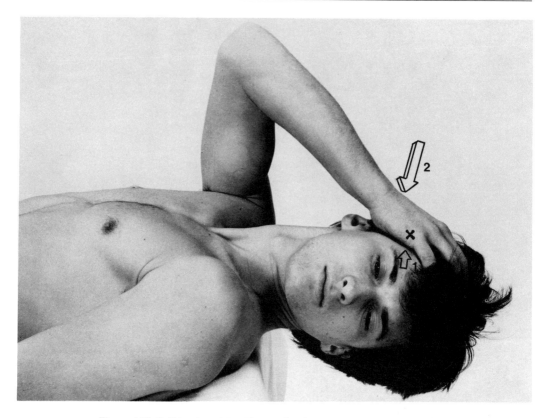

Figure 119 Self-treatment (postisometric relaxation, or PIR) of the scalenus muscle group

posite direction. The entire action must be well coordinated between both hands so that the to-and-fro motions of the head correspond smoothly with the pulling and pushing massage (Figure 121).

Manual traction of the cervical spine provides a transition to mobilizing techniques. Traction can be performed on both the seated and supine patient. With the patient supine, the practitioner stands at the head of the table, grasps the neck with both hands with the fingers pointed toward the posterior, or with one hand under the chin and the other grasping in fork-like shape on the occiput. The therapist shifts his or her body weight backwards to implement the traction impulses. Through variations in the direction of pull and in head position, the most painless direction of traction can be determined (Figures 122 and 123). With the patient seated, the practitioner grasps the head from above with both hands forming a "basket," as it were, so that the occiput and mastoid process are lying on the thumbs and thenar eminence, the lower jaw is resting on the palms of the hands, and the fingers are temporally placed (be cautioned against pushing and pulling on the ear!). The elbows fix the patient's shoulders. A vertical push of the hands leads to traction (Figure 124).

This hand position also provides an orthopedic test for the determination of supposed vertebrogenic origin of the complaint (cervical distraction test).

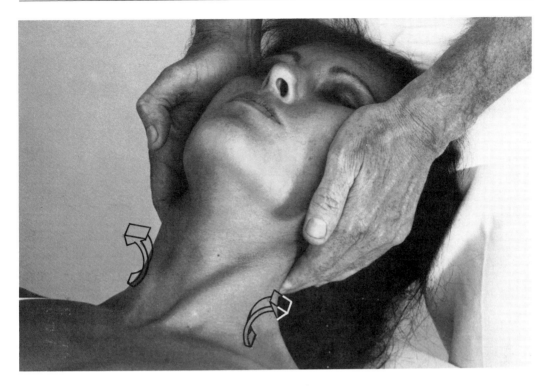

Figure 120 Soft-tissue technique for superficial neck musculature

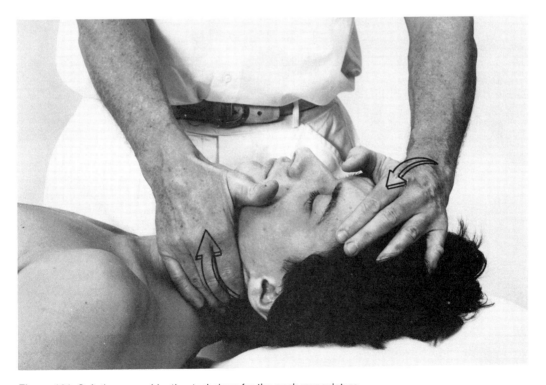

Figure 121 Soft-tissue combination technique for the neck musculature

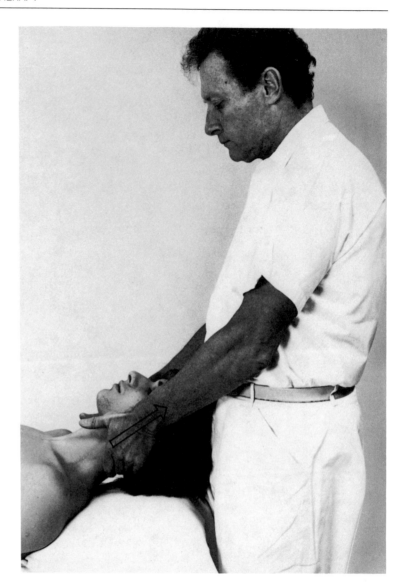

Figure 122 Manual traction of the cervical vertebrae with the patient supine—with pulling on the neck

In the treatment of muscular disruptions, it should always be remembered that an entire series of such muscular conditions may primarily be the result of trauma or overuse, but that muscular hypertonus also frequently emerges as an expression of the segmentally facilitated reaction. The therapist quite often sees the previously mentioned arthromuscular combination, wherein the joint irritation serves as the initiator of the muscular symptoms, which then feed back into exacerbation of the joint function, which must of course be included in the therapeutic approach.

To determine such arthrogenic sources of dysfunction, after the exclusion of radicular lesions, the best tool will again be the segmental functional examination.

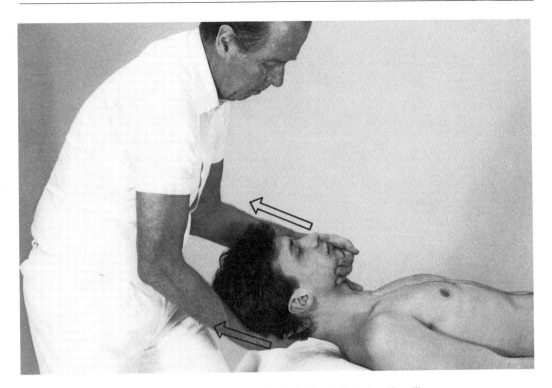

Figure 123 Traction in the supine position (variation)—forked occipital grip with pulling on the chin

7.4.2 Diagnosis and Chiropractic Therapy of Radicular Lesions

To enable one to recognize and define radicular lesions within the realm of lower cervical or cervicobrachial syndromes, an orienting neurological examination of motor and sensory functions should be explored when such a lesion is suspected. Sensory testing that finds hypalgesias (and only these are typical of sensory phenomena) points to a C6 lesion if they are found in the thumb; a C7 lesion, if found on the three middle fingers; and a C8 lesion, if found in the fifth digit. The inability to flex the upper arm against resistance points to suspicion of C5 lesions. When C6 is damaged, the hands held in the lap cannot be guided to the mouth (elbow flexion). C7 lesions manifest themselves through the inability to extend the flexed forearm against resistance. When the abducted little finger gives way under counterpressure, one should suspect a lesion of the C8 nerve root because the indicative myotome of this segment is the abductor digiti quinti (Table 5).

The corresponding therapeutic consequences are dictated according to the acuteness or chronicity of the clinical picture.

Acute nerve-root-compression syndromes with reflexive pain causing total spasm and preventing any free movement of the cervical spine are a contraindication for active forms of therapy. Here, rest (with a soft cervical

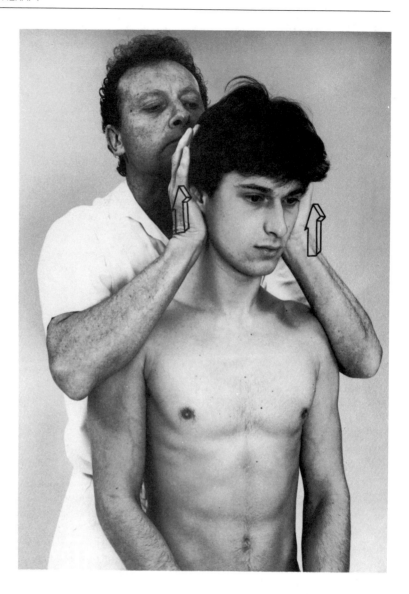

Figure 124 Manual traction of the cervical vertebrae in the seated patient

collar), as well as supporting pain medication therapy, may be indicated. Cases with nonrelenting or worsening neurological findings despite treatment require the therapist to consider surgical consultation. After a lessening of the acute symptomatology and a slight "freeing" of the cervical ranges of motion, chiropractic therapy can be introduced step by step, proceeding from light traction to isometrics, mobilizations, and manipulation.

Differential diagnostic aspects of cervicobrachial syndromes should not be limited to the possibility of a radicular genesis. Such irritative conditions frequently arise from the shoulder joint structures as well. Arm pain can also emerge from epicondylitis or can be an expression of a carpal tunnel syndrome. The differentially diagnostic clarification of vertebrogenic pain syndromes is relatively simple. Characteristic examination data will easily

Table 5 Orientation Table of Radicular Symptomatology

Segment	Dermatome	Myotome	Associated Reflexes
C5	Across the shoulder and the deltoid muscles	Deltoid and biceps	Weakening of the biceps reflex
C6	Radial side of the upper and lower arm to the thumb	Paresis of the biceps brachii and brachioradialis ("hand to mouth")	Loss of the biceps reflex
C7	Laterally (dorsally) dermatome C6 to the 2nd through 4th finger	Paresis of the triceps brachii (eventually, also, pectoralis major, pronator teres, and thenar eminence atrophy)	Possible loss of the triceps reflex
C8	Laterally-dorsally from dermatome C7 to the little finger	Intrinsic muscles (atrophy) finger abduction	Weakening of the triceps reflex

indicate the final diagnosis after the exclusion of aggravating distal visceral pathologies.

7.4.3 Differential Diagnosis of Shoulder Joint Dysfunctions

Many conditions have their etiology in the shoulder joints. Their diagnostic differentiation from vertebrogenic disruptions with similar symptoms is necessary before therapy is possible.

In diseases of the shoulder joint, there are two main forms that must be differentiated: one, the shoulder capsular contraction (the "frozen shoulder"); the other, a pain syndrome of exclusively muscular origin.

The typical symptom of frozen shoulder is widespread movement restriction, which develops according to the joint-specific capsular pattern. The capsular pattern of the shoulder appears as consistent patterns of restriction relationships between external rotation, abduction, and internal rotation (e.g., external rotation restriction of 5° = abduction restriction of 15° = internal rotation restriction of 45°; expressed in the typical ratio of "1:3:9").

In addition, there is a typical progression of the disease that allows corresponding predictions.

The development and progression of "frozen shoulder" is as follows:

$$3 \times 4 = 12 = 1 \text{ year}$$

- first to fourth month:
  Increasing pain; increasing reduction in range of motion
- fifth to eighth month:
  Decreased pain, contracture and range of motion (ROM) remains the same
- ninth to twelfth month:
  Leveling of pain, increasing mobility.

Table 6 Differentiation of Shoulder Dysfunctions

	Capsular Pattern	Active Mobility	Passive Mobility	Exertional Pain
Shoulder contracture	Yes	Painful, restricted	Painful, restricted	No
Supraspinatus tendinosis	No	Painful arc	Painful arc	In abduction against resistance
Infraspinatus tendinosis	No	Painful arc	Painful arc	In outward rotation against resistance
Acute bursitis	No	Totally inhibited by pain	Often pain free	No
Chronic bursitis	No	Painful arc	Painful arc	No
Irritation of the acromioclavicular joint	No	End ranges hindered	Forced adduction is painful	No

The painful arc is critical in the diagnosis of muscular disruptions. This concept is understood as shoulder pain emerging at 80° (Cyriax) of abduction, and disappearing again with further abduction past the horizontal. The pain is caused by the contact of the irritated and sensitive muscular insertions on the major and minor tubercles of the humerus with the coracoacromial ligament. With further abduction of the arm through cooperative rotation of the scapula, this ligament's pressure is released from the irritated structures and the pain stops. The underlying insertion tendinopathy afflicts, above all, the supraspinatus and infraspinatus (as well as the subscapularis). A painful arc may also indicate forms of bursitis. Table 6 indicates the necessary considerations to aid in differentiation.

> The characteristic of capsular disruptions is the capsular pattern; in muscular and bursal syndromes it is the painful arc.

7.4.4 Segmental Functional Analysis

If muscular or radicular disruptions and irritations from the structures of the shoulder-arm area itself have been excluded as the cause of existing difficulties, then arthrogenic pathomechanisms are probably the cause. The segmental functional examination of the cervical spine uncovers the source of disruption.

The examination begins in the C2/C3 motor segment, and the upper cervical joint region (occiput/C1/C2) is examined separately and last.

Once again, the best thing to do is to move the head using the wrap grip described previously. This position allows the testing movements to be directed specifically to the individual motor segment. The palpating fingers contact the joints in the laminar area. For orientation, the practitioner feels for the first palpable processus spinosus, which corresponds to the level of C2. Moving somewhat caudally and laterally, the palpating finger will find the laminar junction. Advancing cranially to caudally, from C2, every single motor segment must be assessed in flexion, extension, rotation, and lateral flexion. Especially valuable are the results of lateral flexion testing because in the cervical spine, lateral flexion is inseparably linked with rotation. Therefore, in this testing, the lack of elastic end-feel signals definite disruption in the motor segment (Figures 125–128).

The translational gliding test also is performed in this region in the sagittal or transverse planes, as for the previously mentioned cervicothoracic transition (Figure 129). Therapy can likewise be implemented from the same hand positions as the examination procedures.

7.4.5 Treatment of Joint Dysfunction

For mobilization treatment of this region, many methods can be used— some in the seated patient, some in the supine patient. Most methods rely on the principle that the caudally lying vertebra is fixed and the cranial one is moved in the restricted direction. Even the manipulative techniques, which must be used when mobilizations prove insufficient, can be carried out from the same basic position of the practitioner's hands. Before treatment is discussed, however, joint-locking techniques will be introduced.

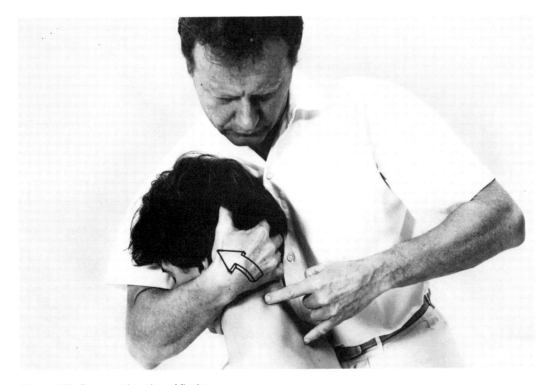

Figure 125 Segmental testing of flexion

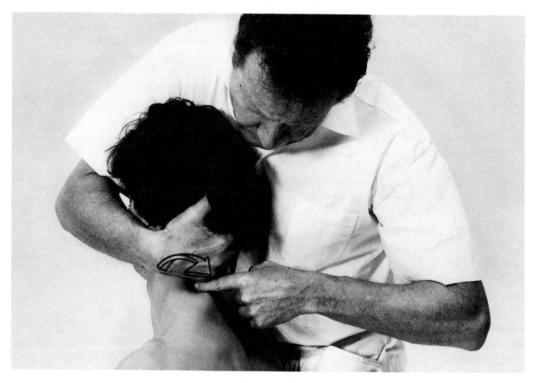

Figure 126 Segmental testing of extension

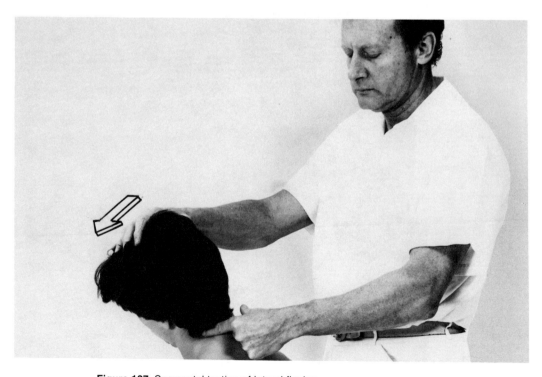

Figure 127 Segmental testing of lateral flexion

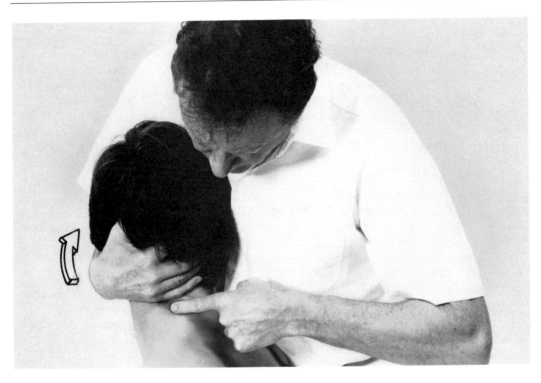

Figure 128 Segmental testing of rotation

Figure 129 Translational glide testing in the cervical spine

7.4.5.1 Joint Locking As a Therapeutic Principle

The term *joint locking* is used repeatedly in connection with manual techniques. This concept is examined in detail here because the associated mechanisms are essential in segmental treatment of the cervical vertebrae. Above all, only a correctly applied positioning of the cervical spinal region can effectively guard against traumatic side effects of manipulation. The joint-locking principle has two components: one is the "facet lock," which involves the joint surface; the other involves "ligament taughtening." To use the cervical spine as an example, lateral flexion and rotation occur in the same direction, corresponding to Lovett's rule (i.e., left lateral flexion implies left rotation, and vice versa). The consequence of this is that a good facet lock is achieved when lateral flexion is linked with an opposite rotation; this causes the joint surfaces to approximate more firmly against each other, as when only a rotational or lateral flexion position is used as a set-up. Further movement becomes impossible, and the motor segments are now locked.

For successful chiropractic therapy, it is of decisive importance that the joint locks be positioned so that the motor segment to be treated is not included in the locked region. If it were included, the treatment impulse would be intercepted, hindering normalization of the joint's function.

The therapist also must determine whether the component to be emphasized is that of rotation or lateral flexion; this differentiation depends on the evaluation of the particular lesion. In rotational restriction, position and treatment impulse should include more of a rotational component; lateral flexion disruptions should include more lateral flexion in the therapeutic approach.

Another essential component of mobilization or manipulative treatment is the secure fixation of the caudal partner of the motor unit, through support or holding of the vertebral arch. In rotational manipulation, the thumb gives resistance from the dorsal direction on the transverse process of the caudal vertebra, that is, the process that lies on the side to which the head is rotated (e.g., rotation to the left—left transverse process). This precaution also enables one to target a disrupted motor segment in isolation and to spare the remaining levels. Moreover, in the treatment of the cervical spine, the therapist may use ligament tightening for the restriction of all segments below C2 by inducing a forced flexion, as applied during the assessment of rotation (discussed previously in the section on diagnosis). All these methods are pertinent to treatment techniques of the cervical spine, which can be carried out in the seated as well as the supine patient.

The next sections show how naturally the diagnostic maneuvers flow into therapeutic possibilities. This progression is demonstrated by serial photographs showing representative lesions. The accompanying text confines itself to special circumstances relating to specific levels because all the basic concepts have been covered in previous sections.

7.4.5.2 Recognition and Treatment of Lateral Flexion Dysfunction

The first example is an assumed restriction of left lateral flexion in the C2/C3 motor segment.

Phase 1 (Figure 130). The right guiding hand brings the patient's head into lateral flexion. A restricted lateral flexion angle and a missing elastic end-feel is recognized by the radial edge of the index finger of the palpating hand, which worked as the fixing fulcrum in the examination procedure.

Phase 2 (Figures 131 a and b). After resistance testing has uncovered a spasm of the right lateral flexion musculature, this disruption must first be lessened through postisometric relaxation.

Without changing the hand position, PIR is accomplished through slight pressure of the patient's head against the practitioner's fixed guiding hand; this action can be facilitated if the patient glances to the upper right. In the relaxation phase, the patient looks toward the side of the restriction (down

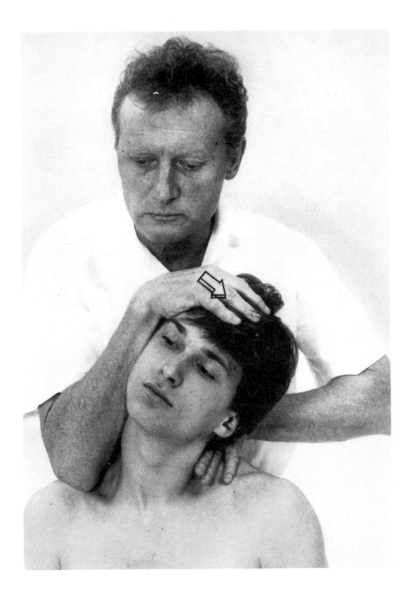

Figure 130 Restriction of left lateral flexion in the C2/C3 motor segment—diagnosis

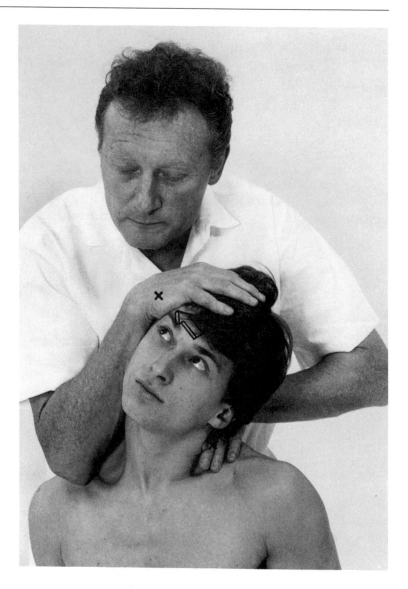

Figure 131a PIR treatment—isometric activation

and to the left), and lateral flexion is increased through the weight of the guiding hand. A few repetitions of this treatment are necessary.

Phase 3 (Figure 132). Restriction of lateral flexion will continue to exist after the muscular component has been alleviated, due to obstructed joint play. Thus, a corresponding mobilization treatment, using slight traction in the direction of the hindrance, is the next step.

The practitioner places one hand, using the forked grip, on the laminae of the lower vertebra, approaching from the healthy side. The other hand makes a side contact on the upper vertebra, using the ulnar edge and the little finger. The patient's head lies with the right half of the face against the practitioner's upper body. Through slight stepping back or a back-

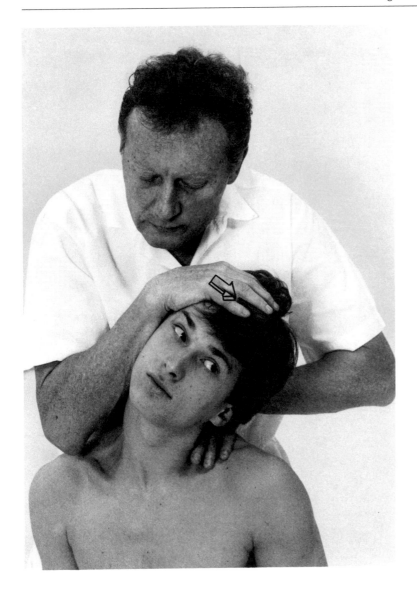

Figure 131b PIR treatment—stretching phase

wards pendular motion, a slight traction and increase of lateral flexion is achieved.

Phase 4 (Figure 133). If a conclusive manipulation is necessary because of a remaining disruption, the manipulation can be achieved with no change in position. Manipulations include the so-called master technique, one of the oldest and most-used manipulation methods for such disruptions of the cervical spine.[2]

---

[2]*U.S. Editor's Note*: The "master technique" should *not* be confused with the idea of a "master cervical" adjustment, which has come to mean a nonspecific mobilization thrust on the cervical spine involving several segments. The technique described by the authors uses joint locking and is aimed at a specific motor segment.

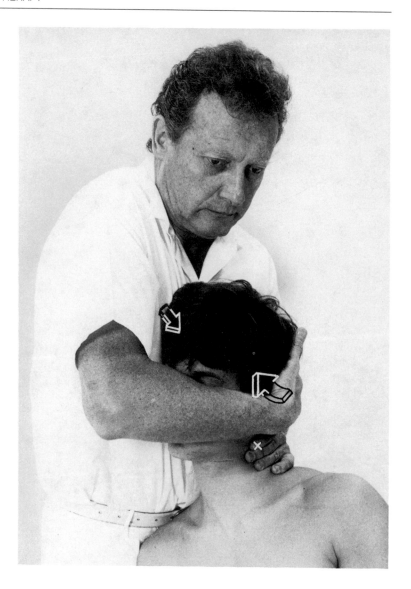

Figure 132 Mobilization
with traction

When using this method, the practitioner places the guiding hand over
the patient's temple and parietal bone; the contact hand lies with the tip of
the middle finger on the uppermost vertebra of the disrupted segment.
The manipulation impulse is a synchronized action of the guiding hand
(increasing lateral flexion) and the contact finger (tractional impulse) under
simultaneous activation of the practitioner's pectoralis and trapezius. That
is, the physician pulls the patient toward him or her, as well as slightly
tractioning the patient vertically.

If the patient must be in a supine position (because the patient is bedridden or cannot relax while seated), the examination and therapy develop in
a correspondingly varied format.

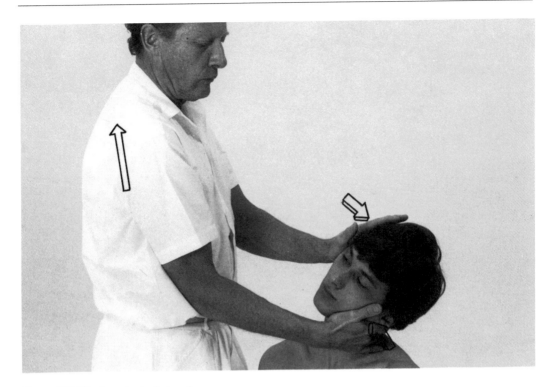

Figure 133 The "master technique"

Phase 1 (Figure 134). A similar left lateral flexion disruption in the C2/C3 motor segment is used as an example.

The patient lies supine. The practitioner stands at the patient's head, with the guiding hand supporting the occiput on the side. The practitioner laterally flexes the head toward the contact hand, the index finger of which again serves as a sensor on the joint on the side of lateral flexion.

Phase 2 (Figures 135 a and b). The muscular disruptive component is first alleviated through PIR, and the procedure is analogous. The patient looks up to the right during activation of the head against resistance of the practitioner's guiding hand. During relaxation, the patient looks down to the left while lateral flexion is increased. This treatment should be repeated until muscular spasm is reduced.

Phase 3 (Figure 136). Rhythmic mobilizations are used in the restricted direction, with gentle accompanying tractional components.

Phase 4 (Figure 137). For manipulation, the practitioner stands to the side of the patient, on the side of restrictive lesion. The patient's head is held with a wrap grip, with the practitioner's fingers encircling the chin; the patient's head rests on the forearm of the guiding hand. An initial slight rotation toward the opposite side locks the segments lying cranially to the disruption. The practitioner's impulse hand makes contact with the lateral

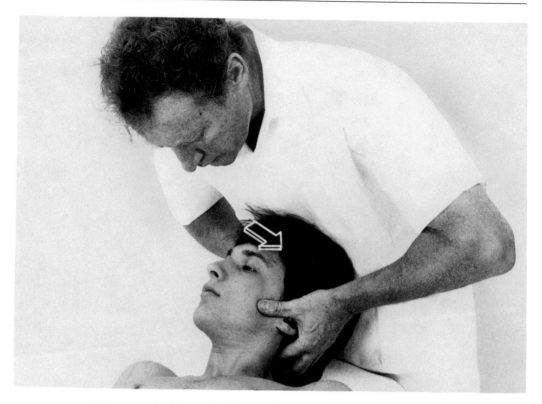

Figure 134 Restriction of left lateral flexion in the C2/C3 motor segment—supine procedure—diagnosis

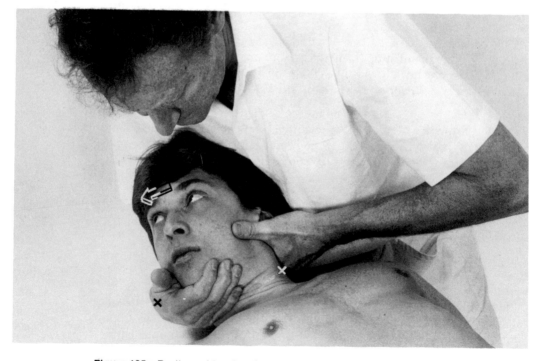

Figure 135a Postisometric relaxation treatment—isometric activation

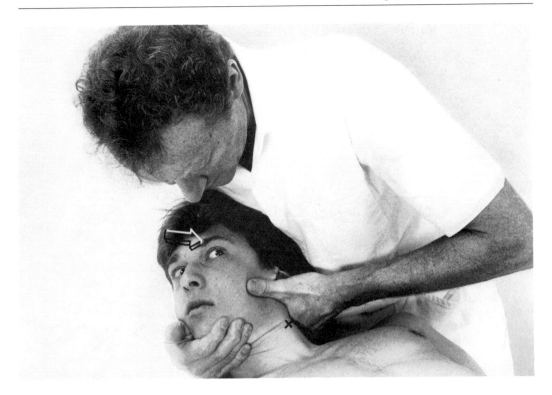

Figure 135b Postisometric relaxation treatment—stretching phase

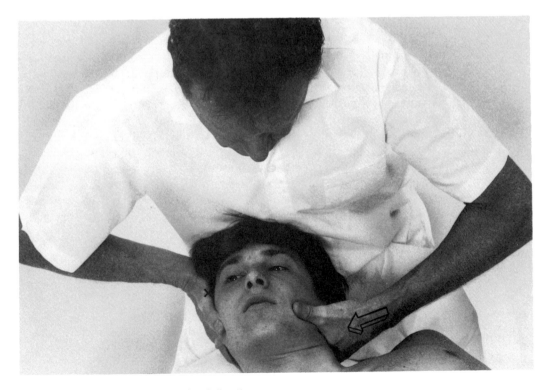

Figure 136 Mobilization in the restricted direction

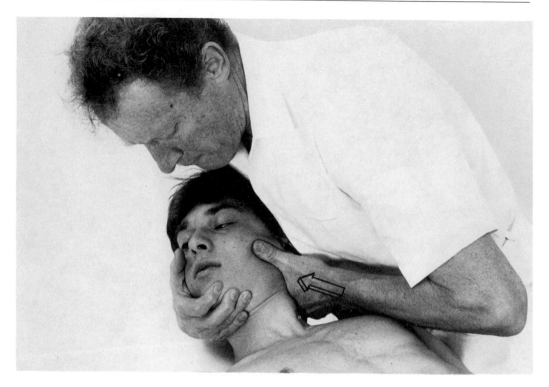

Figure 137 Manipulation—either in pure traction or traction with lateral flexion toward the restricted side

edge of the index finger on the transverse process of the caudal vertebra. The manipulative impulse goes primarily in the direction of pure traction.

If this treatment is not successful, it is recommended that the basic positioning be varied and the head not only rotated to the opposite side, but also laterally flexed toward the side of the lesion. With this position, the treatment impulse with lateral flexion still maintains a tractional force, and the manipulative impulse is carried out in a diagonally cranial direction. One should be careful to use the forearm to facilitate the exact line of drive, while the guiding hand supplements the motion with additional traction. In addition, one must realize that purely tractional manipulations almost never succeed; they probably are most useful for very extensive fixations in which the musculature is relatively relaxed and provides little resistance.

7.4.5.3 Recognition and Treatment of Rotational Dysfunction

The next method demonstrated is the diagnosis and treatment of a disruption of left rotation in the C4/C5 motor segment.

As discussed in Section I, rotation and lateral flexion have a symbiotic relationship to each other; that is, they are inseparably coupled in movement mechanism. For diagnostic and therapeutic purposes, one must evaluate which of the component partial mechanisms has priority. Whereas lateral flexion restriction dominated in the previous example, the method presented below is used when the prevailing lesion is one of rotational disruption.

Phase 1 (Figure 138). The practitioner stands to the left of the seated patient and encircles the patient's head with the guiding hand. The practitioner then rotates the patient's head to the left and, with the index finger on the C4/C5 joint, evaluates the range of motion, the end-feel, and the degree of disruption.

Phase 2 (Figures 139 a and b). When there are concurrent restrictions of the rotators on the right side, PIR can be helpful, as follows:

- Patient's head and cranial vertebra fixed, with the wrap grip in left rotation; the lower vertebra held with the forked grip.
- Patient looks to the right, with resistance.
- Patient looks to the left and relaxes; increase of rotation to the left with light traction.
- Facilitation using respiration assist (inhaling and exhaling).

Phase 3 (Figure 140). Following PIR—or when there is no concomitant muscular restriction—a rhythmic mobilization and light traction can be implemented with no change in the practitioner's hand position.

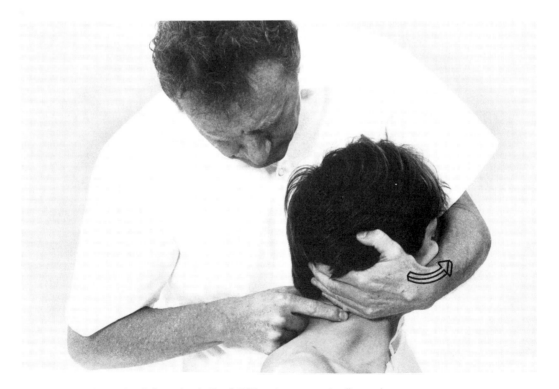

Figure 138 Left rotational disruption in the C4/C5 motor segment—diagnosis

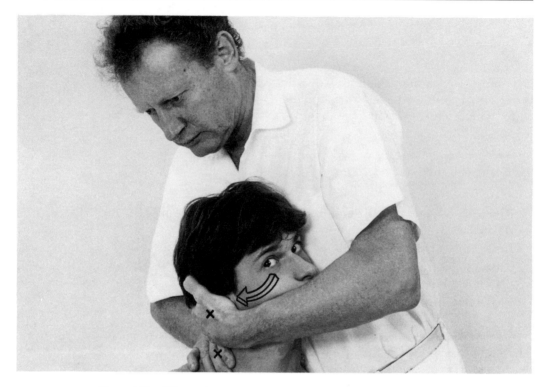

Figure 139a PIR treatment—isometric activation

Phase 4. The manipulation also can proceed with no change in the practitioner's hand position, or grip (Figure 141).

First, the lower vertebra is fixed, and tissue tension is increased with corresponding lateral flexion to the right. The manipulation impulse consists of a short tractional exaggeration of left rotation. In addition, the practitioner may use the master technique. Here, it is varied only to the extent that the contact of the middle finger of the left hand on the transverse process of the upper vertebra is used to provide an impulse slightly cranially and rotationally directed, once maximum tissue tension has been reached. The practitioner stands to the front and left of the patient for normal implementation of this technique (Figure 142).

For a patient in the supine position, one should use the method previously discussed for the treatment of lateral flexion problems. Mobilization should be modified only to pay increased attention in the rotational component. The previously mentioned relationship between lateral flexion and rotation dictates that manipulation techniques for the restoration of lateral flexion are virtually unchanged for the treatment of rotational disruptions.

An alternative to this method is a supine technique, which should be very cautiously applied, because a significant rotational increase is an important component. The practitioner stands at the head of the patient, not at the side (as in the lateral flexion treatment). The patient's head, rotated and slightly laterally fixed, lies on the forearm of the practitioner; the practitioner's hand encircles the chin. The other hand is placed on the cranial

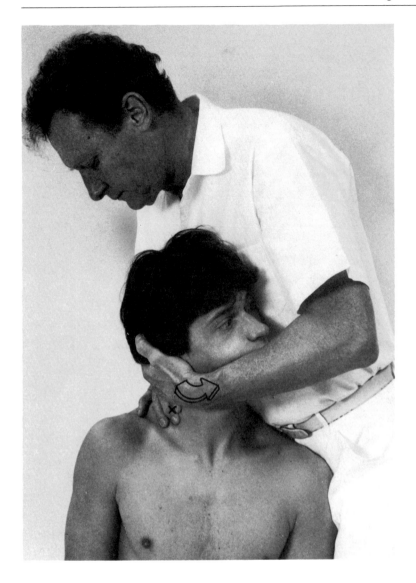

Figure 139b PIR treatment—stretching phase

vertebra with a forked grip and brings the cervical spine into flexion, far enough to lock the caudal segments. The manipulative impulse consists of a short, small (high-velocity, low-amplitude) rotational increase (Figure 143).

For generalized treatment, as well as for the preparation of diffusely disrupted cervical segments for these specific treatment methods, a simple tractional mobilization can be used.

The patient leans his or her forehead onto the chest of the practitioner, who encircles the neck with both hands, forming a basket so that the ulnar edges and little fingers contact and are fixed on the vertebra cranial to the disruption. The practitioner then rhythmically leans back to provide traction. In this way, each segment may be mobilized individually in a caudal-to-cranial sequence (Figure 144).

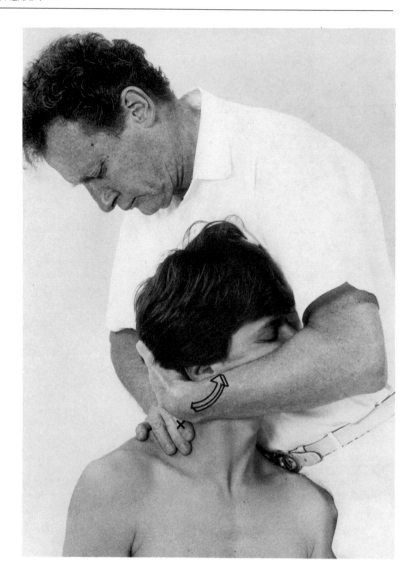

Figure 140 Mobilization
with light traction

7.5 UPPER CERVICAL REGION

Because this text discusses the upper cervical vertebrae separately from
the rest of the cervical spine, the practitioner should be forewarned that
this region must be subject to special circumstances. The diagnostic and
therapeutic importance of this uppermost spinal column sector far exceed
that of the more caudal segments; it is not an overstatement to speak of
"regulatory dominance" of the upper cervical joints. Optimal functioning
of this region is necessary for optimal functioning of the remainder of the
spine. As previously mentioned, this region includes transverse links to
vegetative centers and the abducens nuclei. It also functions as a peripheral
organ of equilibrium and balance. In addition, the influence of the gamma
system in the receptor field of the upper cervical joints is very important

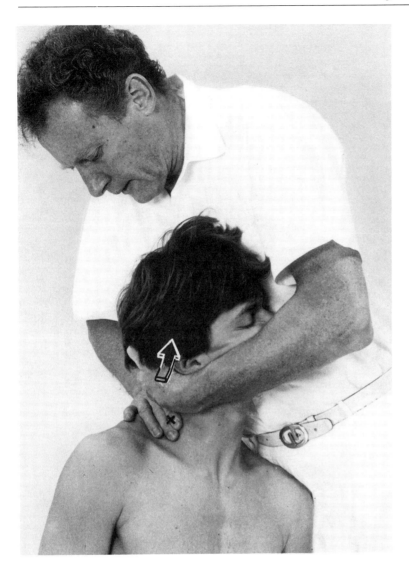

Figure 141 Manipulation with short tractional exaggeration of left rotation

in that the tonus situation of the entire muscular system is tangent to this area.

Irritative conditions of the upper joints, whether fixations or instabilities, not only are frequently responsible for chronic forms of headaches and diffuse conditions of dizziness, but also produce vegetative reactions as well as peripheral symptoms (e.g., dysesthesias, feelings of weakness, and imbalance). These symptoms, above all, can confuse differential diagnosis if the mechanisms of the upper cervical spine are not considered or if the functionally diagnostic concepts of manual medicine are not included in the patient's physical examination.

The importance of the upper cervical region, of course, dictates both subtlety and caution in the physician's approach to this area. Here, as in no other area of the spine, the possibility of iatrogenic damage constantly exists for the careless practitioner.

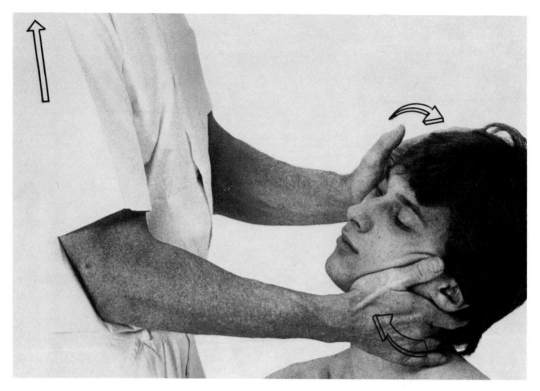

Figure 142 The master technique (in this illustration, a disruption of right rotation)

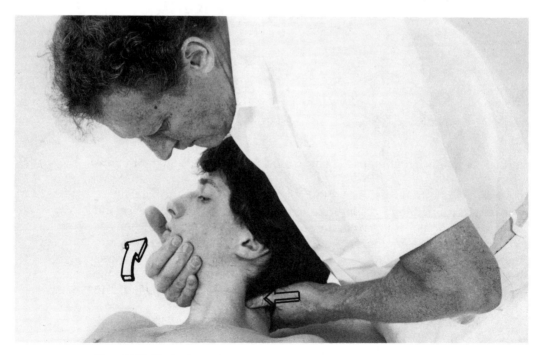

Figure 143 Manipulation with the patient in the supine position—impulse increase in rotation ("short and small") using the chin of the patient (in this illustration, fixation of C4/C5, rotation to the right)

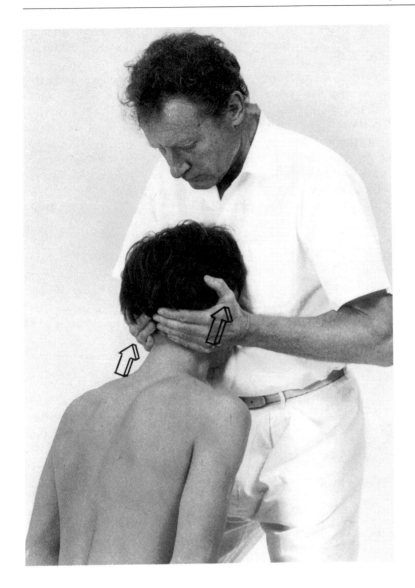

Figure 144 Tractional mobilization of the cervical spine

In the chiropractic examination and treatment of this region, the opportunity for flowing transitions, or phases, is again valid. As a prerequisite, however, the practitioner must recognize and exclude instabilities. These are especially to be assumed if the patient's history reveals traumas or inflammatory rheumatic diseases. Forceful treatments in the upper cervical joints most frequently cause damage of the ligamentous apparatus. The alar and transverse ligaments are most commonly affected. It is quite evident that ligamentous lesions in the C1/C2 motor segment can lead to instability and problems.

7.5.1 Motion Analysis—Results and Consequences

The ligament strength between the atlas and axis can be examined as follows, on the seated patient.

The practitioner stands to the side of the patient. One hand dorsally encircles the patient's axis with the forked grip, and the other is fixed from the opposite side (with contact of the ulnar edge of the little finger) on the transverse process and posterior arch of the atlas. From this starting position, one then attempts to push the axis below the atlas (line of drive a few degrees ventral) to the opposite side. This is performed with the cervical spine slightly flexed to diminish pressure against the dens by the anterior arch of the atlas (Figure 145).

Any significant movement in the direction of pressure must be considered a sign of instability; this motion is an important contraindication for manipulation in this motor segment. A corresponding test can be performed with the patient supine (Figure 146).

The resulting therapeutic consequences are as follows:
- Avoidance of long-lasting flexed position (school, office): writing desks or work stations should be ergonomically optimized.
- Rehabilitative strengthening and balancing of neck musculature is indicated.

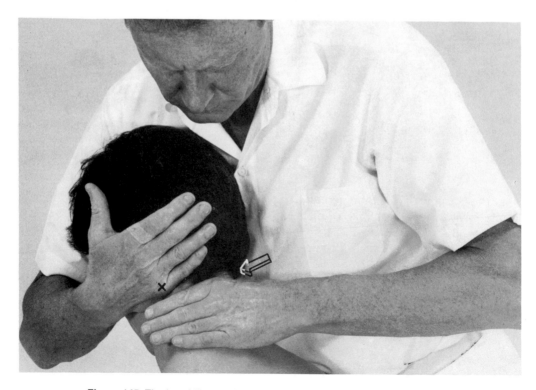

Figure 145 The instability test for the C1/C2 motor segment, with the patient in the seated position

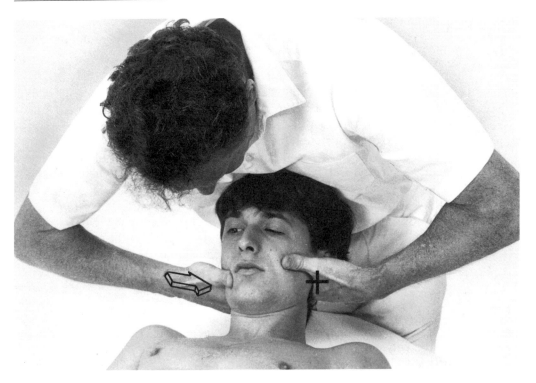

Figure 146 The instability test for the C1/C2 motor segment, with the patient in the supine position

7.5.2 Upper Cervical Joint Fixations—Examination and Treatment

More common than instabilities, fixations in the upper cervical joints are responsible for many complaints. As a matter of principle, the occiput-atlas is commonly susceptible and often is combined with disruptions of the C2/C3 segment. Fixations in the C1/C2 segment are less common, but their manifestations form a more dramatic clinical picture.

To understand this area in a practical sense, one must recall the functional anatomical factors and ask the following questions: Which movements are possible in the occiput/C1 sector, and which are possible in the C1/C2 motor segment?

- Occiput-atlas:
  –Flexion and extension, as well as lateral flexion, are possible.
  –There is no rotation here, only slight rotary joint play.
- Atlas-axis:
  –The main movement is rotation (40° to 50° of the total rotation of the head occur between C1 and C2).
  –Flexion and extension are minimally possible.
  –Again, there is no pure lateral flexion.
  –As an accompanying coupled mechanism, every lateral movement is accompanied by rotation of the axis to the same side.

Characteristics of existing fixations correspond to the mechanics of the elements involved; that is, they often appear as a disruption of more than one function.

7.5.2.1 Techniques for the Seated Patient

Examination and treatment proceed according to the illustrated functional anatomical principles. The first point of reference is the general mobility of the cervical spine, evaluated actively and passively, as well as resistively. The passive mobility test must be conducted not only in the neutral position, but also in complete flexion and extension. Full flexion blocks rotation below C2. Rotational restrictions in this position, therefore, indicate fixation in the upper cervical joints. An additional nodding movement will also lock C1/C2; then the rotation occurs exclusively in the C2/C3 segment. Total extension, on the other hand, locks the upper cervical segments; consequently, rotation disruptions must be localized to the caudal sectors.

To test flexion and extension between the occiput and atlas in the seated patient, the practitioner steps to the side of the patient, encircles the head with the wrap grip, and takes care to hold the patient's head so that a pure nodding movement can occur. The palpation finger of the other hand, placed between the occipital border and the rear arch of the atlas, feels for occipital "impact" or its lack in cases of fixation (Figures 147 and 148).

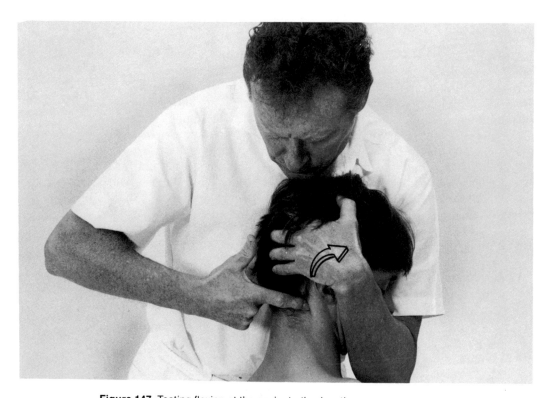

Figure 147 Testing flexion at the occiput-atlas junction

For the evaluation of the C1/C2 segment, the palpation finger moves one segment lower and somewhat more medially. Restrictions in the occiput/C1 segment almost always show accompanying spasm of the deep, small neck muscles (rectus and obliquus capitus), PIR therapy should be used as a first step, once flexion restriction has been noted. Using the wrap grip (as in the examination), the practitioner encircles the posterior arch of the atlas with the other hand in the forked position and places the head in maximum forward nodding position. The further procedure is as follows:

- Patient looks up—breathes in—provides resistance.
- Patient looks down—breathes out—practitioner increases the flexion.

While the patient is still seated, the practitioner tests the rotary joint play between the occiput and atlas (Figure 149).

Standing behind the patient, the practitioner completely rotates the patient's head to one side. With the guiding hand flat on the chin and lower jaw, the practitioner moves the head to the point of end-feel. To avoid a locking between the occiput and atlas and the corresponding false test results, no lateral flexion is allowed to occur. The index finger of the practitioner's other hand lies with its tip on the lateral mass of the atlas, which is then palpated between the ascending branch of the mandible and the mastoid process. It should be cautioned that only slight pressure is used, to avoid resulting irritative conditions of this sensitive area (coughing or

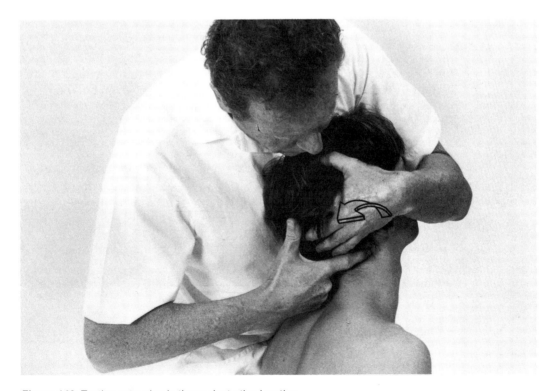

Figure 148 Testing extension in the occiput-atlas junction

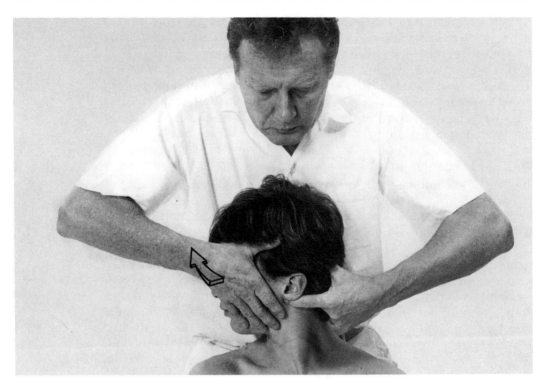

Figure 149 Testing rotary joint play between the occiput and atlas

reflex spasm). Small repeated rotational increases with the guiding hand can be assessed by the palpation finger as soft elastic movement of the occiput over the atlas (the mastoid comes nearer to the lateral mass). This test is especially reliable and informative; failure to perceive elastic end-feel is a sure sign of atlas fixation.

As in previous techniques, it is possible to move to therapy immediately with no change in hand position.

The first step is PIR treatment. The therapist holds the completely rotated head with one hand in the wrap grip; the other hand is fixed with a forked grip on the posterior arch of the atlas. The thumb lies behind the lateral mass on the side of rotation (Figures 150 a and b).

- Patient looks to the opposite side of the rotation—breathes in—provides resistance.
- Patient looks toward the rotation side—breathes out—increases rotation.

The next step is the manipulation.

The use of PIR alone will seldom achieve resolution in the upper cervical area; manipulations usually must be added.

Manipulation also occurs with no change in the position of the hands. It also proceeds from the completely rotated position of the head, because all

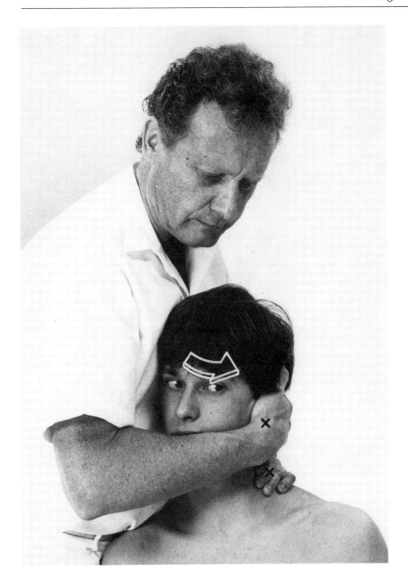

Figure 150a PIR treatment of disrupted rotary joint play— isometric activation

caudally lying segments are thus locked. The thumb of the forked grip must be well placed on the arch of the atlas on the side of rotation (providing counterpressure). The manipulation impulse itself consists of a short, simultaneously tractional increase in rotation after careful building up the tissue tension, and with optimal relaxation of the patient (Figure 151).

With the patient in the seated position, the practitioner also may evaluate flexion of the occiput-atlas junction. Both middle fingers make contact with the lateral masses of the atlas from a diagonal/cranial approach, and the other fingers are supported (with supinated hand position) on the sides of the occiput and upper jaw. The practitioner's forearms follow the long axis of the middle fingers in orientation. Thus, the sinking of the elbows achieves lateral flexion, in which the lateral mass of the atlas seems to approach the middle finger on the side of lateral flexion (Figure 152). If there

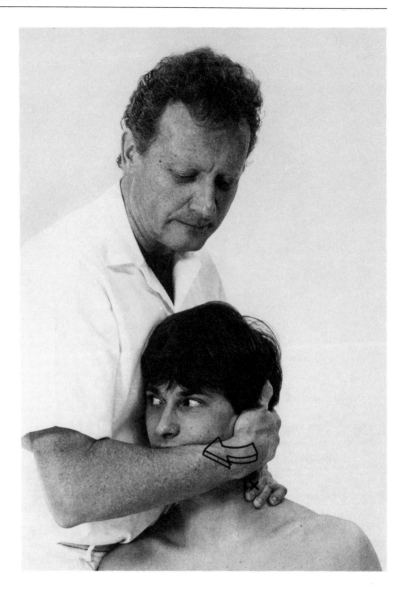

Figure 150b PIR treatment of disrupted rotary joint play— intensification of rotation (stretching phase)

is a corresponding fixation, the patient is treated in the supine position so that the head, placed in the wrap grip, is mobilized (with counterpressure on the atlas) in the restricted direction (Figure 153).

The lateral flexion of the occiput-atlas junction may be more easily tested with the patient in the supine position. The patient's fully rotated head is tested with a passive side-nodding movement (see the next section).

First, the practitioner must accomplish the examination and therapy of the C1/C2 motor segment with the patient in the seated position (Figures 154 and 155).

Massive fixations are less common in this segment; but when the rotational relationship is disrupted, such fixations result in a stubborn and tormenting symptomatology. Recognition of these fixations is based on a

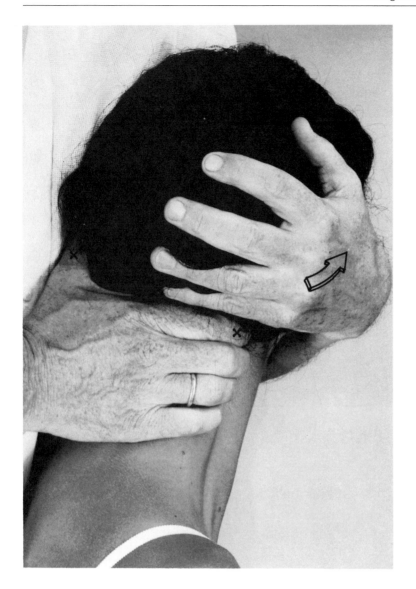

Figure 151 Manipulation through traction intensification of rotation of the occiput-atlas junction

knowledge of functional anatomic relationships. In normal functioning, the atlas and occiput should turn at least 20° solely around the dens. If the axis spinous process moves immediately when the head is passively rotated, this movement indicates a fixation. Moreover, in normal functioning, lateral flexion and rotation toward the same side are coupled. Thus, a lack of co-rotation with passive lateral flexion also indicates fixation. These mechanics are best evaluated by bringing the head into rotation and producing lateral flexion with the guiding hand. The reaction of C2 is evaluated either through palpation of the axis spinous process (it is the first process that can be felt below the occiput) or through placement of the fingers in the forked grip over the axis.

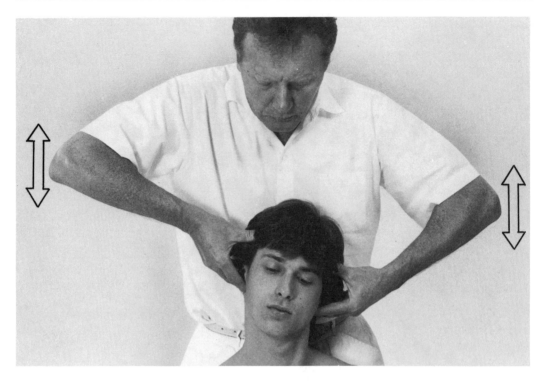

Figure 152 Lateral flexion test of the occiput-atlas junction

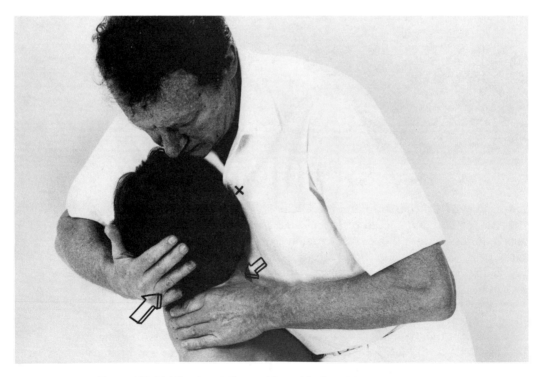

Figure 153 Mobilization of disrupted lateral flexion of the occiput-atlas junction

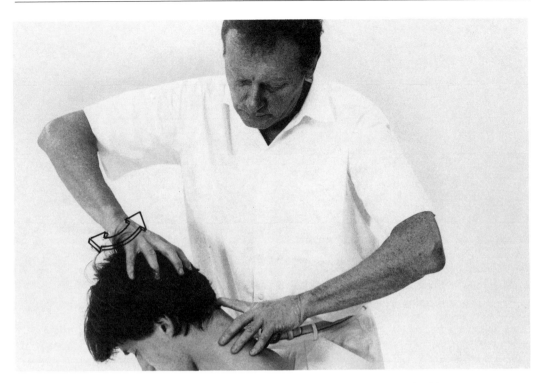

Figure 154 Testing the rotation between atlas and axis (the axis spinous process should only rotate after the first 20°–25°)

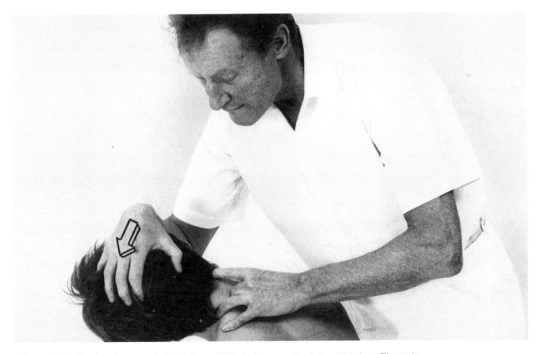

Figure 155 Testing the coupled rotation of C2 during passive lateral flexion. The axis spinous process deviates to the opposite side

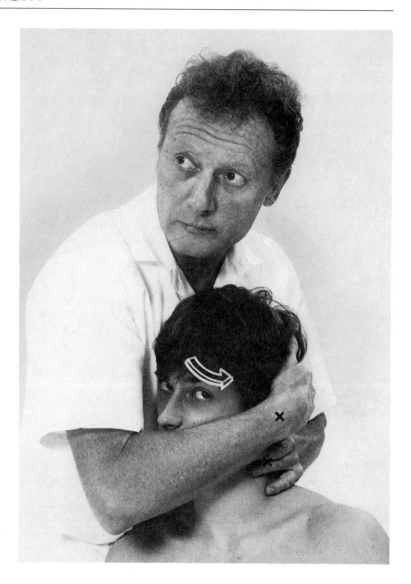

Figure 156a PIR for a right rotational disruption between C1 and C2— isometric activation

The PIR treatment corresponds to the procedure described for the occiput/ C1. In this treatment, the forked grip is simply fixed on C2 (Figures 156 a and b).

The hand position also remains virtually unchanged for manipulation. In the wrap grip, the ulnar edge of the practitioner's hand and little finger lie on the posterior arch of the atlas. The practitioner rotates the atlas in the restricted direction until perceiving the end-feel, while fixing the C2 segment. The practitioner steps back slightly, and the cervical spine is thus flexed somewhat laterally with locking of the caudally located segments. The mobilization impulse should only be in pure traction in this area (Figure 157).

For manipulations of this segment, we recommend that the patient be in the supine position (see Figure 165 in the next section).

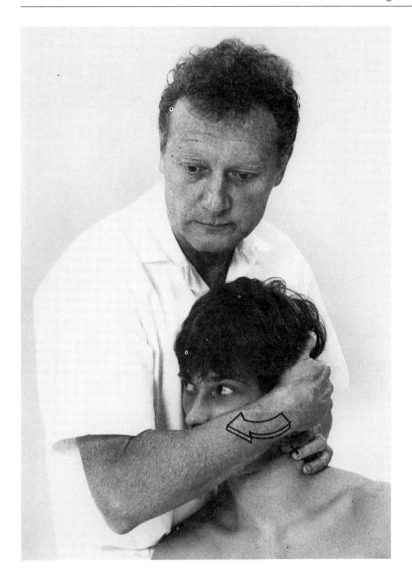

Figure 156b PIR for a right rotational disruption between C1 and C2—intensification of rotation (stretching phase)

7.5.2.2 Techniques for the Supine Patient

Examinations and methods of treatment that are similar to those for the seated patient can, of course, also be used for the supine patient.

To determine a flexion disruption in the occiput/C1 segment, the therapist's left hand grasps the rear of the patient's neck between the lower skull and the posterior of the atlas. The patient's head rests in the physician's hand in a relaxed manner. The physician's right hand lies over the eyebrows on the patient's forehead, the thumb on one temple and fingers on the other. Caudally directed pressure on the forehead causes forward nodding movement during which the elastic end-feel or the lack thereof can be evaluated (Figure 158). If the therapist finds a flexion disruption, the final position of diagnosis is also the starting point for therapy.

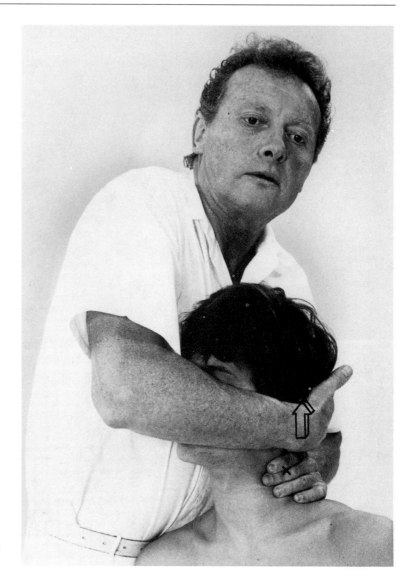

Figure 157 Tractional mobilization of the atlas-axis fixation in the seated patient

The hand lying on the occiput fixes the posterior arch of the atlas once the maximal nodding position has been reached; the other hand fixes the forehead. The following PIR method should be used:

- The patient looks up, breathes in, and gives pressure against the practitioner.
- The patient looks down and breathes out. The practitioner increases the nodding of the head (Figures 159 a and b).

After alleviating muscular restraint, one also may mobilize joint flexion by using rhythmic pressure on the forehead while fixing the atlas with the other hand.

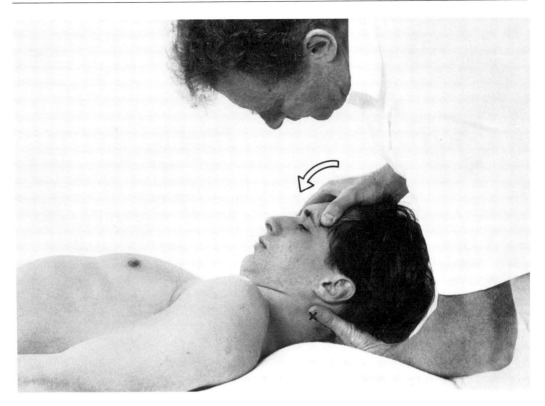

Figure 158 Testing the flexion of the occiput-atlas junction, with the patient in the supine position

For the testing and treatment of extension problems, the head is fully rotated to lock all cervical segments lying caudal to the atlas. The hand closest to the table grasps the chin to implement this rotation and then brings the head into maximal extension. The therapist's other hand is placed with the radial edge of the index finger over the occiput-atlas joint region. The degree of rotation and the elastic end-feel, or lack thereof, are evaluated as an indication of disruption (Figure 160). Muscle energy techniques (METs), mobilization, and manipulation all can be performed in the now well-known method, from the same initial position (Figures 160 a and b).

For the manipulation impulse, the purest direction of traction is to be sought.

Side nodding (joint play) in the occiput-atlas junction can be tested with the patient in the reclining position. First, the therapist fully rotates the patient's head, then, with both hands, brings the head into a sideward, nodding motion. With this test, the therapist compares the right and left motions and assesses the end-feel (Figure 161).

Rhythmic repetitions of the testing movement also can be used for mobilization.

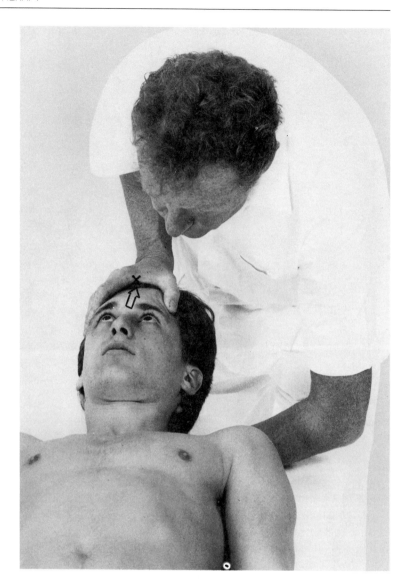

Figure 159a PIR of a flexion disruption between the occiput and atlas—isometric activation

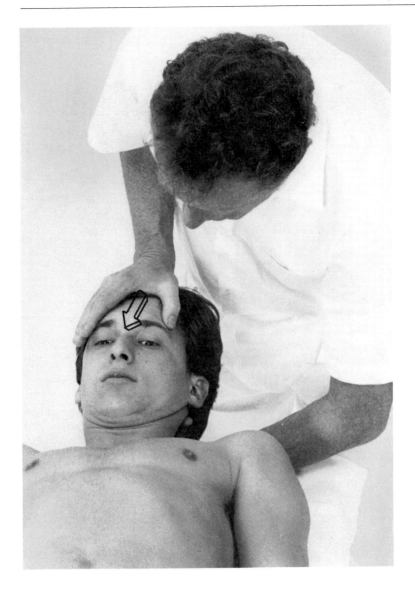

Figure 159b PIR of a flexion disruption between the occiput and atlas—intensification of flexion (stretching phase)

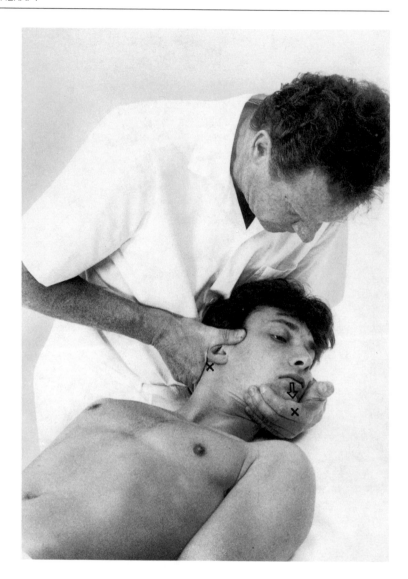

Figure 160a PIR of disrupted extension between the occiput and atlas. Isometric activation—patient looks down

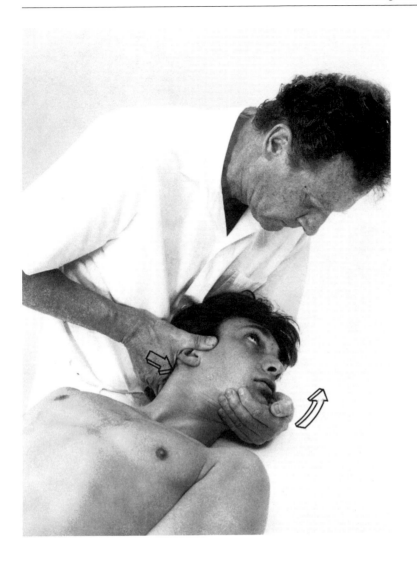

Figure 160b PIR of disrupted extension between the occiput and atlas. Intensification of the extension—patient looks up (stretching phase). With the use of this grip, testing, mobilization, and manipulation can be implemented. Manipulation should be carried out in a purely tractional direction

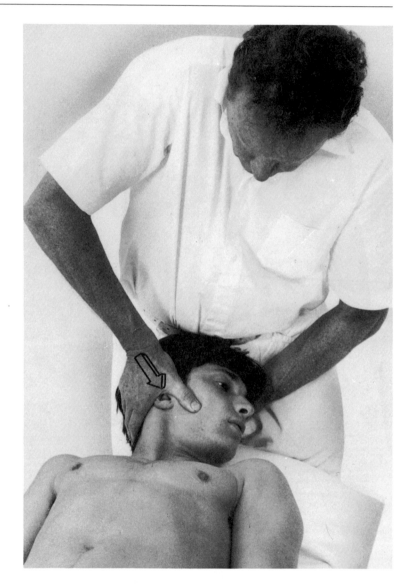

Figure 161 Testing of side nodding (joint play) in the occiput-atlas junction through complete rotation of the head. Repetitions of the testing movement work as mobilization

For the manipulation of atlas fixations, the practitioner must reach around the patient. Standing on the side of the lesion, the practitioner encircles the patient's chin with one hand. The head, resting on the physician's forearm, is rotated toward the opposite side and laterally flexed toward the side of the disruption. The physician's other hand contacts the occiput near the mastoid with the radial edge of the index finger. The forearm points exactly in the direction of the line of drive of the impulse, which must be directed caudocranially and parallel to the axis of the body (Figure 162).

Flexion disruptions between the atlas and axis also can be treated with the patient in the supine position. With one hand, the physician grasps

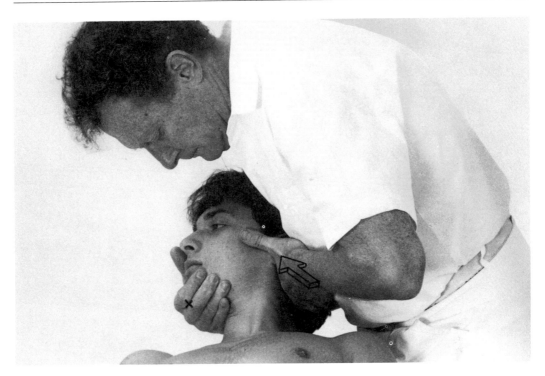

Figure 162 Manipulation of atlas fixation, with the patient in the supine position. With contact on the occiput near the mastoid, the forearm points exactly in the direction of the line of drive (parallel to the body's long axis)

the axis with a forked grip; the wrist is supported by the underlying surface. The other hand encircles the posterior arch of the atlas (with a forked grip) and implements the flexion movement. PIR and mobilization can be similarly implemented with no change in the grip (Figure 163).

With the patient in the reclining position, mobilization of the C1/C2 motor segment is effected by a repeated forcing of lateral flexion. This motion simultaneously includes a rotary component. The practitioner holds the patient's head at the back of the skull with both hands so that the fingertips point toward the table and the radial edges of the index fingers lie as a fulcrum to the left and right in the atlas area (Figure 164).

For the manipulation of C1/C2, the practitioner uses a position similar to that for occiput/C1. The head is merely rotated and laterally flexed slightly. The contact of the impulse hand occurs on the lateral mass of the atlas; and the direction of the impulse is primarily caudocranial, possibly diagonal to the long axis of the body. As in the previous movement, the forearm points exactly in the direction of the impulse line of drive (Figure 165).

The upper cervical joints provide a virtual "parade" of examples of chiropractic therapeutic efficiency.

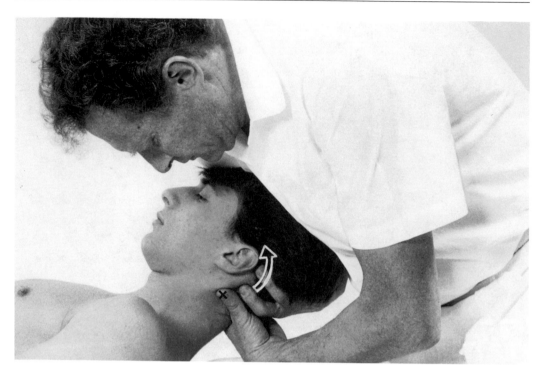

Figure 163 Treatment of a flexion disruption between the atlas and axis through PIR or mobilization

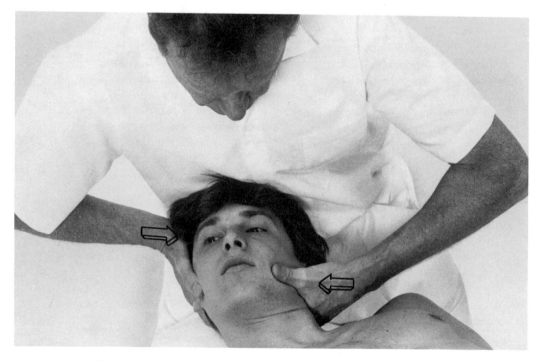

Figure 164 Mobilization of the atlas-axis motor segment, with the patient in the supine position. The radial edge of the index finger works as a fulcrum

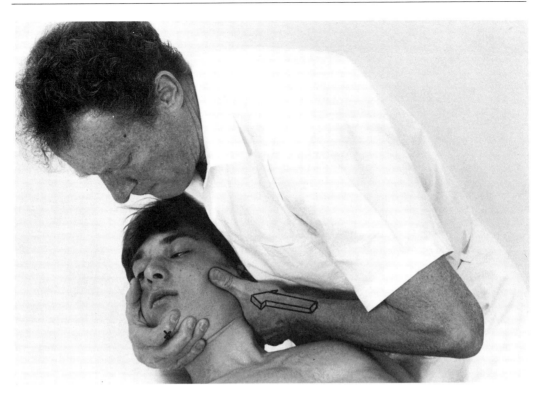

Figure 165 Manipulation of atlas-axis fixation. Contact is on the lateral mass of the atlas, and the direction of the impulse is primarily caudocranial and possibly diagonal to the body's long axis. The forearm points exactly in the direction line of drive

8. Chiropractic Treatment of the Extremities

It has been shown that manual techniques can be successfully used on the spinal regions when other treatments fail. Logically, knowledge obtained in this area should apply to the entire movement apparatus. Therefore, muscular, as well as arthrogenic, disruptions in the extremities also should be considered for chiropractic diagnosis and therapy. After all, in the etiology of disruptions, there are few differences between the axis organs and the extremities. Segmentally facilitated reflexive phenomena and their effects on the viscera are perhaps more profound in the spine, but these effects are by no means absent in the peripheral joints—and there are certainly reflexive cycles between extremities and axis organs. One need only recall the relationships between the cervical spine and shoulder and between the sacroiliac joint and the knee, or the hip and the lumbar spine. If such pathological links exist over a period of time, regardless of where the primary lesion was, they can result in secondary manifestations, which can as easily be autonomic disease, on one hand, as an increase in the primary symptomatology, on the other. This dichotomy is a valid reason to treat the extremities as well as the spinal column.

Moreover, acute and chronic traumas in work or sport frequently lead to functional disruptions of the extremities. Here, both voluntary and non-voluntary motion restrictions, rather than instabilities, dominate as a finding. The classical orthopedic range of motion reduction has always been treated by mobilizing and rehabilitative exercise; but chiropractic therapy techniques can address, in particular, the nonvoluntary movement component and achieve better treatment results through the normalization of important joint play in the peripheral joints.

> The success of the rehabilitation of disruptions of peripheral joints can be enhanced by chiropractic therapy.

In the treatment of the extremities, soft-tissue techniques, mobilizations, isometrics, and manipulations can be used in the same way as in the treatment of spinal regions, but with differing individual emphasis. Although manipulation, once again, provides the greatest therapeutic efficiency, mobilization performs the leading role in the program of therapy for peripheral joint restrictions. For cases in which muscular restriction is prominent, mobilization treatment can be enhanced (or even made possible) through PIR. Specific manipulation itself is only rarely necessary in the extremities, most commonly in fixations of joints of the hand heel; the radial head; and, possibly, the joints of the foot.

In concluding this discussion of chiropractic techniques, we should mention that both the variety of literature and the diverse continuing education courses in different nations provide considerable confusion and often exaggerate possible outcomes of such treatments. It remains the credo of the authors that chiropractic therapy, no matter how perfectly executed, should not be allowed to be entrepreneurially adulterated for self-promotion.

It is still important to address peripheral joint mechanics, the grip to be used, and factors determining the direction of the mobilization. In using mobilization techniques to normalize disrupted movement of peripheral joints, the therapist must consider the angular as well as translational components of the motion of the pertinent joint. Even though commonly used translational techniques include the parallel gliding of both joint partners, the mechanisms of the convex-concave rule for relating angular to translational movement are also valid. This rule states that whether the moving joint partner has a concave or convex configuration will influence the required direction of mobilization. In the extremities, usually only one joint partner (most commonly the distal) is moving, while the other is fixed. If the proximal joint surface is concave and the distal is convex, and if the distal surface is considered to be moving against the proximal, then the translational glide must be applied in an opposite direction to that of the restricted motion. Conversely, if the distal surface is concave, the direction of translational glide is the same as that in which the motion restriction exists (Figure 166).

> Remember that distal convex joint surfaces are mobilized against the direction of the restriction, and distal concave joint surfaces are mobilized in the same direction as the restriction.

Hand position and the direction of the mobilization are further dependent on the acuteness of the condition and degree of pain. One must follow this principle: the more acute and painful the condition, the more gentle the treatment should be. Mobilization should not lead, in any case, to the intensification of pain. In acute cases, treatment should be carefully carried out in pain-free directions of movement. Often, at first, only gentle tractional measures are possible. Forced translational mobilizations are used only after the initial abatement of the joint's irritated condition.

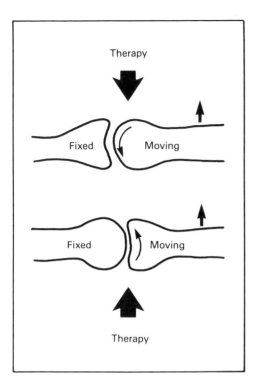

Figure 166 Convex-concave rule: Kaltenborn's method for the determination of the direction of mobilization. *Source:* H. Tilscher and M. Eder, *Textbook of Reflex Therapy.*

The following general regulations are valid for all mobilizations:

- Relaxed positioning of the extremities
- Pure tractional treatments from the neutral position of the joint
- Translational mobilizations under light traction
- Slow, rhythmic implementation of the mobilization
- After eight to ten mobilization repetitions, objective result assessments

An indication for the use of chiropractic therapy of the extremities can be seen in the following disruptions:

Shoulder region:
- Insertion tendinopathy (rotator cuff)—PIR of the afflicted muscles (provocation testing)
- Acromioclavicular irritations (provocation through maximal adduction of the upper arm)—mobilization of the acromioclavicular joint
- Sternoclavicular irritations (pressure pain, insertion of the sternocleidomastoideus)—mobilization of the joint, PIR of the muscle

Elbow region:

• Lateral epicondylitis—mobilization and manipulation of the radiohumeral joint; stretching of the hand extensors, the finger extensors, and the supinator
• Medial epicondylitis—stretching of the hand flexors

Hand and finger joints:

• Post-traumatic joint restrictions, carpal tunnel syndrome (medial/carpal joints)—mobilizations and manipulations

Hip joint region:

• Light to moderate hip arthroses—tractional manipulation, stretching treatment of contracted muscles

Knee joint region:

• Difficulties resulting from traumas, surgeries, or from inflammatory arthroses—mobilization
• "Painful fibular head" (biceps femoris)—mobilization, PIR of the biceps femoris

Foot region:

• Results of trauma with a movement restriction in the area of the ankle and subtalar joints—mobilizations and manipulation
• Fallen arch and plantar-fascial difficulties—mobilization of the tarsometatarsal joints and the metatarsophalangeal joints
• Heel spur difficulties (Insertion tendinopathy of the plantar muscular system)—PIR
• Achilles tendinopathy—stretching of the gastrocnemius-soleus muscular system and PIR

The details of technical implementation have been repeatedly introduced in the literature and can be found in corresponding publications. Which of the numerous technique variations to use in each individual case is less important in treatment of the extremities than in the spine. In treatment of the extremities, it is generally safe to use the technique that is most comfortable for the practitioner. The observation of any indications and contraindications, as well as basic biomechanical principles, is of course important.

Moreover, the previously mentioned concept is valid here, as well: one cannot learn chiropractic therapy technique for the extremities from texts alone. Books are, at best, educational aids; in no case do they replace practical experience and constant practice.

Bibliography

ORIGINAL BIBLIOGRAPHY

Brügger, A., Rhonheimer, Ch.: Pseudoradikuläre Syndrome des Stammes. Huber, Bern 1967

Cyriax, J.: Textbook of Orthopaedic Medicine, 5. Ed., Tindall & Cassel ltd., London, 1970

Dvořák, J., Dvořák, V.: Manuelle Medizin. Thieme, Stuttgart 1983

Dvořák, J., Orelli, F.: Wie gefährlich ist die Manipulation der HWS? Man. Med. 20 (1982) 44–48.

Eder, M.: Grundsätzliches zur Therapie häufiger vertebragener Syndrome. Man. Med. 11/2 (1973) 25–28

Eder, M.: Chirotherapie bei vertebragenen Schmerzsyndromen. Prakt. Arzt Kongreßband (1977) 175–178

Eder, M., Tilscher, H.: Schmerzsyndrome der Wirbelsäule, 3. Aufl. Hippokrates, Stuttgart 1986

Eder, M., Tilscher, H.: Zur Pathogenese und Klinik pseudoradikulärer Schmerzbilder. Man. Med. 19 (1981) 54

Evjenth, O., Hamberg, J.: Muskeldehnung, Teil I u. II. Remed Verlag, Zug 1981

Frisch, H.: Programmierte Untersuchung des Bewegungsapparates. Springer, Berlin/Heidelberg/New York 1983

Gutmann, G.: Funktionelle Pathologie und Klinik der Wirbelsäule, Band I, Teil I. G. Fischer, Stuttgart 1981

Haus, W. H., Gerlach, W.: Rheumatismus and Bindegewebe. Steinkopff, Darmstadt 1966

Head, H.: Die Sensibilitätsstörungen der Haut bei Visceralerkrankungen. Hirschwald, Berlin 1898

Illi, F.: Wirbelsäule, Becken und Chiropraktik. Haug, Saulgau 1953

Janda, V.: Muskelfunktionsdiagnostik. VfM, E. Fischer, acco, Belgien 1979

Junghanns, H.: Die Wirbelbogengelenke. Die Wirbelsäule in Forschung und Praxis, Bd. 87. Hippokrates, Stuttgart 1981

Kellgren, H. H.: On the distribution of pain arising from deep somatic structures with charts of segmental pain areas. Clin. Sci. 4 (1939) 35

Kibler, M.: Segmenttherapie bei Gelenkerkrankungen und inneren Krankheiten. Hippokrates, Stuttgart 1955

Kohlrausch, A.: Reflexzonenmassage in Muskulatur und Bindegewebe. Hippokrates, Stuttgart 1959

Korr, J. M.: The Neurobiologic Mechanism in Manipulative Therapy. Plenum Press, New York 1978

Lampert, H.: Die Bedeutung der vegetativen Ausgangslage für die Therapie. Phys.-Diät. Therapie 2 (1965) 29–32

Lavezzari, R.: Die Osteopathie. Urban & Schwarzenberg, München/Berlin/Wien 1957

Lewit, K.: Manuelle Medizin im Rahmen der ärztlichen Rehabilitation. Urban & Schwarzenberg, Wien 1977

Lewit, K.: Muskelfazilitations- und Inhibitions-techniken in der Manuellen Medizin. Man. Med. 19 (1981) 12–22 u. 40–43

Lewit, K., Gaymanns, F.: Muskelfazilitations- und Inhibitionstechniken in der manuellen Medizin. Man. Med. 18 (1980) 102–110

Melzack, R., Wall, P.D.: Gate Control Theory. In: Pain Proc. Inst. Symp. Pain., hrsg. von A.S. Soulairac et al. Academic Press, London/New York 1968

Mennell, J.M.M.: Joint Play In: Manuelle Medizin und ihre wissenschaftlichen Grundlagen, hrsg. von H.-D. Wolff. Verlag für Medizin, Heidelberg 1970

Mennell, J. M. M.: Joint Play. Churchill LTD, London 1964

Mumenthaler, M., Schliack, H.: Läsionen peripherer Nerven, 2. Aufl. Thieme, Stuttgart 1973

Neumann, H. D.: Manuelle Medizin. Springer, Berlin/Heidelberg/New York 1983

Peper, W.: Technik der Chiropraktik. Haug, Ulm 1958

Sachse, J.: Manuelle Untersuchung u. Mobilisationsbehandlung der Extremitätengelenke. G. Fischer, Stuttgart 1983

Sollmann, A. H.: 5000 Jahre manuelle Medizin. Marczell, Puchheim 1974

Stoddard, A.: Lehrbuch der osteopathischen Technik. Hippokrates, Stuttgart 1961

Sutter, M.: Wesen, Klinik und Bedeutung spondylogener Reflexsyndrome. Schw. Rdsch. Med. 64 (1975) 42

Teirich-Leube, H.: Grundriß der Bindegewebs-massage. G. Fischer, Stuttgart 1983

Terrior, J. C.: Manipulativmassage im Rahmen der physikalischen Therapie. Hippokrates, Stuttgart 1958

Tilscher, H.: Weichteil- und Artikulationstechniken der manuellen Medizin bei der Behandlung von Schmerzsyndromen des Bewegungsapparates. Zeitschr. f. angewandte Bäder- und Klimaheilkunde 4 (1976) 317–320

Tilscher, H.: Ursachen für Lumbalsyndrome. Der Rheumatismus. Steinkopff, Darmstadt 1979

Tilscher, H., Eder, M.: Rehabilitation von Wirbelsäulengestörten. Springer, Berlin/Heidelberg/New York 1983

Tilscher, H., Eder, M.: Lehrbuch der Reflextherapie. Hippokrates, Stuttgart 1986

Tilscher, H., Friedrich, M.: Erfahrungsbericht über 11 Jahre Manualmedizin an der Abteilung für konservative Orthopädie und Rehabilitation. Orthop. Pr. 2 (1983) 97–103

Tilscher, H., Steinbrück, K.: Die Behandlung vertebragener Störungen durch die manuelle Medizin. Orthop. Pr. 5 (1979) 370–373

Tilscher, H., Steinbrück, K.: Symptomatik und manualmedizinische Befunde bei der Hypermobilitt. Orthop. Pr. 2 (1980) 16

Waller, U.: Pathogenese des spondylogenen Reflexsyndroms. Schw. Rdsch. Med. 42 (1975) 127

Wolff, H.-D.: Manuelle Medizin und ihre wissenschaftlichen Grundlage. Kongreßband. VfM, Heidelberg 1979

Wolff, H.-D.: Kimplikationen bei Manueller Therapie der HWS. Man. Med. 4 (1978) 77–81

Wolff, H.-D.: Neurophysiologische Aspekte der manuellen Medizin, 2. Aufl. Springer, Berlin/Heidelberg/New York 1983

Zimmermann, M.: Physiologische Mechanismen von Schmerz und Schmerztherapie. Triangel, 20 (1981) 1–2

TRANSLATED BIBLIOGRAPHY*

Brügger, A., Rhonheimer, Ch. Pseudoradicular Syndromes of the Brain Stem. Bern: Huber 1967.

Cyriax, J. Textbook of Orthopaedic Medicine. London: Tindall & Cassell, 1970.

Dvorak, J., Dvorak, V. Manual Medicine. Stuttgart: Thieme, 1983.

Dvorak, J., Orelli, F. How dangerous is the manipulation of the cervical vertebrae? Man. Med. 20 (1982) pp. 44–48.

Eder, M. Basics of therapy of frequent vertebrogenic syndromes. Pract. Doctor Congress Volume (1977) pp. 175–178.

Eder, M., Tilscher, H. Chiropractic Therapy of Vertebragenic Pain Syndromes, 3rd ed. Stuttgart: Hippokrates, 1986.

Eder, M., Tilscher, H. Pathogensis and clinical picture of pseudoradicular pain presentation. Man. Med. 19 (1981) p. 54.

Evjenth, O., Hamberg, J. Muscle Stretching, Pts. I & II. Zug: Remed Verlag, 1981.

Frisch, H. Programmed Examination of the Motor Apparatus. Berlin: Springer, 1983.

Gutmann, G. Functional Pathology and Clinical Picture of the Spine, Vol. I, Pt. 1. Stuttgart: I.G. Fischer, 1981.

Haus, W.H., Gerlach, W. Rheumatoid Arthritis and the Connective Tissue. Darmstadt: Steinkopff, 1966.

Head, H. The Disruption of Skin Sensitivity by Visceral Disease. Berlin: Hirschwald, 1898.

Illi, F. Spinal Column, Pelvis, and Chiropractic Therapy. Saulgau: Haug, 1953.

Janda, V. Muscle Function Diagnosis. Belgium: VfM, E. Fischer, 1979.

Junghanns, H. The Vertebral Arch Joints: The Spinal Column in Research and Practice, Vol. 87. Stuttgart: Hippokrates, 1981.

Kellgren, H. H. On the distribution of pain arising from deep somatic structures with charts of segmental pain areas. Clin. Sci. 4 (1939), p. 35.

Kibler, M. Segmental Therapy of Joint Diseases and Visceral Illnesses. Stuttgart: Hippokrates, 1955.

Kohlrausch, A. Reflex Zone Massage in the Muscles and Connective Tissue. Stuttgart: Hippokrates, 1959.

Korr, J. M. The Neurobiologic Mechanism in Manipulative Therapy. New York: Plenum Press, 1978.

Lampert, H. The meaning of autonomic discharge for therapy. Phys.-Diat. Therapy 2 (1965), pp. 29–32.

Lavezzari, R. Osteopathy. Munich: Urban & Schwarzenberg, 1957.

Lewit, K. Manual Medicine in the Realm of Medical Rehabilitation. Vienna: Urban & Schwarzenberg, 1977.

Lewit, K. Muscle facilitation and inhibition techniques in manual medicine. Man. Med. 18 (1980), pp. 102–110.

Lewit, K., Gaymanns, F. Muscle facilitation and inhibition techniques in manual medicine. Man. Med. 19 (1981) pp. 12–20, 40–43.

Melzack, R., Wall, P.D. Gate Control Theory. Pain Proc. Inst. Symp. Pain. A.S. Soulairic, Ed. London: Academic Press, 1968.

Mennell, J. M. M. Joint Play. Manual Medicine and Its Scientific Basis. H.D. Wolff, Ed. Heidelberg: Verlag fur Medizin, 1970.

Mennell, J. M. M. Joint Play. London: Churchill LtD., 1964.

---

*Please note: Most of these titles were published in the German language. See the previous "original bibliography" for the German titles.

Mumenthaler, M., Schliack, H. Lesions of Peripheral Nerves. 2nd ed. Stuttgart: Thieme, 1973.

Neumann, H. D. Manual Medicine. Berlin: Springer, 1983.

Peper, W. Techniques of Chiropractic Therapy. Ulm: Haug, 1958.

Sachse, J. Manual Examination and Mobilization Treatment of the Extremity Joints. Stuttgart: G. Fischer, 1983.

Selye, H. The Stress of Life. New York: McGraw-Hill, 1978.

Sollmann, A. H. 5000 Years of Manual Medicine. Puchheim: Marczell, 1974.

Stoddard, A. Textbook of Osteopathic Technique. Stuttgart: Hippokrates, 1961.

Sutter, M. Methods, clinical presentation, and significance of spondylogenic reflex syndromes. Schw. Rdsch. Med. 64 (1975), p. 42.

Teirich-Leube, H. Basics of the Connective Tissue Massage. Stuttgart: G. Fischer, 1983.

Terrier, J.C. Manipulative Massage in the Realm of the Physical Therapy. Stuttgart: Hippokrates, 1958.

Tilscher, H. Soft tissue and articular techniques of manual medicine in the treatment of pain syndromes of the motor apparatus. Periodical for Applied Bath and Climate Cures 4 (1976), pp. 317–320.

Tilscher, H. Causes for Lumbar Syndromes. Rheumatism. Darmstadt: Steinkopff, 1979.

Tilscher, H., Eder, M. The Rehabilitation of Patients With Spinal Column Disruptions. Berlin: Springer, 1983.

Tilscher, H., Eder, M. Textbook of Reflex Therapy. Stuttgart: Hippokrates, 1986.

Tilscher, H., Friedrich, M. Report of experience of 11 years of manual medicine at the Department of Conservative Orthopedics and Rehabilitation. Orthop. Pr. 2 (1983), pp. 97–103.

Tilscher, H., Steinbrueck, K. The treatment of vertebragenic disruptions with manual medicine. Orthop. Pr. 5 (1979), pp. 370–373.

———. Symptomatology and manual medical findings in hypermobility. Orthop. Pr. 2 (1980), p. 16.

Travell, J.G., Simons, D.G. Myofascial Pain and Dysfunction. Baltimore, Md.: Williams & Wilkins, 1983.

Waller, U. Pathogenesis of the spondylogenic reflex syndrome. Schw. Rdsch. Med. 42 (1975), p. 127.

Wolff, H.-D. Manual Medicine and Its Scientific Basis. Congress Volume. Heidelberg: VfM., 1979.

———. Complications of manual therapy of the cervical vertebrae. Man. Med. 4 (1978), pp. 77–81.

——. Neurophysiological Aspects of Manual Medicine. 2nd. ed. Berlin: Springer, 1983.

Zimmermann, M. Physiological mechanisms of pain and pain therapy. Triangel, 20 (1981), pp. 1–2.

Index

About the Authors

Manfred Eder, M.D., was born in Graz, Austria, in 1927 and went on to earn his degree and study medicine there. By 1952, he was practicing in many clinics, and in 1956, he settled in Graz, specializing in diseases of the motor apparatus. He then began to intensely study the theories of manual medicine, physiotherapy, kinesiology, and rehabilitative medicine. His writing talents have resulted in 90 scientific publications, including six texts. A member of the medical faculty of the University of Graz, he was awarded the academic honor Venia Docendi. His interests are diseases of the spinal column, diagnosis, and therapy, especially chiropractic therapy.

Hans Tilscher, M.D., was born in Vienna, Austria, in 1935 and went on to study medicine there. After receiving his degree in 1961, he entered practice and then went on to become a professor of orthopedic studies. Since 1971, he has been in charge of the Department of Rehabilitation and Conservative Orthopaedics at the Orthopaedic Hospital in Vienna, and he also served as the head of the Neuro-Orthopaedic Outpatient clinic of the Neurological University. Trained in manual medicine, he has been teaching courses on the subject since 1969. In 1982, he received the Venia Docendi Award for Conservative Orthopaedics with a concentration on manual medicine. He has written 210 publications, including five texts. His special interests are the origin of lumbar syndromes, focal occurrences, trigger points and acupuncture, and vertebrogenic pain syndromes.

In this text, the authors follow the format of their training programs in manual medicine, which is based on the daily requirements of examination and treatment of patients. The book is introduced with a description of the basis for chiropractic therapy, including structural, neurophysiological, and biomechanical aspects. The main body of the text, however, centers around the integration of examination and the consequences of clinical information derived therefrom with treatment techniques. Because of this unique approach, there is no arbitrary division between diagnosis and therapy in this text. However, phases of management and therapy may consistently be inferred, based on information provided.